Pelican Books
The Phoenicians

Donald Harden was educated at Westminster and Trinity
College, Cambridge, where he graduated in Classics in
1923. In 1925 he assisted in excavations at Carthage
conducted by a Franco-American expedition led by
Professor F. W. Kelsey of the University of Michigan.
Subsequently he visited sites in Sicily, Sardinia, and
North Africa, as well as many museums in these and
other countries containing Phoenician material. In 1955,
when holding a Leverhulme Fellowship, he visited Tyre,
Sidon, Beirut, Byblos and other Phoenician sites, as well
as museums in the Levant. From 1929 until 1956 he was,
first, Assistant Keeper and, later, Keeper of the
Department of Antiquities in the Ashmolean Museum,
Oxford. He then moved to the London Museum, of which
he was Director until his retirement in 1970.

Dr Harden has published articles on Phoenician pottery
(in *Iraq* and *American Journal of Archaeology*) and
Phoenician exploration (in *Antiquity*). He is also an
authority on ancient glass, about which he has written
one major catalogue (*Roman Glass from Karanis*) and
numerous shorter studies. He edited *Oxoniensia*
for many years and is at present editor of *Medieval
Archaeology*.

THE
PHOENICIANS

DONALD HARDEN

PENGUIN BOOKS

Penguin Books Ltd, Harmondsworth,
Middlesex, England
Penguin Books Australia Ltd, Ringwood,
Victoria, Australia

First published by Thames & Hudson 1962
Published in Pelican Books 1971
Copyright © Donald Harden, 1971

Made and printed in Great Britain by
Richard Clay (The Chaucer Press) Ltd
Bungay, Suffolk
Set in Monotype Imprint

Contents

6 *Contents*

Illustrations

Plates

Figures

*All maps are drawn with the north point at the top.

Table

Preface to the Revised Edition, 1963

Inevitably, in a small book covering so wide a field, it is impossible to treat the subject fully enough to satisfy either the author or the reader. Some aspects of the Phoenicians and their culture are not touched on at all; others only in the most summary fashion. I hope, however, that in spite of its limitations the book will provide some general picture of the Phoenicians at the time when this comparatively small group of people was a force to be reckoned with throughout the Mediterranean, and beyond, and that it will help also to indicate their place in the story of the nations.

In the homeland I have tried to differentiate the Phoenicians of the coastal belt from the Canaanites as a whole and have even omitted – very largely – the earlier history of that belt, for it was not until the late Bronze Age that 'Phoenicia' and 'the Phoenicians', as we now understand the terms, came into being. This will explain, if it does not excuse, the small part that the great French excavations at Byblos and Ugarit play in my story. They would take their place more appropriately in a companion volume on the Canaanites, which would cover, too, the prolific finds on key Palestinian sites such as Megiddo and Hazor.

The literature about the Phoenicians is immense and so widely scattered in many languages that it would take a lifetime to digest. The books that I have primarily used are indicated in my bibliography. There are many others that I could well have consulted had time allowed, but I hope I have not missed anything really vital. Not only are there many books, however: they often express many divergent opinions. It is not possible within the space allotted to me to explain these different view-points and leave the reader to form his own judgement. I note some occasionally, either in the text or in the notes, but usually I state one view, omitting controversies. Those who know the literature will recognize how often I have done so; those who come fresh to the subject may be glad not to be wearied with records of arid disputations.

There has been much excavation on Phoenician sites, both east and west, during the past hundred years, not all of it scholarly. The most prolific, and perhaps the best, has been in North Africa, particularly at Carthage, during the present century, where the French Department of Antiquities under Paul Gauckler and his successors and the White Fathers under the late Père Delattre have done much good work. In recent years under the Picards, Pierre Cintas and others the pace in North Africa has not slackened, and there has been much digging also in other areas, particularly in Phoenicia itself and in Sardinia, some of which is not yet published. No doubt its results will invalidate some of my statements and my guesses. But to have waited for all the evidence would have meant that the book would never be written and I make no apology, therefore, for its appearance at this juncture.

My own interest in the Phoenicians was awakened many years ago quite by chance when, as a young student at the British School at Rome, I accepted an invitation from the late Byron de Prorok to join his team at Carthage, where they were going to excavate in the newly discovered precinct of Tanit. Since then Carthage and the Phoenicians have never been far from my thoughts, though often for long years the research has had to be laid aside because of other calls. In those early years I was greatly encouraged not only by de Prorok but also by the late Professor F. W. Kelsey of the University of Michigan, and to both of these enthusiastic workers I owe a very deep debt of gratitude. Among others who helped me in past years I would mention particularly Joseph Whitaker of Palermo and Louis Poinssot of Tunis.

For the maps and other text illustrations in the present book acknowledgement is made elsewhere to Marion Cox and H. A. Shelley, whose great skill is matched by their long-suffering patience in carrying out my most detailed instructions. For photographs and much other help I am grateful to D. M. Bailey,

R. D. Barnett, R. A. G. Carson, R. A. Higgins, G. K. Jenkins and D. J. Wiseman (British Museum); A. S. Trotman (London Museum); Joan du Plat Taylor (London University Institute of Archaeology); B. H. Warmington (Bristol); V. E. G. Kenna (Farringdon, Devon); G. R. Driver, Ann Brown and H. W. Catling (Oxford); P. Dikaios (Cyprus); C. G. Zammit and F. S. Mallia (Malta); M.-T. Barrelet, E. Coche de la Ferté, and Lucienne Laroche (Louvre); P. Cintas (Mission archéologique française, Paris); F. Barreca (Cagliari); V. Tusa (Palermo); S. Chiappisi (Rome); C. Carducci (Turin); A. Blanco Freijeiro, A. F. de Avilés, and A. Garcia y Bellido (Madrid); J. M. Mañá de Angulo (Ibiza); F. Johansen (Copenhagen); H. Abdelnour and M. Chéhab (Beirut); C. Elperin (Tel Aviv); Y. Yadin (Jerusalem); E. E. Peterson (Ann Arbor); W. Stevenson Smith (Boston); Briggs Buchanan (Guilford, Conn.); and B. Cook, D. von Bothmer, and C. Wilkinson (New York). The index would not have been finished in time had it not been for the kindness of Ann Morley, who helped greatly in putting it into order.

But above all I would like to thank Dr and Mrs Glyn Daniel and the directors and staff of Messrs Thames & Hudson for their forbearance and guidance in a task which has dragged on far longer than they wished and which at times they must have felt would never be accomplished; nor would it have been without the ever-present sympathy and encouragement of my wife, who knows better than any the difficulties and trials which beset it.

D. B. HARDEN

London, 1963

Preface to the Present Edition

In revising this book for publication in Pelican my aim has been to retain its basic form, making only such changes as are necessary to correct inaccuracies and to draw attention to some of the more important recent discoveries in the field of Phoenician studies. Some of this fresh information has come from friends and colleagues, whose names are mentioned in the appropriate places in the text and notes. I am most grateful to them all, not only for providing the new material, but also, in some instances, for their even greater kindness in permitting me to include it here in advance of their own publications.

It has seemed to me that to attempt a more drastic revision of the text within the compass of its present length would so alter its character and style that it would cease to bear any resemblance to the original version. The book filled a need, I believe, both for English readers and for others, in 1962. It is my hope that this new edition may continue to provide students and the general public with a useful introduction to the archaeology and history of the Phoenicians.

D. B. HARDEN

London, 1971

Until archaeology came to the rescue in the middle of the nineteenth century our knowledge of the Phoenicians was entirely derived from the writings of other nations, notably the Jews, Greeks and Romans, with whom they were from time to time in contact, not always on a friendly basis; for the Phoenician literature has almost wholly perished. Such a picture was bound to be distorted.

Thus Plutarch, a Greek, writes in the first century AD, long after the fall of Carthage:

They are a people full of bitterness and surly, submissive to rulers, tyrannical to those they rule, abject in fear, fierce when provoked, unshakable in resolve, and so strict as to dislike all humour and kindness.

There are similar strictures in Appian, an Alexandrian Greek, writing about a century later:

In prosperity the Carthaginians are cruel and overweening to all men, but they are very humble in adversity.

It would be quite unfair to lay too great stress on such judgements. Pomponius Mela, a Spaniard, writing in Latin in the first century AD is much more generous:

The Phoenicians were a clever race, who prospered in war and peace. They excelled in writing and literature, and in other arts, in seamanship, in naval warfare, and in ruling an empire.[1]

Archaeological exploration has done much to emphasize the more balanced view. Yet of all the major peoples of antiquity the Phoenicians remain today the least well served by archaeological discoveries. In particular, we have found no written documents on Phoenician sites (as we might well have done) telling us what the Phoenicians themselves thought of their relations with other peoples – particularly the Egyptians, Assyrians and Greeks; giving us accounts of their political and commercial dealings with their neighbours; and even, perhaps, supplying information about their technical and manufacturing achievements in purple dyeing, metal-working and shipbuilding. As it is, we can but judge these things on the circumstantial evidence of archaeological finds and on the information – not always reliable – that writings of other nations provide. Often there are gaps in the evidence; often we have to admit complete ignorance on certain points in the story. Yet despite all this the work of recent scholars and field-workers has revealed a clear enough general picture of this small but gallant people who made such an impact on world history and on the growth of civilization.

As explorers, in antiquity, the Phoenicians were second to none, as colonizers to few, save perhaps the Greeks. As traders and merchants they fetched and carried raw materials and manufactured goods throughout the then known world. Their prowess as doughty fighters was shown, not only in Carthage's long-drawn-out struggle with Rome, but also in the resistance that Tyre and Sidon put up against Mesopotamian and other conquerors and in the services their navy rendered to Persia. But all these things pale before their highest and most enduring memorial, the alphabet. This is where they impinge most strongly on all subsequent civilizations of Old World origin. All Indo-European and Semitic tongues – indeed all subsequent alphabetic scripts – have employed the medium developed by the Phoenicians and rapidly adopted by many other nations round about them, including the Greeks.

The people of whom all this can be said occupied, as homeland, a narrow strip of the Levant coast from Tartus to somewhere south of Mount Carmel [Fig 1].

In the Bible the Bronze Age inhabitants of this strip of coast and its hinterland were called Canaanites. Despite the genealogy in Genesis, which makes Canaan the son of Ham, they were Semitic and spoke a Semitic tongue.

These Canaanites were certainly not autochthonous, and the date of their entry into the country has been disputed. It is usually recognized that there were several waves of migrating Semites, coming, it is thought, from Arabia or the Persian Gulf,[2] but the problem of their origin and timing bristles with difficulties. Many now equate the first main northward migration with the movement which brought the Akkadian overlordship to Mesopotamia about 2350 BC, the second with the influx of the Amorites towards the end of the third millennium, and the third with that of the Aramaeans at the end of the Bronze Age. But if that is so, what about the evidence from Byblos (p. 40)? Must we assume that the earliest Giblites, who were trading with Egypt at or soon after 3000 BC, were not Semitic and not the direct forerunners of the Phoenician Giblites of later years? There is no evidence for a Semitic conquest by force of arms, either at Byblos or elsewhere. Perhaps, then, there were Semites in Byblos from at least the beginning of the Bronze Age. Physical anthropology does not seem to help. To judge from their cranial measurements, it seems that the population of the Levant was pretty thoroughly mixed even by the fourth millennium. Nor does archaeology, for archaeologists are not yet, and may never be, able to equate with complete confidence a given class of pottery or weapons or seals, for example, hereabouts with a given ethnic group. So we are left guessing. What is certain is that by the fourteenth century BC in the el Amarna letters the inhabitants of Canaan were calling themselves in Akkadian Kinahu or Kinanu. This seems to be the earliest occurrence of the word in literature.

Whence came the other name, Phoenicians, by which this branch of the Canaanites is now universally known? They did not invent it themselves. It seems to have been given to them by Greeks, presumably Mycenaeans, who came into trading contact with them in the later second millennium. At first it was no doubt used for all Canaanites; later it would be confined to those who lived in the coastal belt and retained their independence.

The word is first found in Homer (singular *Phoenix*, plural *Phoenikes*) and appears to denote originally a dark red or purple or brown colour, whence it was transferred both to the date-palm and to the brown-skinned Canaanites. The name of the mythical bird – the Phoenix – is thought to be an independent derivation from the same adjective. The Roman name, *Poeni*, for the Carthaginians and other western representatives of this people is a latinized version of the Greek, and the Romans differentiated between the western *Poeni* and the eastern *Phoenices*, though recognizing that they were the same stock. Pagan Greek and Latin authors never use the name Canaanite in any form. But the Phoenicians, even in the west, retained it. In the New Testament where St Mark,[3] writing for gentile readers, speaks of a Syrophoenician woman, St Matthew,[4] writing for the Jews, calls her a woman of Canaan. Even St Augustine in the early fifth century AD says that if you ask the country people in Africa who they are they will reply in the Punic tongue 'Chanani' (p. 105).[5]

The Phoenicians as a people cannot be differentiated from the general mass of Canaanites until somewhere during the later half of the second millennium BC, and it is then that we shall begin our story. They reached their zenith at the beginning of the first millennium BC, when they began to spread their influence by commerce and their stock by colonization throughout the Mediterranean and beyond.

We shall follow their fortunes in the east until 332 BC, when Alexander took Tyre, and in the west until 146 BC, when Rome sacked Carthage: thenceforward east Phoenicia passed into the Greek (Hellenistic) world and west Phoenicia into the Roman.

To the north and east of the Phoenician coastal belt, in the Orontes valley and the area which Greeks and Romans of later ages called Coele-Syria, the Bronze Age people, who were also Canaanites, produced an art and culture which is exceedingly difficult to distinguish from what we find farther south. The difficulty is heightened by the innate disposition of all the Levant people to copy the art and culture of others, particularly Egypt and Mesopotamia, and to fuse them together into an amalgam which, though different from either, is sufficiently allied to one, or both, to cause confusion.

Important cities such as Ugarit (Ras Shamra), Alalakh

(Atchana), Hamath and Damascus had long histories. Indeed, in the sculptures and bronzes from the more northerly Phoenician cities such as Aradus and Tripolis, and even perhaps Byblos, we can recognize strong north Syrian traits from time to time, while at Ugarit much of what Schaeffer found can be closely paralleled by finds farther south, and his alphabetic cuneiform tablets revealed to us for the first time a fine series of Canaanite religious and mythological texts. This is not to say that Ugarit and these other sites were Phoenician in the sense we adopt here, and though we shall use some of the finds from them to illustrate our story, we do not include that area within our direct purview.

Similarly, since, as we have seen, the whole of Palestine was basically Canaanite before the Hebrews arrived, and since the Hebrew conquest was a gradual process which did not finish till the time of Solomon, we may use Palestinian objects, too, to illustrate our theme, though not claiming them as truly Phoenician. Hazor, in particular, remained a strong and important Canaanite stronghold (as Yadin's recent excavations have emphasized) for long after the Hebrew entry under Joshua.

These problems, that give us such difficulty when we are dealing with Phoenicia proper, surrounded by neighbours of basically similar stock, do not arise overseas, except in Cyprus. Elsewhere the peoples whose territories the Phoenicians entered were of wholly alien origin, and we can readily distinguish between the native and the Phoenician. But in Cyprus there had been Semitic contacts if not immigration since the third millennium B C, and Cypriote influences were at the same time spreading to the mainland (p. 52).

We find, too, a further difficulty in Cyprus and to a less extent in Phoenicia. Early Greek art imbibed much oriental influence from the eighth century onwards.[6] In this movement the Phoenicians and their art played a prominent part. Now here, again, there was a two-way traffic. Many centuries earlier, in Mycenaean times, Greek things and Greeks themselves had come to the Levant coast and to Cyprus, and it is difficult thereafter to sort out the Phoenician from the Graeco-Phoenician, especially in the realms of art (pp. 184 ff.). To pick out what is Egyptian and Mesopotamian among finds and culture-traits in Phoenicia is not nearly so hard, for when Levantines copied from Egypt or Mesopotamia their copies were usually sufficiently unlike the originals to be readily recognizable.

2 Geography

As so often happens, it was geographical environment which led the Phoenicians to develop as they did. The configuration of their land made it necessary for them to seek an outlet by sea rather than by land, and their position on the land-route between the two great culture-areas of antiquity laid them open to constant political domination and cultural influences from each.

The Syro-Palestinian or, as we shall call it for short, the Levant coast stretches for 450 miles or so from the Gulf of Iskenderun to the Egyptian borderland [Fig 1]. The Phoenician cities lay in the middle portion of this strip of coast from Antaradus (Tartus) on the north to Dor or even perhaps to Joppa (Jaffa), a distance of just under 200 miles.[7] Their four most important towns were Aradus (Ruad), which was on an island opposite to Tartus, Byblos (Gebeil), Sidon and Tyre. Others were Marathus (Amrit), Berytus (Beirut), Ecdippa (Aczib) and many more, some no larger than villages.

Along this strip the Lebanon chain, attaining in places a height of 9,000 ft or more, lies never more than thirty miles from the coast and usually much less, and though the lowland parts are fertile, they are not extensive, so that, as population grew, the produce soon became insufficient to support the inhabitants.

This is why Phoenicia could never live or prosper by its agriculture or become an exporting country. What it did possess in plenty in antiquity was timber – especially cedar and fir – from the Lebanon forests [Plate 1]. This great natural product brought the region into early contact with Egypt, a land where trees were rare.

The Levant coast possesses a great many small bays flanking

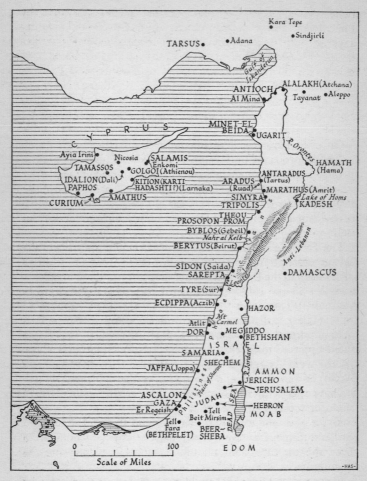

Fig 1 *The Levant coast: Phoenicia and its chief towns*

headlands where people could defend themselves readily
against a landward attack, and at the same time have a good
anchorage on each side for their ships. If, instead of a headland
and isthmus, they could find an island near enough to the coast
to provide ready anchorage on its landward side, so much the

better. When they set out later on their colonial ventures the Phoenicians always sought similar sites, and planted colonies at some of the best and most famous fortress and harbour sites in the Mediterranean such as Cadiz in Spain, Valletta in Malta, Bizerta in Tunisia, Cagliari in Sardinia and Palermo in Sicily. Others of their sites, such as Carthage, Motya in Sicily and Tyre and Sidon themselves, though good for the small ships of antiquity, do not provide good harbourage for the larger vessels of today.

To understand the Phoenician development we must consider some of these sites more closely.

Of the chief homeland sites, Aradus was a small rocky island, only about 1,500 m. in circumference [Plate 4]. According to Strabo [8] it was covered with buildings of great height in several stories. Yet, despite its small size, history records that the city held sway over many of the near-by towns such as Marathus and Simyra. We know no details of its topography. Its cemeteries, and also perhaps its suburbs, may have spread on to the mainland, as happened, for example, at Motya in Sicily. There is a strange story in Strabo that it possessed no wells, and if its cisterns ran dry during a siege, there was a submarine spring between it and the mainland from which the inhabitants drew water by letting it rise through a leather pipe into boats, the pipe having at its lower end a hemisphere of lead to cover the spring-head and exclude the sea-water. The Arvadites were noted sailors. They provided a large contingent in Phoenician fleets and their earliest coins had a galley forming the badge of the city on the reverse [Plate 110,c].

Byblos lies about twenty-eight miles north of Beirut. Its earlier topography, down to the end of the Bronze Age, has been greatly elucidated by the French excavators, but this digging has recovered little or nothing of the Iron Age or later city, except cult sites that occupied the same emplacements as their Bronze Age predecessors and a fortress of the fourth century BC.[9] It is likely that the main Iron Age habitation lay to the north, under the modern village. Dunand notes that in the late Bronze Age private dwellings 'desert the acropolis'. The site is on a cliff from which a ramp led down to the harbour that lay between the Bronze Age and modern settlements.

Byblos was by its own tradition the oldest city in the world,
built by the god El, and the French excavations have shown
an unbroken series of levels down to the Neolithic period. It
was one of the oldest and most important centres of Astarte-
worship and has yielded much valuable information about
Bronze Age cults in the area.

Ancient Sidon lay on the northern slope of a headland.
Roman, medieval and modern towns have retained the same
site and thus there is not much hope that we can ever discover
the general topography of the Phoenician city. There was a
good harbour on the north, protected by a low line of rocks that
ran from the north end of the promontory towards the mainland shore for several hundred metres. On the south there is a
large bay, not well protected, but providing fair anchorage in
some weathers.[10] Here, as at Aradus, Renan thought he could
recognize traces of the Phoenician walls and fortification, but
even if he is right, the traces are so meagre that they give no
real indication of what the elaborate walls of such settlements
looked like. We can tell this better (pp. 114, 157) from Assyrian
reliefs [Plates 48, 51; Fig 37] and Sidonian coins [Plate 110,a].
The cemeteries, temples, and no doubt also the industrial area,
extended along the main shore and up the cliffs.

The plan of Tyre is perhaps better known than that of any
other homeland city, but even so we can only fill in the out-
lines [Fig 2]. It lay on the two largest of a chain of rocks close
inshore. The present peninsula which joins the old island site
to the mainland represents the mole built as a siege-work by
Alexander the Great: before that there was no adit except in
boats. But, as at Aradus, this island, even with tightly packed
houses of several stories,[11] was insufficient to contain a city of
Tyre's size, and there must have been much overflowing on to
the mainland. The topography has been well studied with the
help of air-photographs [Plate 3]. As at Sidon, there was a port
or roadstead on each side of the town. To the north was a
natural harbour, improved by an enclosing sea-wall and a fine
roadstead protected by the northern end of the chain of islets;
on the south or south-east a second artificial harbour supplemented the natural protection which the site itself provided.[12]
Since modern Tyre lies on the same site we have little hope of

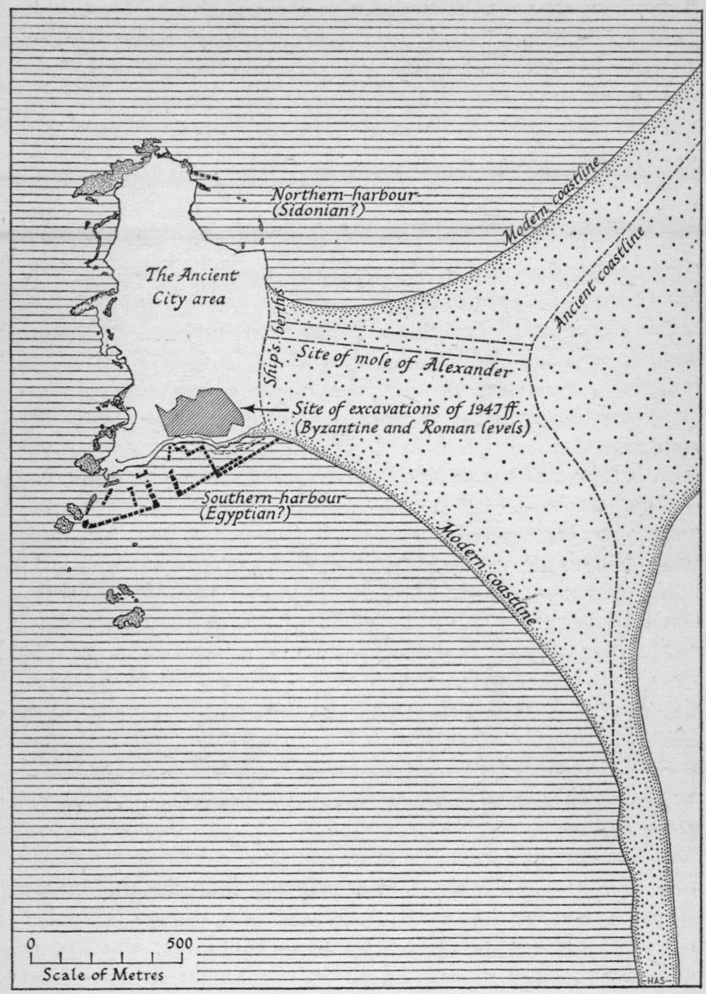

The map shows labels:

- Northern-harbour (Sidonian?)
- Modern coastline
- Ancient coastline
- The Ancient City area
- Ship's berths
- Site of mole of Alexander
- Site of excavations of 1947 ff. (Byzantine and Roman levels)
- Southern-harbour (Egyptian?)
- Modern coastline
- 0 ... 500
- Scale of Metres

Fig 2 *The site of Tyre, with the ancient harbours, and Alexander's siege-mole linking the isle with the mainland*

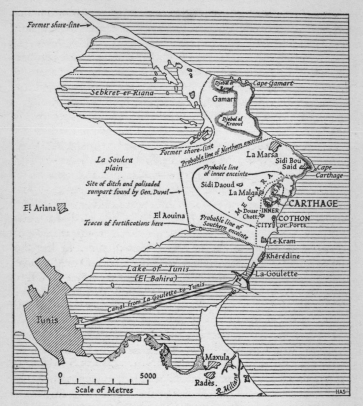

Fig 3 *The peninsula of Carthage, and the probable line of the late Punic defences*

discovering much about the internal details of the city. Wide-spread excavation on the built-up ground to the south-east of the ancient island site has not so far yielded much evidence of pre-Alexandrine habitation.

Fortunately the colonial sites sometimes provide better evidence of the general topography of a Phoenician city. Carthage itself is the most revealing of all, and also of course the biggest and greatest.

In the nineteenth century and earlier one writer or another

placed the city in almost every conceivable position on the peninsula which stretches from Tunis to Cape Gamart, Sidi Bou Said and La Goulette [Fig 3]. Since the 1880s, however, the discovery of a great series of Punic tombs in an arc between the hill of St Louis and that of Ste Monique showed that the Punic city must have lain between Sidi Bou Said and La Goulette [Plate 6]. Even then there was room for great difference of opinion on topographical details, and, in particular, it has been hotly disputed whether the two lagoons north of Le Kram [Plate 5] represent the circular and rectangular Punic ports or cothon that are so vividly (but not altogether clearly) described by Appian, Strabo and other ancient writers.[13]

One difficulty has been that the Sebkret er Riana on the north of the isthmus, now a land-locked bay owing to the deposition of silt by the river Bagradas (mod. Medjerda), was in Punic times open to the sea; while on the south the lake of Tunis, though its shore-line has remained more or less the same, has become shallower. Nowadays it will take little more than a rowing-boat: formerly it could provide water for larger craft, and Punic ships could ride at anchor both here and in the Sebkret er Riana.[14] The eastern coast-line between Sidi Bou Said and La Goulette has remained more or less constant.

In 1918 Gsell summarized the archaeological and literary evidence and concluded that Byrsa was on the hill of St Louis and that the lagoons near Le Kram marked the site of the rectangular and circular ports about which ancient writers tell us.[15] We need worry less about the smallness of the lagoons if we remember that a Punic cothon was a wet dock rather than a real harbour, and that normally ships would ride at anchor near by or be drawn up on a beach. True, ancient texts say that during the third Punic war Carthage built a fleet of 120 ships in the circular port, and that it contained docks for up to 220 vessels:[16] but possibilities exist by which such statements may be reconciled with the potential area of whatever circular port might have existed here (p. 120). That the circular lagoon has a paved bottom shows that it, at least, is artificial, and also that it is not just a medieval salt-pan.[17]

It seems, then, that the main Punic city spread from Le Kram to Bordj Djedid and inwards to La Malga or thereabouts

[Fig 4]. The forum (following ancient texts) would have been on the lower ground between the hill of St Louis and the ports. Of the rest of the inner topography we can say very little with two exceptions – the Tanit precinct, which lay to the west of the rectangular lagoon (pp. 86 ff.), and the cemeteries (p. 31). Nearly

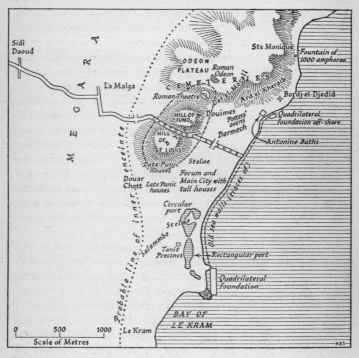

Fig 4 *The inner city of Carthage*

all the other ancient buildings of which traces remain on the site are Roman or Byzantine. Remains of late Punic houses and streets (p. 124 f.) have recently been found on the south slope of the hill of St Louis [Plate 9], and other traces of Punic houses are known at Dermech and Douar Chott. Carton found a late sanctuary at Salammbo station and Merlin another one at Sidi Bou Said. But not a single temple emplacement is known, and though some of the many cisterns may be Punic in origin, most, such as the great cisterns at La Malga and Bordj Djedid, are, in their present form, undoubtedly Roman.[18] The well-chamber, however, called 'Fountain of a thousand amphorae', at the foot of the Bordj Djedid cliff was originally constructed in Punic times and still shows some good Punic stone-work, although its vault and arches are not earlier than Roman [Plate 8].

In the third Punic war the city, we are told, was encircled with a wall twenty-one miles in circuit. This would be about the right length for an enceinte running north across the isthmus at its narrowest point, then east to the coast, north of La Marsa and back along the sea-coast via Sidi Bou Said and Le Kram [Fig 3]; and such is, indeed, traceable in scattered detachments: (1) foundations off-shore from Bordj Djedid to near the rectangular lagoon; (2) evidence of ditches, palisade and other works found in 1949 [Plate 7][19] where the enceinte would cross the isthmus (p. 119) and (3) walling on the lake shore, 13–16 feet thick, two miles west of Le Kram. The type of stone and its size and regularity indicate that these fortifications must be Punic or early Imperial, and as Roman Carthage was not fortified until the fifth century AD we can accept them as Punic.

The earliest interments so far found in the cemeteries cannot be shown to be earlier than the later eighth century BC. These and their successors of the next two centuries are situated on the slopes of the hills of St Louis and Juno and in the Douimes and Dermech regions, between Byrsa and the Bordj Djedid. By the fifth century the burial-ground had spread on to the southern slopes of the Bordj Djedid. In the fourth century the land between the Odeon hill and the Bordj Djedid (Dar-el-Morali and Ard-el-Kheraib) was in use, and finally the third- and second-century cemeteries lay on the Odeon and Ste Monique hills, farther north and north-east, though strangely enough the St Louis and Juno slopes also came back into use. Thus in general there is a spread north-eastward as century succeeded century [Plate 6; Fig 4].

There can be no doubt, from all this evidence, that the earliest settlement at Carthage was at and near Le Kram. The existence of the Tanit precinct beside the rectangular port

[Fig 21][20] as early as the eighth century (pp. 86 ff.) clinches the matter, for it is highly improbable that such a precinct, which enshrined all that was deepest in Carthaginian religious feeling and observance, would have lain outside the settlement area. A settlement here could control La Goulette peninsula and would have the lake of Tunis near enough to provide good sheltered anchorage. As the years went by, we can picture the Punic city gradually spreading from the port area northward, but we can do no more than make a guess at the date when the Byrsa hills [15] became the citadel area and were crowned with the temple of Eshmun (p. 78). It may not have taken more than a century or two for the town to develop so far.[21]

The nearest Phoenician city to Carthage was Utica, situated about 35 km. N.N.W. on rising ground at the mouth of the Bagradas, the principal river of Tunisia, which flowed down from some of the richest agricultural land in the region.

To look at the site today causes us to wonder why the Phoenicians settled there, for the Bagradas during the centuries since Roman times has so shifted its lower course and so silted up the land near Utica that the site of the Phoenician and Roman city lies now on rising ground surrounded by alluvium, 10 km. from the sea.[22] We can recognize the acropolis on a hill which was once a promontory, with a former island to the east, separated from it originally by a narrow channel. As at Carthage, there are many Roman ruins still existing, but no building that can be proved to be Punic. The earliest tombs, however, may go back to the late eighth century, and occur on both sides of the channel separating the 'island' from the 'promontory'; the later tombs are farther west and north.

Elsewhere in north Africa both to the south and east and to the west of Carthage there is an equal dearth of architectural remains on Punic sites, and for the most part their topography has to be worked out from geographical probabilities and the location of the Punic cemeteries. Cintas, who has undertaken much exploration for Punic sites in north Africa, explains clearly what we should look for. First, a suitably sheltered anchorage with a beach (not necessarily large) for drawing up the ships; second, a good source of fresh water; and third, a rocky limestone area, generally on an eminence, where the rock-

tombs so beloved (pp. 97 ff.) by the Phoenicians could be cut
and where traces of quarrying may, therefore, still exist. The
Punic anchorages along the coast were normally set at a day's
sea journey of about 40 km. from each other, for it was the
sailors' habit to travel by day and stop each night *en route*.[23]

Let us look at just one of these sites, the farthest one so far
discovered along the western route from Carthage. Just south
of Mogador on the Moroccan coast between Casablanca and
Agadir the river Ksob debouches into a small bay partly shut
off from the open sea by a small island about 3 km. long by
$1\frac{1}{2}$ km. wide lying $1\frac{1}{2}$–3 km. from the mainland – just the
kind of situation the Phoenicians loved [Fig 5].[24] Here
Koeberlé and Cintas dug and found firm traces of Phoenician
occupation (pp. 59, 156), and the results of their trial excavations in 1950–52 were confirmed and amplified by Jodin's
further work in 1956–8.[25]

Of the important western sites outside Africa we take first
Motya in Sicily. This was the main base from which Carthage
prosecuted her Sicilian wars, until it was besieged and destroyed by Dionysius of Syracuse in 398. Here again the settlement was on a small and low-lying off-shore island [Figs 6, 7].
From the sixth century onwards, it was surrounded by a fine
town wall, about $2\frac{1}{2}$ km. in circumference and enclosing an area
of 50 hectares, or about 125 acres, many good sections of which,
including remains of staircases, guard-houses and gates, are
still extant [Plates 13, 14]. The masonry is of various styles and
dates and there are traces of twenty towers. The wall follows
the line of the shore fairly closely. As yet there is no evidence
of any permanent spread of habitation to the mainland, but a
large cemetery with inhumations in coffins beginning in the
sixth century exists at Birgi, and a causeway, the foundations
of which are clearly visible under water, ran directly from this
area to the north gate of the town.[26] A cemetery has also been
found on the island, as well as a sacrificial precinct with urns and
stelae.[27] A cothon on the island, if one existed (p. 120 f), would
have been too small to hold many ships, even of ancient type
[Fig 36], and we must assume that the lagoon between the
island and the mainland served as the main harbour or
roadstead.

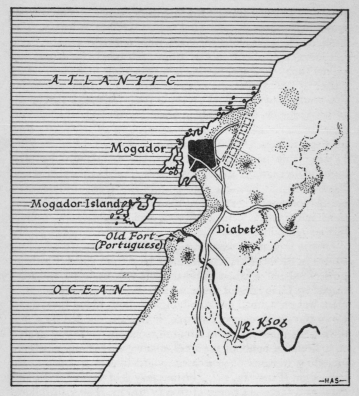

Fig 5 *The island of Mogador (Morocco), the site of a Punic settlement*

Of internal buildings we have only two [Fig 7], a fine house of Greek style near the south-east shore (p. 123), and the foundations of what must have been a temple or other public building at the spot called Cappiddazzu. Several rebuildings of this structure occurred, the last, in the fifth century, being of fine ashlar masonry.

In Sardinia there were four main Phoenician cities – Sulcis (S. Antioco), Caralis (Cagliari), Nora and Tharros [Fig 14]. All were on promontories except Sulcis, which lay on the landward side of the modern Isola di S. Antioco, beside a

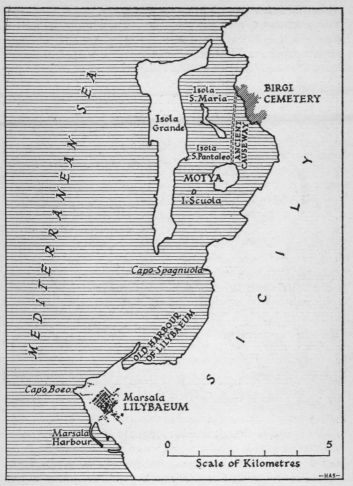

Fig 6 *Motya (Sicily), and neighbourhood*

causeway which now joins the island to the mainland, but which probably did not exist in Punic days. Sulcis has yielded few traces of its Phoenician topography, but it has produced Phoenician pottery of the eighth century BC, the earliest so far known in Sardinia, and a series of stelae wholly comparable in styles and date to those from the Tanit precinct at Carthage. The sanctuary, which the presence of these stelae indicated, has recently been excavated. At Cagliari, where later building has obscured the Phoenician topography, the original settlement was most likely on or near the S. Elia promontory to the

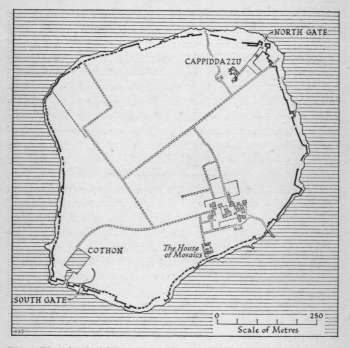

Fig 7 *The island of Motya, with the town walls and principal remains*

south-east, in which case the salt lake east of Cagliari probably represents the ancient port. No early tombs have been found here; tombs of the fifth century and later spread along the hillside north-west of the modern city [Plate 12].

The site of Nora stands at the end of a low-lying peninsula, with good anchorage to the north [Plate 11]. It has been unoccupied since Roman days, except for a medieval fortress on the high headland which previously carried the Phoenician acropolis. Tombs of the sixth century and later were found many years ago, as well as another sanctuary of Tanit with numerous stelae and urns. There has been recent excavation also, concentrated on the town and its defences. If the records of the earlier excavations at Nora are not as full as we should like, those of the even more extensive nineteenth-century excavations at Tharros on the west of the island are completely lacking, for the site was plundered for objects. It lies on the headland of San Marco, jutting out far into the sea on the north side of the Gulf of Oristano. Excavations have taken place recently, revealing, *inter alia*, a precinct of Tanit.[28]

There is as yet no trace of any Phoenician town in Malta. Many late Punic tombs from the fifth century BC onwards and a few quite early ones exist, some going back to the eighth or perhaps even the ninth century. There are also some inscriptions, including [Plate 36] two late bilingual *cippi* (p. 110). We may assume that the main colony was where Valletta now stands, hidden deep below Valletta's present houses and fortifications. Phoenician things have also been found on the islands of Gaulos (Gozo) and Kossyra (Pantelleria).[29]

In Spanish lands the three chief Phoenician or Punic sites were Gades (Cadiz), Ebusus (Ibiza), and Hasdrubal's late foundation of Carthago Nova (Cartagena).

Gades, the earliest settlement, lay on the north end of an island some 20 km. long and nowhere more than 1 km. wide, which formed a bar across a fine bay at the mouth of the Guadalete river [Fig 8]. Between this island and the mainland was a smaller island on the site of the modern San Fernando. At the southern tip of the outer island lay the famous temple of Heracles (Melqart). The general topography is well described by Strabo.[30] Coastal changes have since joined both the islands to the mainland and to each other, but have cut off the site of the temple, which is now the Isla de Sancti Petri. The sea has also eroded much of the west (seaward) side of old Gades, so that parts of the ancient town and its necropolis no longer exist. As the rest lies under medieval and modern Cadiz, we know little of the Punic topography, but a large cemetery stretching across the peninsula immediately south of the medieval town has yielded more than 150 tombs of the late

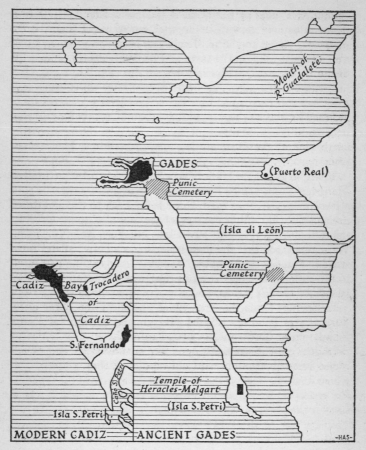

Fig 8 *The site of Gades, showing changes in the coast line since ancient times*

sixth to the third century B C with fairly rich furniture. Another (late) Punic cemetery, extending into Roman times, existed on the smaller island, which was probably not occupied by the earlier colonists.

The settlement on Ibiza was founded from Carthage in 654–3 B C. Once more the sea has altered the topography since

Punic days. The first settlement was on an island which protected a bay. This site, which is still called Isla Plana, though
it is now joined to the main island, has produced remains of
the seventh century, including [Plate 76] some surprisingly
primitive snow-man figurines of clay (p. 188). Here, too, but
probably of later date, are traces of buildings which may have
been used for dye manufacture (there was a large heap of
murex shells, cf. p. 135 f.) or fish-curing. On the main island,
at Puig d'es Molins, lay the main cemetery dating from the
sixth century to Roman times, and elsewhere on it are the
remains of a small settlement (not the chief Punic one) and a
hill-sanctuary of Tanit at Cueva d'es Cuyram belonging to the
fifth to the first century BC (p. 192).

Carthago Nova, though a much later settlement, founded
for political and military purposes and not as a genuine colony
of the earlier type, was none the less a typical Phoenician
settlement, in that it occupied a promontory between an almost
land-locked bay and an inner lagoon, the bay being protected
some distance out by an island (Isla Escombrera). Time has
again altered the topography, for the lagoon is now dry land,
and modern Cartagena, on the site of the Punic city, is no
longer a promontory. Archaeology has given us few Punic
objects from here, and no evidence for the town's layout or
buildings: but its topography is well described by Polybius,[31]
when relating Scipio's siege and capture of it in 209 BC.

3 History of the Phoenicians in their Homeland

Byblos is, so far, the only site in the Phoenician homeland that has yielded a large quantity of material that can be dated before 1500 BC. In the early Bronze Age, Giblite connections with Old Kingdom Egypt are already manifest in a cylinder-seal of Egyptian style found in a cache under a later temple.[32] Under Sneferu of the fourth dynasty an Egyptian text records the arrival in Egypt of forty ships from Gebal laden with cedars, while both Sahure (fifth dynasty) and Phiops (Pepi) I (sixth dynasty) in the second half of the third millennium record expeditions of a warlike character which they made into Asia by sea as well as by land.[33]

At the same time Mesopotamian activity, at first only trading and commercial, but later under Sargon of Agade military as well, was also manifest in the Levant. Thus the stage was already fully set. The Levant coast remained thereafter the political and cultural battleground of these two great African and Asiatic centres of civilization [Fig 9].

Even after the beginning of the second millennium BC Byblos is still the only city in the Phoenician homeland of whose doings we have any knowledge. By now it was certainly Canaanite. We have the Semitic name of one of its princes, Ypshemuabi, inscribed in hieroglyphic characters on two objects – a bronze *harpé*, or ceremonial axe, and a gold pectoral in the form of a shell, decorated in cloisonné work. These were found by Montet in the second of a series of deep well-tombs, contemporary with the later years of the twelfth dynasty in Egypt, which also contained a gold-mounted obsidian casket [Fig 10,a], made in Egypt, and bearing the cartouche of Ammenemes IV (1800–1792 BC). The first tomb of the same series, that of Ypshemuabi's father Abishemu, contained an Egyptian gold-mounted obsidian unguent vase [Fig 10,b] with the cartouche of the preceding Egyptian king Ammenemes III (1850–1800 BC). From another point of view also, letters and economic tablets in cuneiform found at Mari on the Euphrates tell us something of Byblos and other Canaanite towns of the period, including Hazor. In a word, we have good evidence from different sources of Giblite culture of the time. That we have no direct evidence from other sites on the Phoenician coast is probably because they have not yet been excavated to sufficiently low levels.

An Egyptian literary text, the tale of the adventures of Sinuhe,[34] well illustrates the nomadic life of this area during the twelfth dynasty, and confirms much that is found in the patriarchal stories in Genesis. Sinuhe fled from Egypt after the death of Ammenemes I in *c.* 1970 BC, and, meaning to go to Gebal (Eg. Keben), stayed instead for many years in the country of the upper Retenu, whose chief was Ammi-enshi. Here Sinuhe prospered, marrying the chief's eldest daughter, and the tale ends with his return to Egypt many years later, under Sesostris I, coming 'as a Bedu, in the guise of the Asiatics'.

During the eighteenth and early seventeenth centuries BC, while Egyptian power was in decline between the Middle and New Kingdoms the Canaanites at first developed their military and economic strength without outside interference, and excavations have shown that the Canaanite rulers of the time lived prosperously in fine houses. Later in the seventeenth century Indo-Europeans (Hittites) and Hurrians (Horites) advanced southward into the area [Fig 9]. This movement was connected, in part at least, with that of the Hyksos princes who, during the seventeenth century, advanced from Asia into Egypt and set up a capital in the Delta from which to rule both Egypt and Canaan. We may assume that at this time the coastal cities were building up their power quietly enough, being more strongly placed than the inland ones to ward off attacks from invaders and local petty chiefs. It took all the might of an Alexander to capture Tyre by storm.

The period of relief and independence ended suddenly in 1580, when Amosis drove the Hyksos out of Egypt and

Fig 9 *The ancient near east in the late second and early first millennium* BC

CASPIAN SEA

URARTU

ASSYRIA

Khorsabad
NINEVEH (Kouyunjik)
Balawat
CALAH (Nimrud)

R. Tigris

BABY
LONIA

BABYLON

R. Euphrates

ELAM

SUSA

PERSEPOLIS

A
B
I
A

PERSIAN

GULF

0   200   400   600

Scale of Miles

HAS

founded the eighteenth dynasty. From then on the Egyptian tide of conquest flowed through the Levant towards the upper Euphrates, and the Phoenician cities, many of which we now hear of for the first time, were engulfed in it. Tuthmosis I, *c.* 1525, exacted tribute from them and Tuthmosis III, after the battle of Megiddo, reduced them all to vassalage. Simyra, Aradus, Berytus, Sarepta, Byblos, Tyre and Sidon [Fig 1] are all mentioned by name in Egyptian inscriptions of the time,

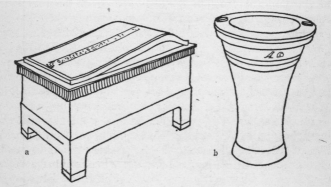

Fig 10, a, b *Gold-embellished obsidian box (L. 0·045 m.) and unguent-vase (H. 0·12 m.) with royal cartouches of Ammenemes IV and III respectively, from Byblos. Twelfth dynasty*

and it is clear that a recognizable enclave of 'Phoenician' states had at last begun to build up their own special brand of Canaanite culture and civilization.[35] But for the time being Egypt was still too powerful to allow them to develop their independence, and control of the eastern Mediterranean by Aegeans still blocked the way to Phoenician colonization.

Thus during the eighteenth dynasty Phoenicia was a land of petty local states, subservient to Egypt and relying on her, often in vain, for protection from Asiatic conquerors such as the Amorites and Hittites of northern Syria. They were still an integral part of the Canaanite complex, speaking closely related Semitic dialects and having a common religion, which extended from the mouth of the Orontes to the Egyptian border and inland across the Jordan and Orontes valleys. The invasions which were to bring about a contraction of these Canaanite boundaries were still to come. Culturally they lived in an Asiatic milieu: they wrote, even to their Egyptian overlords, on clay tablets in Babylonian cuneiform. Their art objects – cylinder-seals, statuettes and jewellery – were mainly influenced by Mesopotamian and Syrian models, though Egyptian motifs and elements of design break through at times.

Tablets found at el Amarna in Egypt provide a good picture of the political situation in the first half of the fourteenth century under Amenophis III and Akhenaton. There are, for example, many letters from Ribaddi, governor of Byblos, begging for help from Egypt in his attempt to hold the town for the king [Plate 40]. There are others from Abimilki of Tyre pleading in vain for a small contingent to help against Zimrida of Sidon, who had turned against Egypt and was attacking him, and complaining that, besieged in his island city, his plight was terrible, with no wood, no water, and no ground in which to bury the dead. On the other hand there is one from Zimrida himself protesting eternal loyalty and asking for help to enable him to free towns that had fallen into the hands of brigands, so that he could continue to serve the king, his master! It was left to the powerful kings of the nineteenth dynasty, Sethos I and Ramesses II, at the end of the fourteenth and the beginning of the thirteenth century to rescue their vassals from the northern yoke. In 1298 Ramesses had an inscription carved on the cliff at the mouth of the Nahr-el-Kelb, above the defile between the sea and the Lebanon foothills north of Beirut [Plate 2]. Three years later he fought an indecisive battle at Kadesh on the Orontes, and finally signed a treaty with the Hittites in 1279, which retained the Phoenician coast within the Egyptian sphere.

Meanwhile new influences and new people appeared in the Levant. From the west in the fourteenth century came Mycenaeans, who for wellnigh two centuries were in command of all trade and commerce in the eastern half of the Mediterranean. These not only traded, but established enclaves of merchants within the Canaanite cities. Their pottery became a commonplace on all sites of the period and was imitated locally in great quantities as well. Their artistic motifs, notably the Aegean

spiral and plant forms, also took hold. They were specially
prominent at Ugarit and Alalakh in north Syria, and, by the
thirteenth century, even more strongly entrenched in Cyprus.
In the south, also, one of the numerous groups of Sea Peoples,
who overran so much of the eastern Mediterranean at the end
of the Bronze Age, the Philistines (Pulusati), occupied a broad
strip of the coastal plain probably in the late thirteenth century.
They are usually thought to have been Aegeans, but they were
not basically seafarers, and founded their cities somewhat
inland.

The Exodus, too, brought the Israelites under Joshua into
Canaan. Its exact date was long a matter of great dispute, but
it is now usually ascribed to the thirteenth century. With
the Canaanites of the south being squeezed by Philistines and
Hebrews and those of the north hard-pressed by Hittites and
Amorites the only independent Canaanite area by about 1200
was the central coastal strip – Phoenicia proper.

It was at this time that Egypt entered upon a long period
of decline, the Hittite empire was destroyed, Assyria was
only beginning to arise as a world power and the Mycenaeans in their own home had been conquered by northern
invaders. There was indeed no great power left and the way
was at last open for a revivified and independent Phoenicia to
come into its own, and spread its influence far and wide.

That it was ready to do so then and not before demands some
explanation. As they had always been seafarers, why had they
not long ago sent out colonizing expeditions, at least to near-by
lands such as Cyprus and Rhodes? Experience of coastal
traffic with Egypt over two millennia and more might well
have shown them the way. Some infusion of new ideas and of
new blood must be postulated to account for their sudden
maritime activity, and this probably came from Mycenaeans,
who had been settling in some numbers among the Canaanites
of the Levant coast for many years past.[36] The story of Elissa
or Dido (p. 60) may illustrate this suggestion. She was sister of
Pygmalion, king of Tyre, and wife of Acharbas, the king's
uncle and the high priest, whom Pygmalion murdered. Can
we see here not only a political, but also a cultural conflict
within the city between Aegean and Canaanite elements? In

support we may note Justin's statement that Pygmalion was raised to power by the people in violation of the testament of his great-grandfather Ithobaal.[37] If there were such a mingling of Mycenaeans and Canaanites it would indicate whence the Canaanites derived their urge for colonization and perhaps even some knowledge of the places they would reach during their journeyings.

Be this as it may, their power and influence did expand from now on, and it remained strong till about 600 BC. Throughout all that period Tyre was the chief city of the homeland, Byblos, Sidon and the rest taking a lesser place, and it was not until Nebuchadnezzar destroyed Tyre's power in 574 that Sidon inherited the leadership.

Now, during the late eleventh and earlier tenth centuries the Hebrews were consolidating their rule in south Palestine under Saul, David and Solomon, and defeating the Philistines. Hiram the Great of Tyre (*c.* 970–36) was an ally of David (*c.* 1000–960) and Solomon (*c.* 960–20) and archaeology confirms the Biblical indications that the two nations (for so we may now call them) were in close touch and mutually helpful. The two powers reached their zenith during the reigns of Hiram and Solomon. Not yet – though raids of Tiglath-Pileser I, who occupied Aradus temporarily *c.* 1100, gave warning of what was to come – had the Assyrian come down like a wolf on the fold, and made life unsafe throughout these lands of the Levant coast.

Hiram, at Solomon's appeal, provided materials and workmen to help build the temple in Jerusalem (p. 83). The Bible also tells of Hiram's building and improvement of the harbour works at Tyre itself, and of how he aided Solomon in maritime ventures (p. 150), all of which provides a picture of the flourishing condition of Tyre at the time, when its maritime and colonial drive was in progress (p. 151).

During the ninth century the relations between the royal houses of Tyre, Israel and Judah were still close. Ithobaal of Tyre married his daughter Jezebel to Ahab of Israel, son of Omri, and Jezebel's daughter Athaliah married Joram of Judah. Since Elissa of Carthage was Ithobaal's great-grand-daughter, Jezebel was her great-aunt. Phoenician builders were

Omri
K Israel
886–75

Ithobaal*
(Bibl. Ethbaal)
K Tyre
891–59

Jezebel = Ahab
K Israel
875–53

Athaliah = Joram
Q Judah   K Judah
843–37   848–4

Badezor
K Tyre
859–3

Ahaziah
K Israel
853–1

Jehoram**
K Israel
851–43

Ahaziah** = Zibiah
K Judah   of Beer-
844–3   sheba

Jehosheba

Joash
K Judah
837–797

Mattan
K Tyre
853–21

Elissa
(Dido) = Acharbas
(fled to
Carthage 814)

Pygmalion
K Tyre
821–774

* According to the
traditional history
in Josephus,
Ithobaal, priest of
Astarte, seized the
throne after
murdering Phales,
the last king of the
line of Hiram the
Great (970–36)

** Jehoram of
Israel and Ahaziah
of Judah were slain
by Jehu, who
usurped the throne
of Israel in 843.
Athaliah then
seized the throne of
Judah, but after six
years was slain by
Jehoiada, the priest,
who restored the
throne to Joash,
still a minor of
seven years (2
Kings, ix–xi)

still helping the Israelite kings. We see their work in the time
of Omri and Ahab at Samaria, for example, as well as at
Megiddo, where the famous stables, once thought to be
Solomon's, are now ascribed to Omri.[38]

Meanwhile the Assyrian menace had arrived. Assyria
needed an opening to the sea and also the products of the
Levant, particularly timber, if she was to become really great.
In 876 Assurnasirpal, as we learn from his own inscriptions,[39]
took tribute from Tyre, Sidon, Byblos and Aradus, among
other places – including silver, gold, fine polychrome cloths
and ivory. In the next reign (Shalmaneser III, 859–24) we
hear of further tribute from Phoenician cities and a defeat of
the king of Aradus in battle. The gates of Balawat and the
Black Obelisk, both monuments of this king, now in the British
Museum, illustrate this. On the former [Plate 48], Phoenician
boats bring tribute from Tyre to the mainland (p. 122), and
on the latter many kings of the Levant, including Jehu of
Israel, do obeisance before the Assyrian monarch.

By 741 the kingships of Tyre and Sidon seem to have been
joined, for the Hiram of Tyre who in that year is mentioned as
a tributary of Tiglath-Pileser III appears to be the same person
who is named on a well-known fragment of a bronze bowl
from Cyprus (p. 109) as king of the Sidonians.[40] Shortly afterwards, under the next Assyrian king, Shalmaneser V, Luli is
also described as king of both these cities.[41] This Luli reigned
for some twenty or thirty years and was in conflict not only
with Shalmaneser V but also with Sargon II (722–705) and
Sennacherib (705–680). He was an active and powerful ruler
who made alliances, as the records tell us, with Judah and
Egypt against the Assyrians and he was besieged in Tyre more
than once without success. Ultimately in 701 Sennacherib
forced him to flee to Cyprus, and Barnett has recognized an
Assyrian relief of that king [Plate 51] as illustrating Luli's
escape from the city (p. 122).

In the early seventh century, when Egypt was once more
reasonably powerful under its twenty-fifth dynasty, Tyre makes
common cause with her in 672 against Esarhaddon. But Tyre
and Egypt were no more successful than the others, for a stele
found at Sinjirli in Turkey [Fig 11] shows the Assyrian king

holding the kings of Tyre and Egypt on leashes! Yet, as we know, the city of Tyre was not captured.[42] Inland towns and even coastal towns were fairly easy prey to the Assyrian scaling-ladders: island fortresses were less so, for a land force such as theirs. Assurbanipal, the last powerful king of Assyria, laid siege to it in 668 but could not take it, though the Tyrians had to give in and provide hostages.

Nineveh fell in 612 to the Babylonians and their famous king Nebuchadnezzar (604–561) was the power who captured Jerusalem and enslaved the Jews in 587. Thirteen years later he defeated Tyre after a long siege (p. 114) and so finally brought the whole Phoenician and Palestinian region into the dominion of the rulers of the land of the two rivers. The Babylonian monarchy was overthrown by the Persians in 539, under whom Phoenicia, Syria and Cyprus formed the fifth satrapy (province) of their empire.

Fig 11 *Stele of Esarhaddon of Assyria, with the kings of Tyre and Egypt on leashes, c. 672 BC, from Sinjirli. H. 3·04 m.*

Though Phoenicia lost her independence, her influence did not vanish with the conquest. Her naval power was such that her fleets became one of the mainstays of the Persian sea campaigns, in particular in Persia's wars against Greece – a foe whom the Phoenicians, their commercial rivals, were by no means reluctant to attack. But though they fought the Greeks from time to time they themselves during the fifth and fourth centuries fell more and more under Greek influence culturally and artistically, just as their colony Carthage began to do at the same time (pp. 76, 81, 135, 191 f.).

Sidon, now the chief town of Phoenicia, was for a time the seat of a palace of the Persian king, some capitals from which have been found, which are in Susan Persian style, in the form of bull-protomai [Fig 12]. This fact is also no doubt reflected in

the figure of the Persian king [Plate 110,a] which appears on Sidonian coins of the period (p. 158). But Tyre was still impor-
tant, having recovered from the blows of Nebuchadnezzar, and it was Tyre, not Sidon, that in 332 put up the only Phoenician resistance to Alexander. Alexander's siege of the town is described in full by Diodorus:[43] in particular how he constructed the famous causeway between the island and the mainland [Fig 2], which still exists today (p. 26 f.), so that Tyre has never since been the island it once was.

With the siege and capture of Tyre and the passage of the whole coast into Greek hands the Phoenician cities became henceforth but units, first in the Seleucid kingdom, then in the Roman province of Syria. The Phoenician name and character still lived on, but there was no longer a Phoenician nation. Even the Canaanite language (p. 105) had already given place to a large extent to Aramaic, which from the middle of the first millennium onwards gradually ousted the old

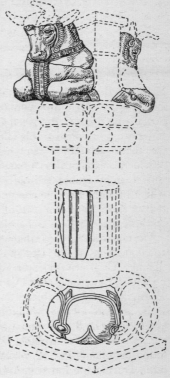

Fig 12 *Reconstruction of a column, the capital in the form of bull-protomai, Sidon. Fifth or fourth century* BC.

Canaanitic dialects, though it was itself, from Seleucid times, much overshadowed by Greek, which became the *lingua franca* of the eastern Mediterranean.

Greek mythology has many tales to tell of Phoenician expansion [Fig 13], even into mainland Greece, such as, for instance, how the mythical Cadmus led a band of Phoenicians to Boeotia. If we are to rationalize this tale, which occurs in Herodotus,[44] we must attach it to some prehistoric Asiatic influx into Greece, of which, as archaeology has shown, there was more than one. But we may ignore the more obviously mythological stories which brought Phoenicians to almost all the eastern Mediterranean shores, and even within the Black Sea, and concentrate on those places where archaeology confirms the ancient stories.

We take first Cyprus, the eastern tip of which lies less than 100 km. from the nearest point of the Syrian coast at Ras Shamra. Cypriote trading relations with the mainland began, no doubt, quite early, but it is not until the fifteenth and fourteenth centuries that pottery and other items, such as cylinder-seals, indicate a close admixture of styles between the island and the mainland – an admixture so close, indeed, that archaeologists are in doubt whether some types of pottery which are found commonly in both places were made in one only, or in both. During the fourteenth and thirteenth centuries Aegean Mycenaeans were arriving in the island, at first as merchants, but towards the end of this period as settlers also,[45] and they were also settling in some numbers, as we have seen (p. 45 f.), not only in north Syria at Ugarit, Alalakh and elsewhere, but in Phoenicia proper and farther south as well.

Thus some of the interconnections between Phoenicia and Cyprus from the thirteenth century onwards may have been due more to the existence of Mycenaeans in both, than of Phoenicians. Yet mythology, and even history, gainsay this. We have the existence of the Astarte/Venus cult in many cities,

especially Paphos [Plates 100, 101]; there is the Elissa story –
how she went to Cyprus and picked up extra followers on her
way to Carthage in the late ninth century (p. 60); and we have
the tale of Luli's flight (p. 49). Philological evidence also exists,
e.g. the Semitic name of Kition. Yet all these might merely
indicate migrations or flights of dispossessed inhabitants (like
Luli) from the mainland at the time of the Hittite, Amorite and
Assyrian wars rather than real colonial ventures.

Myres long ago found evidence at Bamboula hill, Kition
(Larnaka) of a small settlement, which he believed to be
Phoenician of *c*. 1000–750 BC, succeeded by a much larger
and well-fortified one, which he thought began about 700.[46]
Since 1959 however the story of Kition has acquired a completely new aspect, following many seasons of work by V. Karageorghis. It now appears that on the site of modern Larnaka,
apart from even earlier settlement, there was a fortified
late Bronze Age town from at least the fourteenth century,
which received two waves of Achaean colonists in the late
thirteenth and late twelfth centuries and was not abandoned
until *c*. 1000. Thereafter the town centre moved nearer to the
sea, and it was at this new centre, in Karageorghis's view, that
the first Phoenician settlers founded a colony during the ninth
century (he puts it no earlier); although quite recently he has
also found evidence that at least one Mycenaean temple on the
old site, abandoned in the eleventh century, was renovated by
the incoming Phoenicians as a temple of Astarte and remained
in use down to the end of the fourth century BC.[47] This
colony must be the Qartihadashti of the Assyrian records,
whose king joined with eight other Cypriote potentates in
doing homage to Sargon in 709–8, and was, according to other
sources, in close touch with Tyre at that time. It is clear that
from the ninth century the site was the main Phoenician base
in the island in contrast to Hellenic Salamis.

Henceforth Cypro-Phoenician connections were strong and
Cyprus was a useful staging-post for Phoenician vessels going
farther afield. Much of the so-called Cypro-Phoenician pottery
of the ninth century and later is really descended from
Mycenaean wares (p. 185), though in some of its shapes, such
as jugs with beaked lips and others with neck-carinations, it has

Fig 13 *Phoenician colonization in the Mediterranean*

adopted Phoenician characteristics. There is, too, a special type of red-slip, burnished ware [Plate 111,a], which occurred, for example, at the Bamboula site, and is closely parallel to similar red-slip, burnished wares from many eastern and western Phoenician sites (p. 139 f.).

There must have been Phoenician staging-posts along the coast of southern Asia Minor from Cilicia westward, but outside mythology there is no suggestion of direct colonization, whether we look for it in ancient texts or modern field-work. The bilingual inscriptions (p. 111 f.) in Hittite hieroglyphs and Phoenician of the late eighth century from Kara-Tepe [Plate 37] are no proof of a colony, though they presumably indicate the presence of groups of Phoenician traders or business-men. It is thought that the Asitawandas who set them up was linguistically a Hittite and not a Phoenician.[48]

At the other end of the Levant coast, in southern Palestine, we may also record the existence of Phoenician trading-posts.

The typical Phoenician red-burnished pottery of the ninth to eighth centuries (p. 139) has occurred on several sites such as Bethpelet and er-Regeish, near Gaza.[49] Intermediate staging- or trading-posts of this kind are only to be expected between Egypt and Phoenicia: but they were not real colonies. In Egypt itself, too, history records that Phoenician traders had settlements not only in the Delta but at Memphis, where Herodotus[50] mentions an area of the city called the 'Tyrian Camp', in which a temple of Ashtart (Aphrodite 'the Stranger') was founded – so the story went – in connection with Helen's arrival after the Trojan War. Archaeology confirms their presence in Egypt, for early red-burnished pottery has been found at er-Retabeh and other Delta sites [Plate 111,b]. But these settlements would, again, be market centres rather than real colonies. Indeed, the Phoenicians could not found colonies in countries where good government and civilization already existed; besides they were only too ready to be satisfied with the role of traders wherever they found an equally civilized people to trade with.

We come next to the Aegean. It seems clear that in Rhodes, especially in its two chief towns Cameiros and Ialysos, Phoenician influence was the successor to Mycenaean. Myth tells that Phalas or Phalanthus (an early Greek name: might he have been of Mycenaean descent?) led Phoenician colonists hither about the time of the Trojan War, and that they were expelled by Greeks under Iphiclus or by Carians – the sources differ. Certain it is that much of the material of early geometric style found in Rhodes is more akin to the Phoenician stock-in-trade than to the Greek: yet by the sixth century Greek influence predominates and any Phoenician colonial endeavour must have wholly ceased.[51]

Crete, as one of the original centres from which the Aegeans, who brought Mycenaean civilization to the Phoenician seaboard, expanded, must also have welcomed their Phoenician trading successors. One town in the east, Itanos, is traditionally a Phoenician foundation. We have no archaeological knowledge of any true colonization here by Phoenicians, yet objects of Phoenician art of the ninth or eighth centuries have been found in the island, so that Phoenician artists may have settled there by then.[52]

When all is said, the Greeks themselves were so well established in the Aegean region that it is unlikely that Phoenician colonists would seek to settle there. Yet their traders frequented it, as we know from Homer (p. 151 f.), and their metal-work in particular was an object of luxury which made them welcome.

Passing west of Greece, recent research has shown that Mycenaean pottery, and presumably therefore Mycenaean traders, had reached Sicily and the islands and coasts of the Tyrrhenian sea in the fourteenth century BC, if not before. It perhaps was one of these traders who owned the Syrian copper figurine of Melqart of the fourteenth or thirteenth century BC that was recently found in the sea off the south coast of Sicily [Plate 93].[53]

Dunbabin[54] believed that there may have been Aegean trading stations at Syracuse and Thapsos, and perhaps elsewhere. These sites seem to correspond closely with Thucydides' description of the 'islets and capes round the coast' where, he says, Phoenicians first settled, before they retreated west to Palermo and other places when the Greek colonists began to arrive in the later eighth century. But if the Phoenicians were settled in the east of the island, they could surely have held such settlements against any attack that the Greeks of the time could mount.[55] May we not rather assume that the Phoenicians left Sicily, and especially eastern Sicily, severely alone until they saw the Greeks settling in the island and then decided to take the western sites to prevent further Greek expansion? This would accord with the archaeological evidence that Phoenician Motya on the west coast was not settled before the eighth century, and the close kinship of some early Motyan pottery with contemporary wares at Carthage seems to indicate that Carthage took a large share in her foundation.[56] Panormus (Palermo) and Soloeis (Pizzo Cannita[57]) were the other main Phoenician towns in the island.

There is no indication in ancient authors or from archaeological finds that the Phoenicians planted independent colonies on the Italian mainland. It was the Greeks and Etruscans (if we accept the view that Etruscans were not autochthonous) who followed in Mycenaean footsteps here – the former in the eighth century, the latter perhaps a bit earlier. Phoenician trading contacts with the Italian mainland were, however, strong and there was a settlement of Phoenician traders at Pyrgi, at least, and perhaps at Rome, too, as we shall see (p. 154 f.).

In north Africa, apart from Carthage, whose history is discussed in the next chapter, there was a traditionally very early settlement at Utica (*c.* 1100), and there is mention of other early ones at Hadrumetum (Sousse), Lepcis Magna, and elsewhere. There had been a big push to the far west also – to Gades, traditionally founded in the twelfth century, and thus reputedly the earliest foundation of all, except the mythical first foundation of Carthage (p. 60).[58] Archaeology suggests that Malta was settled by the early eighth century at latest, and perhaps even sooner, and the inscription on the Nora stone in Sardinia is now given a ninth-century date by at least some scholars.[59] Thus by *c.* 800 the pattern of western settlement had been fixed: later colonists merely filled it in and

consolidated it. The key-points of Carthage, Utica, Motya and
Malta controlled the narrow central Mediterranean passage to
Gades and beyond. The Sardinian settlements – Nora, Tharros
Sulcis and Caralis – kept the Greeks out of the southern half
of that island, while the Etruscans prevented them from
settling in the north and in Corsica. The Greeks won the race
for south France, where the Phocaean colony of Massalia was
founded *c.* 600, and they also controlled much of Sicily and
south Italy, and had an important colony at Cyrene on the
African coast between Egypt and Syrtica. Later, *c.* 500, an
imaginary line of demarcation between the Greek and Punic
spheres in north Africa was drawn at Arae Philenorum, some
kilometres west of modern El Agheila. Thenceforward until
after the second Punic war, Carthage held sway along all the
African coast west of this point, permitting no encroachment
by others.

Long before this, however, Carthage, as her first recorded
overseas venture, had, in 654–3, as Diodorus[60] tells us, planted
a colony in Ibiza, the main island in the Pityusae group, east of
Spain, where there was a good port in a situation which it was
important to save from Greek and other rivals. It is not
recorded when or to what extent the two Balearic Islands were
occupied by Phoenicians, nor does archaeology help. The name
Port Mahon (anc. Mago) in Minorca is Phoenician and, as it is
one of the best harbours in the Mediterranean, it would be a
matter of much surprise if it was not occupied by them quite
early. They were certainly there at the time of the Punic wars
and used Balearic mercenaries as early as the end of the fifth
century.

In Spain Gades was the key site – the best harbour from
which to collect and export the metal ores of Tartessos (i.e.
Tarshish, if we accept the identification; see p. 151).[61] Much
eastern Phoenician influence from at least the eighth century
BC can be recognized among finds in south and south-east
Spain, but so far not earlier. Sceptics therefore cast doubts on
the traditional twelfth-century date for the foundation of Gades
with some justification, just as they also doubt the almost
equally early date for Utica. Indeed, if we are wise we shall not
push any Phoenician colonies back behind 1000 and will be

chary of accepting even a tenth-century date for any colony in
the west. If the Nora stone (pp. 57, 110) is ninth-century, it is
the earliest real evidence we have. Finds on the whole do not
take us back beyond the eighth century.

There were other eastern Phoenician settlements in Spain,
besides Gades, at an early date, for there are red burnished
wares of eighth-century type such as the jug [Fig 41] from
Torre del Mar near Malaga (cf. those from Kition and er-
Retabeh), which have been found on numerous sites on the
southern Spanish coast and in its hinterland, such as Al-
múñécar (anc. Sexi), Toscanos, Trayamar and others near
Torre del Mar, and Riotinto, Aljaraque and others near
Huelva.[62] These are too early to be derived from Carthage,
whose influence in Spain cannot have begun until after the
foundation of Ibiza. At some time thereafter she founded or
refounded colonies at Abdera, Sexi, Mainake (formerly a
Phocaean colony, see p. 152) and elsewhere in southern Spain
and kept her rivals at bay, and she also had strong influence in
Iberian centres such as Villaricos, where much Punic material
of the fifth century and later has been found. The first Punic
war nearly killed her domination in Spain, but Hamilcar began
to resuscitate it in 237 (p. 64), and some years later Carthago
Nova and Akra Leuke were founded as Carthaginian bases.
Defeat in the second Punic war, however, finally destroyed her
Spanish empire and left Spain to the Romans.

Considerable evidence now exists to show (pp. 33, 156) that
Phoenicians settled in many places on the Moroccan coast,
notably Lixos, Mogador, Tangier and Tamuda, during the
seventh century BC. Since these settlements took place at such
an early date, it was probably from east Phoenicia or Gades
and not from Carthage that the settlers came, as, indeed, the
types of pottery and other objects on which the evidence rests
clearly suggest.[63] It is most likely that Carthage's own power
on that coast began with the colonies [Fig 50] founded for her
by Hanno, *c.* 425 BC (pp. 163 ff.). These spread down to Cerne,
the site of which is highly disputable (p. 168). No colonies re-
sulted from Himilco's similar voyage northward, so far as
history relates, nor does archaeology as yet suggest that such
existed, despite some possible Phoenician finds in Portugal.

Of all the Phoenician cities Carthage is the most important for our story. History makes her more renowned than her mother-land of Tyre, and her leadership of all the west Phoenicians was undisputed from the seventh century, if not the eighth, until her fall in 146 BC. Besides, there is more archaeological and literary evidence about Carthage than about any other Phoenician city.

The traditional date for her foundation is 814–13. A putative earlier foundation in the late thirteenth century by Zor and Carchedon, which is mentioned in a passage of Philistus (a Sicilian historian cited by Eusebius) is manifestly an epony-mous myth – Zor being Tyre and Carchedon the Greek for Carthage. But the 814–13 tradition is soundly based and, despite the doubts of some modern scholars, seems to fit the archaeo-logical and historical facts reasonably well.[64] The earliest pottery found in Punic tombs and in the lowest stratum of the Tanit precinct (pp. 86, 140), including Cintas's 'little chapel' (p. 89), can be placed in the eighth century without any distortion of typology [Plate 58,a–f; Fig 27]. Historically Elissa (Dido) and her brother are no mere myths (p. 47 f.). Since Elissa's great-aunt Jezebel married Ahab in the second quarter of the ninth century, we need not be surprised that Elissa's departure for Carthage is ascribed to the end of the same century. Along with a band of Tyrian aristocrats who disliked the king, she went, according to the story, first[65] to Cyprus. The priest of Juno, with his family, joined her there and she also seized some eighty maidens and set sail westward, making straight for Carthage, where they bargained to acquire a piece of ground as big as an ox-hide would cover and obtained as large a piece as possible by having the hide cut up into the thinnest strips! The ground she acquired was therefore called Byrsa (i.e. hide) in Greek, but (some have suggested) with a second meaning, as that word might also be a Greek adaptation of a Semitic word denoting a fortress.[66] Somewhat later, it would seem, the name Byrsa came to be used for the citadel of Carthage, and is now applied to the hill of St Louis, the traditional citadel hill.[67] Reason suggests that the earliest settlement would not be as far inland as that, but rather at a point on the seashore near a convenient beach, and there is no doubt (p. 31 f.) that it was in fact on the flat ground near the two lagoons north of Le Kram. The details of the historical topography of Carthage, however, are very complicated and uncertain (pp. 28 ff.).

Carthage, once founded, flourished greatly and seems soon to have become the leader of the Phoenicians in the central Mediterranean, including Motya and Utica, ready to meet and counter the Greek westward thrust in the later eighth century [Fig 14]. Yet the first action taken by Carthage which any ancient historian records is the foundation of a colony at Ibiza in 654–3 BC (p. 58). Half a century later, in 600, she made a vain attempt to prevent the Phocaeans from founding Massalia. Half a century later again her general Malchus ('Milk', lord) defeated the Greeks in Sicily, but, vanquished in his turn in Sardinia, was banished. He later returned and seized power in Carthage and was followed by Magon,[68] who with his sons Hasdrubal and Hamilcar had further conflicts with the Greeks. In 535 an Etruscan and Carthaginian fleet got the better of the Phocaeans in a sea battle near Alalia in Corsica,[69] a result which put a stop to any attempts by the Greeks to settle in either Corsica or Sardinia.

But the Etruscan power was on the decline. Rome thrust out the Tarquin (Etruscan) kings in 510 and became an independent republic, and the very next year – and how surprising and significant this is – she made a treaty with Carthage (p. 154) defining mutual spheres of influence. Carthage no doubt saw that the new state was likely to prosper, though she cannot yet have suspected that serious rivalry for world power would break out between them in the future. Her real enemies were still the Greeks. The Phoenician homeland (p. 50 f.) was by

Fig 14 *The central Mediterranean, illustrating Carthage's wars with the Greeks*

now under Persian domination and the Persians were deter-
mined to attack mainland Greece. At the time of the second
Persian expedition under Xerxes in 480 the Carthaginians,
urged perhaps by Persia or their mother city, fitted out an
expedition which landed at Panormus and was heavily defeated
at Himera by a Syracusan and Agrigentine force, on the same
day, according to tradition, as that on which the Greeks
defeated the Persian navy, which included a large Phoenician
contingent, at Salamis.

Thus defeated the Carthaginians turned westward with all the greater determination. Colonies along the north African coast were founded or strengthened, and about 425 (p. 162) Hanno's and Himilco's journeys (pp. 163 ff.) indicate Carthage's new interest in far-distant lands outside the Pillars of Heracles [Fig 50]. Clearly, if any credence is to be placed in these stories (and they surely must have some basis in fact, despite justifiable strictures on the text of Hanno's *Periplus*[70]) we must see them as indicating a strong attempt by Carthage to develop western trade and obtain for herself access by sea not only to the products of the African hinterland but also to the tin trade of Brittany and Cornwall, from the trans-gallic approach to which she was cut off by the Greeks on the southern coasts of Gaul.

To open up these routes she had to be in contact with the indigenous peoples in north Africa, and we hear, indeed, that the tribute which the original colonists agreed to pay to the Libyans for the site they occupied ceased to be paid about this time, Carthage being then strong enough to take the Libyans under her sway and acquire a wide inland *territorium* (p. 70), spreading over parts of the fertile Tunisian hinterland, particularly the Bagradas valley and the coastal plain behind Hadrumetum (Sousse) [Fig 14]. This helped to provide food for her growing population. She also needed the Libyans as fighters in her wars.

In the last decade of the fifth century war broke out again in earnest between Carthage and the Sicilian Greeks, led by Dionysius of Syracuse. Carthage was at first victorious, but in 398 Dionysius sacked Motya, which never fully recovered, its inhabitants being moved to a new town, Lilybaeum (modern Marsala), near by.[71] Until 338, when peace was made with the Greek general, Timoleon, fighting was frequent. An uneasy lull for nearly twenty years followed, until Agathocles, tyrant of Syracuse, declared war once more and after being defeated in Sicily had the effrontery to invade Carthaginian territory in Africa, landing at Cape Bon. This fighting continued until Agathocles' death in 289, without either side winning. Ten years afterwards Pyrrhus of Epirus, while fighting the Romans, who had by this time spread their sway towards the south of

Italy, wished also to tackle Carthage, but died too soon. There was no more direct warfare between Carthage and the Greeks.

Meanwhile Rome was rising quickly, and during the second half of the fourth century Carthage found it advisable to make commercial treaties with her in 348 and 306. A further treaty in 279 was a pact against the common enemy Pyrrhus. The eclipse and death of Pyrrhus in 272 left Rome in command of most of the Italian peninsula, including the Greek south. She naturally turned next to Sicily and eight years later in 264 the inevitable conflict with Carthage, basically for possession of that island, broke out. This first Punic war ended in 241 with the Roman naval victory in the battle of the Aegates Islands. Carthage had to accept peace terms which were severe, depriving her of all control in Sicily and imposing a crippling indemnity, spread over twenty years.

Carthaginian sway thenceforward was more confined than ever to north Africa and Spain. But north Africa soon became a trouble spot. Utica and other places wished to throw off the Carthaginian yoke and the Libyans were also disaffected. Carthage made the fatal mistake (no doubt forced on her by the Roman indemnity) of failing to pay her mercenaries and all this led to the Mercenary war, which lasted three and a half years and so weakened Carthage that when it ended in 238 Rome, as the price of staying neutral, obtained the cession of Sardinia and a further money payment.

Carthage's one hope of salvation now was to develop her Spanish empire to redress the balance of her losses elsewhere, and Hamilcar Barca, her foremost general, fresh from his defeat of the mercenaries, had himself chosen for the task. With him in 237 he brought his son Hannibal, then nine years old, after bidding him swear undying hatred of Rome. When Hamilcar was killed in 229 his son-in-law Hasdrubal, who succeeded him, founded Carthago Nova in 228, and in 226 a treaty was made with Rome, who had mineral and other interests in the north-east, making the Ebro the official boundary between the two spheres and thus consolidating the wide conquests the Carthaginian generals had made. Hasdrubal, assassinated in 221, was succeeded by Hannibal, then only twenty-five, but already a man of influence not only with the army in Spain, but even in Carthage itself. It has been suggested that these generals are all (p. 159) depicted on contemporary coins of Carthago Nova [Plate 110,k–m]. If this is true these likenesses would be among the very few Punic portraits known.

Within three years Hannibal picked a quarrel with Rome over Saguntum and the second Punic war had broken out. Hannibal set out for Italy [Fig 15] with a grand army and elephants, marching over the Alps – as is common knowledge – and, though many of his men and nearly all his elephants perished during the rigorous journey, he soon defeated the Roman armies opposed to him, especially at Lake Trasimene (217) and Cannae (216). Roman armies in Spain were also defeated and their generals, the Scipios, slain. It was not until Marcellus took Syracuse (which had sided with Carthage) in 214 that the tide began to turn. The young P. Cornelius Scipio Africanus, appointed by the people to take command in Spain in 210, stormed Carthago Nova in 209 and conquered the whole of Baetica, including Gades, by 206. In 204 he invaded Africa. Hannibal was recalled and the final battle of the war took place at Zama in 202. Of the two chief Libyan rulers Syphax sided with Carthage and Massinissa with Rome. The peace terms were once more severe. Carthage's fleet was burnt, her domain was henceforth to be confined to her *territorium* in eastern Tunisia (p. 63), and Massinissa was confirmed as king of the Numidians with his capital at Cirta (Constantine). The indemnity was again enormous, and worst of all, Carthage must undertake no foreign war without Rome's consent.

We have no certain knowledge of the activities of Carthage during the next fifty years. She cannot, of course, have founded any more colonies, but will have kept contact on a commercial basis with those that existed, particularly westward along the north African coast. Eastward, too, she clearly kept up commercial relations, for she was imbued more and more with Hellenistic art and culture (pp. 152, 195). Agriculture in the fertile Tunisian country prospered, as ancient writers tell us, and her development of farming and arboriculture in all its forms (p. 129) must have been one of the chief planks in her recovery platform. Massinissa, too, whose kingdom prospered

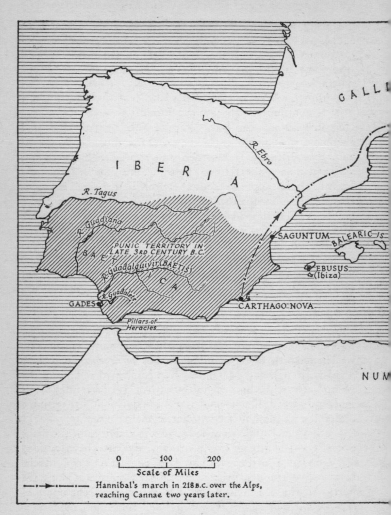

Fig 15 *The Carthaginian* territorium *and empire at the time of the second Punic war*

R.Rhone
R.Isere
GALLIA
PLACENTIA
R.Durance
CISALPINA
R.Ticinus
CREMONA
R.Po
R.Trebia
R.Po
ASSALIA
LIGURIA
ETRURIA
R.Metaurus
L.Trasimene
R.Tiber
CORSICA
ROME
LATIUM CAPUA
CANNAE
CAMPANIA
SARDINIA
TARENTUM
MYLAE
LIPARI.IS.
DREPANUM
PANORMUS
AEGATES.IS.
MESSANA
RHEGIUM
LILYBAEUM
HIMERA
UTICA
ECNOMUS
CARTHAGE
AGRIGENTUM
SYRACUSE
Bône
&COSSYRA
CIRTA
R.Medjerda
CLYPEA
DIA
PUNIC
ZAMA
GOZO
TERRITORIUM
HADRUMETUM
MALTA
Sfax

HAS.

under the new conditions, allowed Punic culture to expand within it, thus laying the foundation of the later prosperity of that part of north Africa.

But Massinissa also nibbled at the Carthaginian domain, under the shelter of the peace treaty. Finally the worm turned. Carthage attacked him in 150 to try to put a stop to his depredations, but was defeated and mulcted of a further indemnity, and – what was worse – Rome declared war upon her in 149 for violating the treaty. The result was inevitable, though her determination and the strength of her defences kept Rome at bay until 146. When she at last fell (the last defenders, along with some Roman deserters, are said to have immolated themselves in the temple of Eshmun), the whole of the city was pillaged and burnt to the ground and the site 'ploughed over' by the victorious Romans commanded by Scipio Aemilianus, the adopted grandson of Scipio Africanus, Hannibal's conqueror. A layer of burning, often many centimetres thick, exists in the port area and at Dermech and elsewhere to testify to the truth of the fire:[72] ploughing up is another matter. It is true that few buildings of any sort at Carthage can be ascribed to the Punic city. But the site cannot have been entirely razed if we take Plutarch's remark[73] about Marius 'sitting amongst the ruins of Carthage' literally, as perhaps we may.

Rome created the Carthaginian territory a province, but not for over a hundred years did a Roman town rise on the ruins of Carthage itself. Until then Roman culture scarcely penetrated into Africa and the Numidian kingdom's long dependence on Carthage and her culture for its advancement ensured that a strong Punic element – henceforth called neo-punic, so far at least as the language was concerned – lived on. Thus when the Roman city did arise it was to a large extent peopled by Africans speaking the neo-punic tongue and worshipping the old Punic deities, Baal-Hammon, Tanit, Eshmun and Melqart, under their Roman names of Saturn, Caelestis, Aesculapius and Hercules.

6 Government, Constitution, Social Structure

Normally the eastern Phoenician cities remained politically independent of each other, each looking after its own immediate interests and having territory round it which formed its 'kingdom'. This territory was usually quite small – no more than the land needed to provide food and raise stock for its inhabitants. No doubt the major cities, and especially Tyre and Sidon, enjoyed some hegemony over others, at least at times. There was never, however, a Phoenician confederacy, still less a Phoenician nation. Herodotus mentions that there were three chief officers in the Phoenician contingent in Xerxes' fleet in 480, Tetramnestos of Sidon, Mattan of Tyre and Marbalos of Aradus.[74] Had there been a real confederacy, all the Phoenician ships would surely have been under one commander-in-chief. This makes it all the more surprising that the Phoenicians succeeded in becoming, commercially at least, a world power. Had they attained political unity as well they might have accomplished greater things at a time when their rivals, the Greeks, were equally disinclined to form themselves into large political groups. The Athenian empire shows what the Greeks could accomplish when united. For the greater part of the fifth century BC it dominated a large part of the eastern and central Mediterranean: Carthage, at the height of her power, showed what the Phoenicians could do in like case.

And yet even Carthage was not imperial in the strict sense. She dominated all other western Phoenician cities by commercial and warlike strength, but so far as we know she did not look upon the other major cities as her possessions, nor were their citizens considered to be her citizens. The Sicilian cities struck their own money even before Carthage herself had coins, and Gades and Ibiza developed mints during the third century

BC, while Carthage was still powerful (p. 159). A Maltese inscription mentions a constitution in that island consisting of suffetes (chief magistrates), senate and people, such as Carthage had also (p. 72), and there is reference to suffetes elsewhere too, e.g. at Tharros and Gades. On the other hand, though these independent cities possessed walls and other basic means of defence, they do not seem to have had their own armies and navies, but (like Motya in 398) trusted normally to Carthage to come quickly to their aid when attacked. It seems that none of them, except, perhaps, Gades, had even a merchant marine of its own capable of standing in rivalry to that of Carthage.[75]

Like all the rest, Carthage herself, at first, had only a small *territorium*. By the fifth century (p. 63) this had been extended to cover a wide area of north-eastern Tunisia, embracing Utica, Hadrumetum and a number of other independent cities [Fig 14]. At some stage this *territorium* was delimited by a great ditch.[76] It is regrettable that the location of this ditch is not known, for the boundary of the *territorium* is historically important since it roughly corresponded with what Carthage was permitted to retain under the peace treaty of 201 (p. 65).

Possession of this territory in itself did not turn Carthage from a city state into a country. But it gave her direct rule over a large expanse of very fertile land and provided her with a source of victuals of all sorts sufficient to keep her from starvation if properly husbanded. Few of the inhabitants of this area, except in the Phoenician cities which it embraced, were full-blooded Phoenicians. The others will have been largely Berbers of indigenous stock, with many slaves (negroes and others) as well.[77]

It was only in Sardinia and Spain, it seems, that Carthage exercised any direct rule outside her north African *territorium*. In Sardinia, while leaving the central massif alone, she annexed as a sort of province the plains of the south and west, bringing Africans in to cultivate them and keeping foreign merchants out. She insisted that the good land should remain under cereal cultivation, but she must also have developed the mineral resources, especially lead and silver.[78] After the first Punic war something similar happened in Spain, as a result of the conquests of Hamilcar Barca, Hasdrubal and Hannibal (p.

64). How far this Spanish domain extended is not known, but it covered a very large area and was ruled from the new capital, Carthago Nova. It paid taxes to Carthage and supplied wartime levies just as the north African *territorium* did.

Elsewhere in the west we should conceive of Carthage's sway being indirect. Yet until her power began to be broken by Rome, her control over the whole of western Phoenicia must have been such that no other city dared to act overtly against her – not even Utica, who, it seems, was always ostensibly independent of her powerful neighbour.[79] But, since it was founded on influence alone and no holding garrisons or other direct forms of control were imposed, the Carthaginian empire had no cohesion and soon disintegrated when evil days befell.

The Semites, once they advanced from patriarchal nomadism to a settled form of urban life, normally adopted a regal form of government. From the el Amarna letters of the fourteenth century BC down to the Assyrian records and beyond we find frequent references to kings in the Phoenician coastal cities. This kingship was hereditary in principle, even if it was not always so in practice, owing to revolution and other upheavals. Dynastic lists – far from complete – can be made out for several cities, and not a few of the kings, such as Hiram the Great of Tyre and his dynasty, Luli of Sidon (and Tyre), and the Tabnit dynasty of Sidon (p. 102 f.), are far more than mere names to us, thanks to some of their own inscriptions and to the Biblical and Assyrian records and classical chroniclers. Elissa, a princess of Ithobaal's royal line at Tyre, must have founded a royal house at Carthage. We have no record of its rulers, but we do know that 'kingship' existed at Carthage long afterwards and many well-known Carthaginians, including members of the Magonid family (p. 61) in the sixth and fifth centuries such as Hamilcar (who commanded the Sicilian expedition in 480) and the explorer Hanno (who may have been Hamilcar's son), are called 'kings' in the ancient texts.

It seems, however, that in all Phoenician cities hereditary royalty ceased at some stage and an oligarchy took its place. Under Persian rule – and perhaps earlier – councils of elders formed of rich merchants, which had no doubt existed before

as advisers of the monarchy, began to attain full power. At
Tyre a dual magistracy arose to undertake executive functions.
This happened at Carthage, too, perhaps in the fifth century,
when the Magonid domination ceased, for Aristotle, writing in
the fourth century, says that the constitutional power rested in
the hands of two magistrates (elected annually perhaps, and
called kings or suffetes), a senate of 300 members appointed for
life, another body of 104 members forming a sort of 'committee
of public safety' (whose relation to the senate is not entirely
clear, but who were – according to Justin, a historian of the
second century AD – the body before which generals had to
answer for their stewardship) and a general assembly of the
people. Writing two hundred years after Aristotle, Polybius
gives a somewhat different account. But it is clear that even in
his day the basic divisions of magistrates, senate and general
assembly still existed. No doubt this constitution was due in
some part to Greek influence, for it greatly resembles the
typical Greek tripartite set-up at Athens and elsewhere, and,
indeed, also the Roman plan of consuls, senate and public
assemblies. The choice of magistrates and entry to the senate
seems to have been largely based on wealth rather than on
hereditary qualifications, at least after the sixth century. Therein
the Carthaginians were true to their Semitic ancestry.

It would seem, indeed, that among the Phoenicians in
general the rich merchant classes normally wielded the real
power in the state. But neither in the east nor in the west do
we hear of much internal unrest and rivalry amongst the citizens of various social grades – not nearly so much as we read of
in Greek states or Rome. In Bronze Age Canaan extant
remains show that there was a great social and economic gulf in
housing and in the general level of living between the upper
and lower classes. We do not know whether such a gulf per-
sisted in the later times which concern us here. If it did, it was
rather between the citizenry and those of subject races, or, still
more, the slaves. The Libyans living in the *territorium* were far
from contented and not infrequently revolted, or lent assistance
to invaders such as Agathocles. They also threw in their lot
with the mercenaries in 241 (p. 64). Yet many of these Libyans
must in time have attained the Punic franchise and it was

these people rather than descendants of full-blooded Phoenicians who kept the Punic language and culture alive in the Numidian kingdom after the fall of Carthage.

But when we speak of full-blooded Phoenicians what do we mean? The Phoenician homeland was a meeting-ground of peoples. The inhabitants of cities such as Tyre and Sidon must have been almost as great an amalgam of races and tongues as can now be seen in one of their descendants, Beirut. The number of languages found on inscriptions in the area, e.g. on tablets from Ugarit, shows this. Thus the Phoenicians who went westward cannot have had xenophobia ingrained in them, and this made them successful in commerce and encouraged men of many nations to settle within their borders. Not only Africans of various kinds, but also Italians and Etruscans, Greeks and maybe even Egyptians came to Carthage to ply their trade or craft. Their presence, and particularly that of the Greeks, had an abiding influence on Punic culture, just as the presence of Egyptians, Syrians and to an even greater degree Mycenaean Greeks had a marked influence on the art and outlook of the people in their motherland. Instances abound of people of pure Phoenician stock marrying foreigners; Hasdrubal and Hannibal, when in Spain, both married native women, and mixed marriages at the highest level with Libyans were common.

7   Religion

Excavations at Ugarit, Byblos and many Palestinian sites have revealed much about early Canaanite religion in all its aspects. We can see it in its sanctuaries and shrines, in its larger temples, and in numerous statuettes, cylinder-seals and other objects of religious scope that have been found.

But beyond all this the paramount new evidence for Canaanite religion comes from the wonderfully revealing series of texts of the fourteenth century BC in a Canaanite tongue written on clay tablets in alphabetic cuneiform script that were found at Ugarit by Claude Schaeffer [Fig 16]. This great archive includes many magical and religious texts dealing, e.g., with fertility cults and the cult of the dead, as well as a number of patriarchal stories, many of which run in parallel with the early Biblical tales and their Sumerian and Babylonian counterparts.[80]

Fig 16 *Cuneiform alphabetic script on a tablet from Ugarit. H. c.0.08 m. Fourteenth century* BC

We learn much of the gods and goddesses of the Canaanite pantheon. There was first El, the supreme god and king, personified at times as a bull. El lived in the west, in the fields of El, and appears, too, as a sun-god. He had a wife, Asherat-of the-sea, conceived of, besides, as the mother-goddess. Their son was Baal, the god of mountains, storms and rain, a god in the prime of life whose statuettes show him horned, brandishing a club and holding a thunderbolt.

One of the tablets gives a most interesting account of the building of a temple to Baal by the gods at the instigation of Asherat-of-the-sea. It describes how Baal felled the cedars for the structure, (Baal)Aliyan[81] made the skylight and Asherat's handmaid fashioned the bricks. We are even told how Asherat collected funds for the work and founded a temple treasury. Schaeffer's excavations at Ugarit revealed a temple dedicated to Baal, which goes back at least to the early second millennium, and was still flourishing when the town fell before the Sea Peoples in the late thirteenth century. This temple, like the similar one near by, dedicated to Dagon, consisted of an outer and an inner shrine preceded by an open court in which was an altar.

The tablets also describe the fertility and chthonic attributes of Baal Aliyan. After struggling with Mot – the summer heat – he descends into the womb of the earth. Anat, his sister and wife, goes wandering to seek him. 'Days followed days,' the text says,[82] 'truly Anat is in love. She is filled with affection. As the heart of an antelope yearns for its fawn and the heart of an ewe for its lamb, so is the heart of Anat.' She finally finds his body in the abode of the dead and carries it up to the heights of Saphon and buries him there with many sacrifices. Then she seeks out Mot and kills him. 'With a sickle she cuts him, with a winnow she winnows him – she scatters his flesh in the field . . .'[83] (an obvious reference to the annual harvest), and then she brings Baal Aliyan back to life and sets him on Mot's throne. The succession of seasons can start again.

Before the discovery of these texts the only ancient evidence for the Phoenician deities and cults came from references in Babylonian, Greek, Egyptian and especially Hebrew literature and from fragments of a work of Philo of Byblos (first century AD) preserved in later writers. Philo's book purported to be a translation of a book by one Sanchoniathon, a Phoenician priest born at Berytus in the eleventh century BC (though modern scholarship does not accept such an early date). This evidence can now be checked, at least in part, by archaeological finds and, more particularly, by the numerous religious inscriptions found during the last century and earlier, which are published in the *Corpus Inscriptionum Semiticarum*. Yet when all these are considered, we know less about Phoenician cults and religious practices than we do about those of most other peoples of antiquity – largely because the Phoenicians' own literature has not been preserved for us.

Another difficulty in assessing Phoenician religion, particularly in the east, is that we cannot always differentiate between true Phoenician elements and borrowings from other cults. The long-standing Egyptian influence – and at times domination – in the Syrian coastal cities brought with it much contact with Egyptian religion. Cult figurines bear Egyptian attributes and dress, and Phoenician deities were equated in the popular belief with their Egyptian counterparts. The Baalat (goddess) of Byblos,[84] for example, was identified with Isis/Hathor. Phoenician religious architecture also borrowed much from Egypt, as we can see clearly from the Egyptian architectural motifs which appear on many Phoenician stelae [Plates, 30, 34; Fig 24], both in the east and in the west.

Similarly, and less surprisingly when we consider the common Semitic origins of the Babylonians and the Canaanites, there is much borrowing – more perhaps in cult practices than in architecture – from Mesopotamia. Cult scenes on seal-stones show this well, as do some details of dress and attributes on statuettes.

From Mycenaean times there must also have been some Aegean element in Phoenician religion, but it was not till much later, in the second half of the first millennium B C, that classical Greek influences began to predominate. From then on cult objects, figurines, architecture and even coffins are mainly Greek in spirit and – no doubt – mainly made by Greek artists. This happens at Carthage, too, from the fourth century onwards, and is an earnest of how all-pervading Greek influence was and how impossible it proved for any nation to withstand its onslaught. Rome itself was to experience the same attack:

> Graecia capta ferum uictorem cepit et artes
> Intulit agresti Latio.[85]

By the time of the Phoenician expansion, then, we can discern not only Canaanite elements in their religion, but also much borrowing from neighbouring cults. Yet the religion remained basically Canaanite in spirit. The Phoenician colonists brought it with them overseas and thus in Carthage, in Motya, in Gades and elsewhere the same gods were worshipped (though not always under the same names) and the same religious practices were performed as were current in the Phoenician homeland. If at times it may seem that the west introduced new ones, it is probably because our information is incomplete. Future discoveries may, indeed, show that a practice, such as infant sacrifice, which is now known to have been widespread in the west (p. 86), was far more current in the mother cities than even the Biblical evidence (ibid.) suggests. It would be surprising if it were otherwise.

THE GODS

In the Ugarit texts the chief god was El, but this name is merely the Semitic word for god, as appears, for example, in the Biblical Elohim (a plural). Other general words were Baal and Baalat, 'lord' and 'lady'; Milk, 'king' or 'ruler'; and Adon (Hebrew Adonai), 'master'. These titles could be used alone or in conjunction with a specific deity's name. Thus the chief god of Tyre, Melqart, who, because of Tyre's supremacy, was also a chief god of the Phoenicians in general, and particularly of Tyre's daughter city, Carthage, was commonly called Baal Melqart. The name Melqart, too, includes the word *milk*, and means 'ruler of the city (*qart* [86])'. Melqart, whom the Greeks assimilated with Heracles, was originally a solar deity, but later – no doubt when the Phoenicians developed their seafaring interests – he acquired marine attributes as well. His importance at Carthage, which for long years sent annual homage and tithes to Melqart's shrine at Tyre, is indicated by the number of names like Hamilcar and Bomilcar that occurred there.

Melqart's cult was also prominent at Gades, where there was a temple to him, founded by Phoenicians from Tyre as early – traditionally – as the twelfth century BC, [87] and his image occurs much later on Gaditan coins. Silius Italicus (a native of Italica, near Seville), in the first century AD, describes this temple at Gades, which 'had remained unimpaired', and was

still served by priests in the ancient Phoenician manner, bare-
foot and clad in linen. There was an ever-burning fire, without
any cult image.[88] Melqart also had a temple near Lixos on the
Atlantic coast.

Just as Tyre had its Melqart, so Sidon had its Eshmun,
assimilated by the Greeks with Asklepios.[89] He was originally
a chthonic deity, but, like Asklepios, he also presided over
health and healing. Now the chthonic fertility and harvest
myth recounted above from the Ugarit texts was current
throughout the Near East. It is known in literature as that of
Venus and Adonis, or, to use the traditional Phoenician names,
Astarte and Eshmun, the same pair in Babylonia appearing as
Ishtar and Tammuz, and in Egypt as Isis and Osiris.

Thus Eshmun was far more than a mere local Sidonian deity.
He later, by all accounts, became a more powerful god at
Carthage than Melqart. It was in his temple in the citadel, or
Byrsa (but probably on the Odeon hill, rather than on the
hill of St Louis, since a dedication to his Roman counterpart
Aesculapius has been found there)[90] that the last act of the
defenders took place in 146 BC (p. 68).

There were other important eastern Phoenician deities.
Resheph [Fig 51] was god of lightning and light, assimilated
with Apollo, but not apparently equivalent to the Syrian Hadad
and Teshub farther north. He, too, was worshipped at Carthage in a temple (of 'Apollo' as ancient texts say) lying between
the ports and Byrsa. Another is Dagon, whose temple (p. 75)
has been found at Ugarit. He was a corn-god and is not to be
identified (as has sometimes been suggested) with the fish-tailed
deity (p. 157) on Aradus coins [Plate 110,c], nor with the
Poseidon to whom Hanno set up a temple far away on the
north African coast (p. 166).

In the west we find another chief god, Baal Hammon [Plate
42]. In Roman days this Carthaginian deity, who occurs in
other western colonies also, was assimilated with Saturn
(Kronos), whose temple at Carthage is mentioned by Hanno
and others. Earlier he may also have been assimilated with
Zeus (father of Heracles/Melqart), for the principal deity
mentioned in connection with Hannibal's oath of undying
enmity to Rome was Zeus, before whose altar the oath was

sworn. Many west Phoenician stelae are dedicated to Baal Hammon and Tanit Pene Baal (p. 110) together, and on them he appears as the lesser deity of the pair. But he also appears alone on stelae, and he had his own sanctuaries as, e.g., on the Djebel Bou Kornein, the mountain which dominated Carthage from across the bay [Plate 5]. He may represent the assimilation of an east Phoenician Baal with an African (Libyan) god akin to Zeus Ammon of Siwa oasis. Gsell[91] explains why, for philological reasons, he cannot just be Ammon transliterated into Phoenician, though like him he was often represented with ram's horns and bearded.

On the female side there was really but one deity throughout Phoenicia, the mother and fertility goddess Astarte (Hebrew, Ashtoreth), known generally in the Punic west as Tanit. Gsell is very certain that the two were identical. Yet it is strange that, despite the prevalence of the name Tanit for the goddess, personal names such as Bodashtart and Abdashtart are frequent and few names bringing in Tanit are known.[92] Equally Tanit does not seem to occur as the name of a goddess in the east, at least at any early date. Astarte as fertility goddess was equated with Ishtar and Aphrodite, but she was more many-sided than that and was also assimilated with Hera, queen of heaven, and with the mother-goddess, Cybele. In Tanit, who came to be identified in Roman days with Juno Caelestis, the queenly and matronly aspects predominated over those of fruitfulness. In inscriptions she is constantly called Tanit Pene Baal (lit. Tanit Face of Baal) and great dispute about this name has arisen. Some believe it means 'reflection' or 'aspect' of Baal, others (though this is unacceptable) take it to be a local name, Tanit of Pene Baal, citing as a parallel the Greek name Prosopon Theou (Face of God) for a cape north of Byblos.

But we are still far from knowing why Astarte in the east became Tanit in the west. The absence of any early eastern evidence for Tanit becomes more remarkable in the light of a stele of *c.* 200 found above a tomb-shaft on the hill of Ste Monique at Carthage, which was erected in honour of 'Astarte and Tanit of Libanon' and mentions sanctuaries dedicated to these two goddesses.[93] Tanit of Libanon ('the white mountain', but not necessarily the Syrian Lebanon) must be a different goddess from Tanit Pene Baal, and Astarte, too, is probably a real transference of the Tyrian deity and not to be equated with Tanit Pene Baal. Other Astartes (e.g. Astarte of Eryx) had shrines at Carthage also. But however they were named and multiplied there was apparently little distinction in essence between such goddesses and we can look upon them all as different manifestations of the main female deity of the Phoenicians.

Tanit Pene Baal was a celestial goddess, perhaps basically lunar. The crescent and disk [Figs 24,f; 25,a,b], which are so frequently seen on many kinds of objects from west Phoenician sites, were probably always meant to indicate this goddess and her consort Baal Hammon. But other symbols are also to be seen on her stelae, notably the upraised right hand, the 'caduceus', and the 'sign of Tanit'. The hand [Fig 25,g] is clearly benedictional and protective and is a symbol which exists today in amuletic form in all Arabic lands, including Tunisia. The caduceus [Fig 25,e,h,n,p,r,t] has nothing in common except the name with the Greek and Roman symbol of Hermes/Mercury, but takes the form of a crescent and disk surmounting a staff, often beribboned. The sign of Tanit [Figs 24,b,f; 25] is an enigmatic symbol, much discussed. Basically it consists of a triangle topped by a disk, from which it is divided by a horizontal arm; but many elaborations of this simple form exist. The cross-arm is not the crescent, which, when present, is normally placed points downward above the disk; but the arm often has upright ends, making the whole symbol very like a stylized human figure. It has been connected by some with the Egyptian *ankh*; but evidence is lacking. The sign is primarily western and does not seem to occur there much, if at all, before the fifth century BC. The much rarer eastern examples of it are all late, and are probably to be explained as western derivatives or imports.[94]

Picard believes we can recognize a great change in Semitic religion at Carthage during the fifth century, in which the eastern pair, Melqart and Astarte, give way before Baal Hammon and Tanit Pene Baal, citing in support dedications to Baal alone which occur on some early stelae.[95] Such a change would indicate a severance of the religious connection with the mother city and the influx of Libyan religious ideas, corresponding in time with an equivalent change in the political alignments within the city. The devotion which the aristocratic Barcid family continued to manifest to Melqart would then be a sign of their religious and political conservatism. But we must not exaggerate these guesses. It is, on the other hand, certain that there was an influx of the Demeter/Kore cult not long after 400 BC. This we know from ancient texts as well as from figurines of these goddesses found in numbers thereafter at Carthage [Fig 65]. Diodorus[96] tells us that the cult was

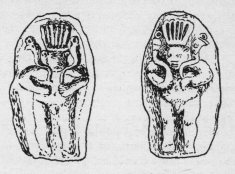

Fig 17 *Terracotta mould for a late Punic Bes figure from Dermech, Carthage, and a modern cast. H. c. 0·06 m.*

introduced to expiate the destruction of a Demeter/Kore sanctuary outside Syracuse by the Carthaginian army in 396. Some think that Demeter and Tanit Pene Baal were equated. But the assimilation of the former with Ceres and the latter with Juno Caelestis in Roman days argues against this, and in any case it seems certain that it was not only Demeter and Kore that were adopted but also their Greek rites. Equally we must not assume that this influx meant any appreciable hellenization of Carthaginian religion in general. We may follow Gsell[97] in rejecting Gauckler's view that there occurred 'a religious revolution which reorientated on a Hellenic pattern the oriental and Semitic traditions of Punic religion'. A much greater upheaval would have been needed for that. But the worship of the two goddesses continued, as is shown, for example, by the fine stele to Persephone in Hellenistic style [Plate 45] dedicated at Carthage by Milkyaton, a suffete (p. 192).

On the basis of theophoric names and much other evidence it would be possible to enquire into the existence of many other deities both in the east and west. But we must content ourselves with those we have been discussing. As always in antiquity local cults abounded. It is proper, however, to draw attention

to the many Egyptian deities represented among the amulets and figurines found on Phoenician sites, though it would be wrong to conclude from their presence that such deities were an integral part of the Phoenician pantheon. There are Hathor-head columns in Phoenician architecture, and Egyptian deities, such as Osiris and Isis, on Carthaginian copper razors [Fig 72] and on many scarabs [Plate 109,c,e,f]. The most frequent of all is Bes, the dwarf demi-god, who seems to have been particularly popular with the Phoenicians. Many tiny Bes amulets came from Egypt, but a mould for a Bes figurine of terracotta [Fig 17] found at the kilns at Dermech (p. 143f.) indicates that such things were also made locally, as is corroborated by a wholly non-Egyptian variety of Bes in clay

Fig 18 *Terracotta figurine of Bes from Tharros, Sardinia. H. 0·10 m. Fifth or fourth century BC*

from Tharros [Fig 18] which must have been made either there or at Carthage.

TEMPLES AND SANCTUARIES

The scanty remains of Phoenician temples that we possess are not very informative. We can get a little help on architectural types from models of shrines and from the coarse limestone stelae [Fig 24] used in Phoenician sanctuaries. We can see something of the façades and plans also, at least in their later guises, from the reverses of some coins of Roman date [Plates 101, 102].

The well-known temples of Byblos and Ugarit are basically

middle Bronze Age and too early to be brought into the present discussion, but valuable evidence of late Bronze Age Canaanite temples of the thirteenth century BC, which must have greatly resembled those of Iron Age Phoenicia, was found at Bethshan, Alalakh and Hazor [Plate 28], and Bethshan has also yielded Iron Age examples. A 'Phoenician' sanctuary of the same type, which was in active use during the fifth and fourth

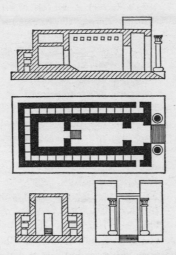

Fig 19 *Reconstruction of Solomon's temple (plan, sections and elevation)*

centuries BC, has recently been found at Tel Makmish in the plain of Sharon.[98] The method of dressing and laying the large stones of the walls of these buildings, together with their general plan, sufficiently indicates Phoenician influence.

The full description in the Bible[99] of Solomon's temple at Jerusalem, which was built by Phoenician workmen, gives some indication of what an important Phoenician temple looked like. Solomon's temple was a triple building [Fig 19] with a holy of holies, a hall, and a porch in front, and it also had side chambers in three stories. In front were two brazen pillars, Jachin and Boaz, either standing free (as some have thought) or forming part of the architectural façade, as Myres has suggested.[100] The temple found in area H at Hazor shows the same triple form with the porch somewhat narrower than the rest [Plate 28]. There were also three wings. Two round pillar-bases of basalt stood in the porch on either side of the entrance to the main hall. [101] This may be compared with a less well-preserved temple of similar plan found by Woolley in thirteenth-century levels at Alalakh, and with a ninth-century temple at Tell Tayanat in Syria, which has the same main structure, but no side chambers. There can be no doubt that

Fig 20 *Phoenician shrine within a* temenos, *Marathus. Sixth or fifth century* BC

similar buildings existed in most, if not all, Phoenician cities. They would usually be surrounded with an open court. The two pillars or columns in front seem to have been normal. Herodotus [102] mentions that the temple of Melqart at Tyre had them, 'one of gold and one of emerald'.

But there were also much smaller shrines enclosed within enceinte walls. One at Marathus of the later sixth or fifth century BC [103] consisted of a little edifice on a high podium about 5 m. square, crowned by an Egyptian cornice and standing on an islet in a sacred lake enclosed by a *temenos*-wall about 50 m. square [Fig 20]. There were similar shrines in Cyprus, e.g. at Paphos, and a terracotta model of one with two lotus-capped columns in front and votaresses at the window is from Idalion [Plate 25]. Late coins, both Cypriote and Phoenician, show elaborate shrines with columnar façades, under which is the cult statue, prominently placed. A coin of Byblos of the third

century AD [Plate 102] shows a precinct approached by steps
with a tall conical betyl (sacred stone) in the centre, and beside
this a gabled shrine with cult statue (?). We may assume that
the shrine was within the precinct, though the artist found it
easier to depict the two side by side. Cypriote coins and a gold
plaque [Plates 100, 101] show that the Paphian sanctuary was
rather different. It has two lesser sanctuaries on either side of
the main one and all three contain conical betyls or other cult
objects; on the side roofs are doves or rosettes; and the main
roof is capped by a crescent and disk. Many stelae found on
western sites take the form of small square or rectangular
shrines with a cult statue or betyl within and they often have
Egyptian architectural details with bands of uraei, etc. [Plates
30, 34; Fig 24]; but architectural remains of shrines in the west
are all late – mostly after the fall of Carthage. One of the earliest
is probably a small distyle-prostyle *naos* at Thuburbo Maius
in the Carthaginian *territorium*, which is believed to belong to
the first half of the second century BC.[104]

The high places so frequently referred to in the Old Testament as Canaanite sanctuaries were different from temples,
being open-air sites centring round altars or betyls. Such high
places must have been frequent in Phoenicia too, and remained
long in use, though, not surprisingly, they have left few recognizable remains. Even in the first century AD Vespasian,[105] in
going to consult the oracle at Mt Carmel, found neither statue
nor temple, but only an open-air altar. Many of these sanctuaries, like this one on Mt Carmel, stood on hills, especially
when dedicated to deities concerned with the weather and
natural phenomena. An example in the west is the famous
sanctuary of Baal Hammon on the Djebel Bou Kornein (p.
79). Here the succeeding Roman sanctuary of Saturn Bal-
caranensis continued to be an open site without any major
buildings. But in the west, in contrast to the east, such sanctuaries were often on low ground by the coast, near the harbours, for the obvious reason that the colonists did not usually
acquire much country, being content with a small area to settle
on and conduct their trade.

Canaanite and Phoenician sanctuaries of this sort usually
had many stelae set up within them. This occurred in a

thirteenth-century sanctuary recently found at Hazor [Plate 29], and, much earlier, in the middle Bronze Age *temenos* at Byblos. There were examples in the west also, such as the neo-punic sanctuary of Saturn at Ain Tounga, and at Carthage itself thousands of stelae, some *in situ* and some in dumps, have been found at Dermech and elsewhere between Byrsa and the sea. Many were set up for themselves alone, others marked the place of burial of objects or of cremated human infants or animals in pots.

This brings us to the last type of sanctuary, the sacrificial precinct, or 'topheth' as the example mentioned in the Bible is called, which stood in the valley of the children of Hinnom outside Jerusalem.[106] Examples have been found at Nora, Sulcis and elsewhere in Sardinia, at Motya, and at several sites in north Africa, notably at Hadrumetum (Sousse), where one in several strata dating from the sixth century BC to Roman times was excavated by Cintas.[107] But the most important of all is the precinct of Tanit at Salammbo, Carthage.[108] Here for the first time sufficient evidence accumulated to show conclusively that the ancient stories of Phoenician and Canaanite infant sacrifice to 'Molech' were only too true, and that the Jerusalem topheth which Josiah defiled while destroying idolatrous practices in Judah was indeed a place where a man 'might make his son or his daughter to pass through the fire to Molech'. It is now clear that other peoples' detestation of the Phoenicians for such a practice was founded on fact.

In this very large precinct (not yet fully excavated) thousands of urns containing the cremated remains of small children, some as much as twelve years old, but mostly under two, and sometimes of birds and small animals as substitute sacrifices, have been found [Plate 58]. This precinct, which lies [Fig 21] only some 50 m. west of the rectangular port (p. 29), lasted throughout the life of the Punic city, and is in three or (as some believe) four strata [Plate 27; Fig 23]. The lowest, lying on bed-rock at and below present water-level [Plate 26], which belongs to the eighth and early seventh centuries, consists of urns of early types, principally burnished red with black linear decoration (p. 140). The urns contained cremated bones of infants and were laid individually on the rock and covered by little cairns

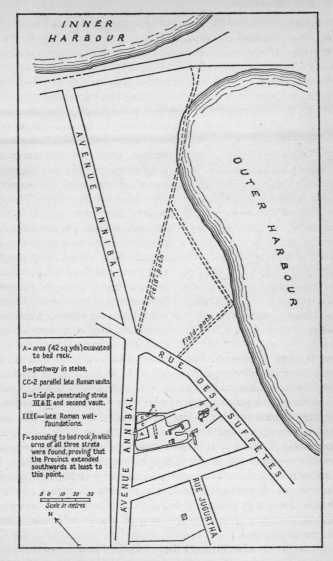

Fig 21 *Site of the precinct of Tanit, Salammbo, Carthage, with excavations up to 1925*

of stones. Occasionally figurines [Fig 22] were placed near by (p. 188). The next stratum, separated from the first by a layer of sticky yellow clay, is wholly different, and on ceramic evidence the change from one to the other occurred during the seventh century. In it the urns are four or five times more numerous, and these – no longer of the red-burnished variety, but plainer and coarser – were laid (p. 192) under coarse lime-stone cippi in the shape of thrones or (later) aedicules, or of simple rectangular gravestones [Plates 30, 33; Fig 24]. Some-times several urns lay under one stele [Plate 27]. These stelae were not usually in-scribed, though an occasional dedication occurs – in one in-stance [Plate 31] a fine-grained limestone inscribed slab record-ing no fewer than seventeen generations of priests of Tanit was let into the front of a coarse limestone stele – but they often bore crude representations of

Fig 22 *Pottery 'feeding'-bottle in the form of a cow, from the lowest stratum in the precinct of Tanit, Carthage. L. 0·15 m. Eighth or early seventh century* BC. (*Hatching indicates red paint*)

betyls or of the sign of Tanit (p. 80) and the like incised or in sunken relief [Plate 33; Fig 24,b,c,f]. At some time during the history of this stratum there was a change to fine-grained hard limestone stelae (p. 193) normally formed like obelisks, roughly shaped on three sides and polished on the fourth, on which side they often bore an inscription, symbols, or other decoration [Plates 32, 35; Figs 25, 28, 67]. This change began about the end of the fifth century, to judge from the pottery, and with it some excavators recognize a new stratum, making four in all. But these burials under hard limestone stelae, though usually at a slightly higher level, were laid in among the earlier types [Plate 27] and no real change in burial level can be recognized.

Near the top of stratum II there occurred in places a layer of burnt debris, ash, etc., though it was neither constant nor uni-formly thick, and did not form a firm dividing-line between this and the next stratum. It may represent the remains of funeral pyres in parts of the precinct temporarily abandoned for burials, rather than a uniform levelling up. Stratum III probably began shortly before the year 300 and represents the last 150 years of the Punic city. It contained smaller urns and

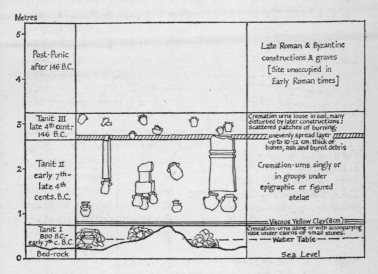

Fig 23 *Schematic chart of stratification in the precinct of Tanit, Carthage*

few stelae, but it was much disturbed by later activity on the site [Fig 23], including Roman vaults for quay-side stores, and, as broken stelae occurred in the debris, many others may have been robbed for building-stone. The precinct remained in use till the fall of Carthage.

The position of this precinct so close to the ports is significant. Cintas, who excavated part of it, found on virgin soil, below urn burials belonging to the lowest stratum, a little building which he believes was the earliest central shrine of the cult [Fig 26], the sailors' chapel of the first colonists, though the objects he found in association with the chapel [Fig 27] are not, as he originally claimed, tenth-century, but belong to the end

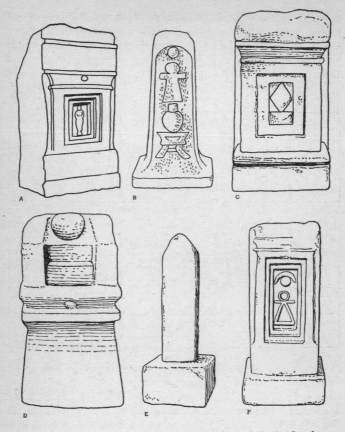

Fig 24,a–f *Six stelae of coarse limestone, precinct of Tanit, Carthage. Seventh to fourth century* BC. *Various scales*

of the ninth century at earliest, and mainly to the second half of the eighth, which must be the date of its deposit.[109]

The long Punic life of this sanctuary is without parallel, as yet. Even the Sousse sanctuary, as we have seen, began later, and other north African sanctuaries, such as those at Bir Bou Knissia, Siagu, Constantine and elsewhere, mostly began

Fig 25 *Twenty stelae of hard, fine-grained limestone, Carthage. Fourth to second century* BC. *Various scales*

during the Punic wars though they often continued (as that at Sousse did) into the neo-punic period. [110]

PRIESTS, OFFICIALS, RITUAL

All these sanctuaries and temples needed priests and other ministrants and officials. Inscriptions mention both priests and

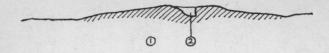

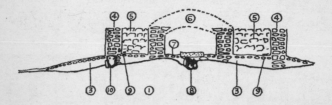

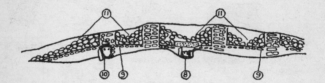

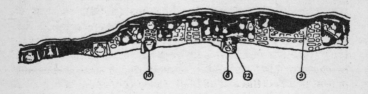

Fig 26 *Schematic sections through the early shrine, precinct of Tanit, Carthage. Second half of eighth century* BC. *1. Bedrock; 2. Natural hollows; 3. Made-up pebbly foundation; 4. Outside walls of shrine; 5. Small court; 6. Central vaulted monument; 7. Pavement of flat stones; 8. Pottery deposit; 9. Offerings (lamps); 10. Foundation deposit; 11. Material from demolished walls; 12. Reuse of chamber*

Fig 27 *Pottery (Punic, Cypriote and Greek) from the early shrine, precinct of Tanit, Carthage. Various scales*

priestesses, and show that at times specific priesthoods remained the perquisite of a particular family for several generations. From Carthage, apart from the stone [Plate 31] which mentions seventeen generations (p. 98), there is an epitaph mentioning five generations buried in one tomb,[111] and we also find priests married to priestesses. The priests were solely religious ministers and were not, as in some countries, *ex officio* magistrates also. Yet at times, it seems, the same person doubled these roles, and Phoenician kings and queens (when and where they existed) had sacerdotal functions. So did aristocratic generals, such as Malchus at Carthage in the sixth century. Picard suggests[112] that the priests, besides having religious duties, were also the main upholders of intellectual life and Phoenician traditions, and that it was through the priesthood that Phoenician customs and language were fostered so long in north Africa. Such a view is quite plausible.

Silius Italicus, speaking about the priest of Melqart at Gades (p. 77 f.), refers to his wearing a cap and being clad in a simple, close-fitting ungirdled tunic. Three limestone stelae from Carthage provide an even better picture. On one a bearded priest with a head-scarf, a stole over his left shoulder, and a transparent linen tunic, holds a *patera* and a flask [Fig 28]; on another a priest with shaven head (this custom is mentioned by Silius Italicus) gives a benediction; on the third a priest in transparent robe carries an infant, perhaps doomed to be sacrificed, in

his left arm [Plate 35]. The priestly figure on the coffin (p. 195) found in a tomb on the hill of Ste Monique also wears headband and stole, but his robe is fuller and seems to show some Greek influence in its cut. The stele of Baalyaton in Copenhagen (p. 184),[113] from Phoenicia, shows a priest similarly dressed [Plate 44]. We may also note the priestess on a coffin lid from Ste Monique, with legs enveloped in birds' wings (p. 195). None of these, however, is early and they mostly do not antedate the third century.

Fig 28 *Stele of limestone showing a priest sacrificing, precinct of Tanit, Carthage. W c. 0·19m. Fourth century* BC

Other officials – scribes, servers, musicians and sacred barbers – are mentioned in inscriptions. The barbers indicate that religious shaving and depilation were part of the ritual, and we shall see (pp. 197 ff.) examples of sacred razors that have been found in Punic tombs. The servers included religious prostitutes, both women and boys. Such a practice was common form in Phoenician sanctuaries [Plate 103], at least in the east. Herodotus[114] records it in Cyprus, and the early fathers have much to say of it in Phoenicia. It also existed in the west, for representations of 'temple boys' occur more than once on Carthage stelae [Fig 25,q].[115]

Phoenician ritual is illustrated by an alabaster statuette from Tutugi (Galera), near Granada in Spain [Plate 73]. From its artistic style it must be eastern of the seventh or sixth century BC, but the tomb in which it was found was perhaps not earlier than the fourth. It represents Astarte seated on a throne flanked by sphinxes. She holds a large bowl outstretched under her breasts, which are pierced. This is clearly a miracle-working statuette, which at an appropriate time in the cult ceremony enabled milk to flow through the breasts into the bowl from a hollow that could be filled through the head. Until the miracle was to happen the holes in the breasts were blocked with wax, or other material, removable by gentle heating.

There is information, too, about sacrificial practices. Many things were sacrificed at times – food and drink, birds and animals, and even humans. Two inscriptions from the Tanit precinct at Carthage expressly mention infant sacrifices.[116] Diodorus' story[117] of the bronze statue into whose hands the victims were placed so that they might fall into the flames, what time the relatives (this is an addition of Minucius Felix and Tertullian) caressed the infants to prevent them crying, is well known, if only through Flaubert's *Salammbô*. It would be nice to think that as time went on the infant sacrifices became rarer and substitutions of small animals and birds[118] were more common, and we may hope that that is what the contents of the Tanit urns will indicate when they have been fully studied. All we can say at present is that bones of birds and small animals do occur in the urns alongside a great predominance of bones of human infants. Adult sacrifices in Phoenician lands were rarer, but history relates some, e.g. the sacrifice of 3,000 prisoners at Himera in 409 to expiate the death of Hamilcar at the battle there in 480 (unless this was merely delayed vengeance), and the immolation annually of one human victim to Melqart at Carthage. Compare, too, the Moabite stone (p. 111), which states that Chemosh killed 7,000 people of Nebo because he 'had devoted it to destruction for Astarte-Chemosh'.

Sacrificial tariffs in Punic exist. There is a fragment of one in the British Museum from Carthage [Plate 25]. That found at Marseilles, referring, however, to the temple of Baal Saphon at Carthage, is the most complete, but is in parallel with fragments found at Carthage. They resemble the Biblical rules in the early chapters of Leviticus, and tell us the varying payments the priests shall get for different sacrifices. The Marseilles text begins:[119] 'Temple of Baal Saphon. Account of the dues which the controllers of dues have fixed . . . for each ox, whether the sacrifice be a sin offering or a peace offering, or a burnt offering the priests shall have 10 pieces of silver for each and for the sin offering in addition a weight of 300 of the flesh . . .' And so it goes on through the smaller animals and fowl, down to oil, fat, and milk. The stelae illustrate these sacrifices, with their designs showing various animals and sacrificial implements.[120]

BURIAL CUSTOMS, TOMBS AND COFFINS

The main Phoenician burial rite was inhumation, but crema- tion occurs, too, for ordinary burials, as well as for the sacri- ficial burials we have been discussing. This custom reached the eastern Mediterranean countries with the barbaric invasions in the twelfth century, and at Hama, Carchemish, Deve Huyuk and elsewhere in Syria and Turkey there are many cremation- cemeteries of various dates between the twelfth and the seventh centuries. On the Palestine coast at Atlit, Ecdippa, er-Regeish and elsewhere there were others of the eighth–seventh cen- turies.[121] Thus we need not be surprised that cremation, as a rite, appears alongside inhumation in seventh-century or earlier interments at Carthage and that at Motya the burials in the early cemetery on the island were predominantly cremations. The custom went into disuse at Atlit, Carthage and Motya in the sixth century at latest, but was reintroduced, no doubt under Greek influence, at Carthage and other western sites, though not apparently in the east, in the third century BC. Even so, inhumation remained predominant at Carthage down to the city's end in 146. Merlin and others suggest that the mixture of rites in early Carthage indicates a mixed origin for the population, and this may be so. The crematers at Atlit and elsewhere in the east may have been non-Semitic newcomers in the Levant[122] who joined in their lot with the Phoenicians and even emigrated westward with them.

Whichever rite he used, the Phoenician liked a good tomb, or at least a cist, coffin or urn, and was not usually content with a mere hollow in the ground. The Phoenician tomb was to some extent influenced by Egyptian patterns. Byblos tombs contemporary with the late twelfth dynasty in Egypt (*c.* 1800) were large chambers cut in the rock 6 m. or more deep, and approached by a sloping *dromos* leading from a vertical access shaft; the chambers contained coffins and funeral offerings. Such were the prototypes of the classic Phoenician tomb. Ahiram's (early tenth century) was not dissimilar, and at Sidon in the Persian period the type continues, only now the

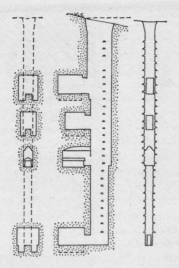

Fig 29 *Vertical sections of a tomb, 20 m. deep, at Carthage. Note the steps cut in the side. Third century* BC

chamber opens directly off the access shaft without an intervening *dromos*, or else the coffin is placed at the bottom of the access shaft itself. Such tombs, too, were normal in the fifth and following centuries in the large cemeteries at Bordj Djedid, Ste Monique, and elsewhere at Carthage. These often were between 20 and 30 m. deep [Fig 29] – a considerable feat of construction, the reason for which is not apparent, unless to prevent tomb-robbing, for there were often not more than two or three chambers leading off the shaft at the bottom. These very deep tombs had vertical shafts with footholds cut in the sides. Shallower tombs often had a staircase in the access shaft, but this could only be when the tomb was rock-cut, providing suitable material for steps, as at Djebel Mlezza on Cape Bon [Figs 30, 31,a,b] .

Built, or semi-built, tombs also occurred. Eshmunazar II at Sidon (pp. 103, 111) had a fairly shallow rock-cut tomb with a

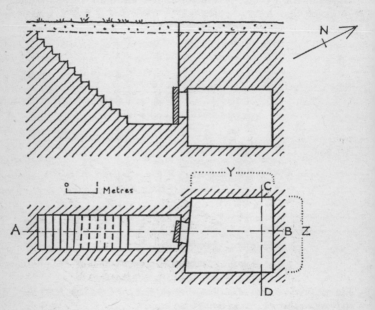

Fig 30 *Plan and section of tomb 8, Djebel Mlezza, Cape Bon. Fourth century* BC

stone-built entrance chamber above ground-level. Many early tombs at Carthage were built chambers set in shallow cuttings in the ground [Fig 32], and the normal Phoenician tomb in Malta has a shallow rock-cut access shaft leading to a chamber closed by a stone slab. Elsewhere, especially if rocky cliffs or headlands were available, tombs were cut high up on the hillside. There are good examples at Cagliari of the fourth century and later [Plate 12], and many instances in north Africa, too,

Fig 31,a *Decoration on west wall (Y in Fig 30), tomb 8, Djebel Mlezza*

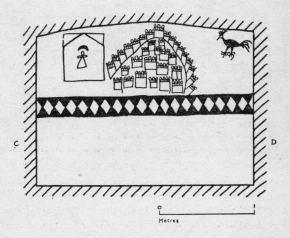

Fig 31,b *Decoration on north wall (Z in Fig 30), tomb 8, Djebel Mlezza*

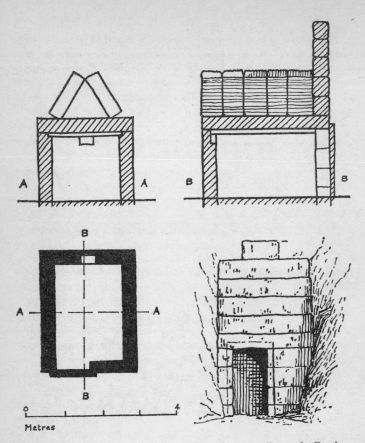

Fig 32 *Plan, sections, and elevation of tomb no. 25, Dermech, Carthage. Seventh century* BC

though not at Carthage itself. At outlying sites tombs are often simple rectangular cists cut in rock outcrops.

But though the Phoenician preferred rock-cut tombs, he also used simple graves at times, especially if rock was not readily available. At Carthage and Utica many of the early burials were of this type, and at Motya, too, where rock tombs were not practicable, inhumation-burials were in shallow graves with coffins – usually monolithic.

It is probable that normally, especially in earlier periods, these tombs were not marked by grave monuments above ground, for fear of tomb-robbers. If they were marked, the monuments were probably of wood or other perishable material, for it is not until later times, and perhaps under the influence of Greek habits, that gravestones begin to occur (p. 194 f.), as in the Ste Monique cemetery at Carthage [Plates 19, 20; Fig 68].

In later years, too, tombs of the monumental type occur in which the chamber, underground and approached by a *dromos*, was surmounted above ground by a funerary monument. In the homeland the best known are three at Marathus, one cylindrical in three stories, another in the form of a slightly tapering cylinder surmounting a four-sided pedestal and topped by a five-sided pyramid, the third also pyramidal at the top, but prismatic below and standing on a pedestal of two steps. The first is the earliest and perhaps belongs to the fifth or fourth century BC, since its architectural details show Persian affinities; the others may be a century or two later.[123] A similar funerary monument exists in the west, the well-known one at Dougga in Tunisia [Plate 116], the inscription from which records in Libyan and Punic that it was the monument of 'Ateban, son of Iepmatath, son of Palu, built by a Punic architect, Abarish son of Abdashtart, and his two assistants, Zamar and Mangi, as well as joiners and smiths. The funerary chamber was in the lowest story, with its entrance on the north side of the monument. This 'Ateban must have been a Numidian king or prince during the late third or earlier second century BC. Massinissa himself seems to have had a similar tomb at Kroubs, near Cirta (Constantine), his capital.[124]

On the east and west walls of the Djebel Mlezza tomb (pp. 98, 123) two two-storied buildings are depicted, each with an altar beside it [Fig 31,a].[125] Are these, as the excavators thought, meant to represent tombs, or are they shrines? It may be that the distinction is not very great, for Phoenician mausolea may normally have been shrines as well.

One would expect Phoenician tombs always to have been outside the inhabited areas, and if so the St Louis and Juno hills at Carthage [Fig 4], which contained some of the earliest tombs (p. 31), cannot have been incorporated in the city area until after the seventh century. Yet the tradition that the hill of St Louis was included in the citadel from early days is very persistent. At Motya the early cemetery on the island may have been outside the original inhabited area, for the enceinte wall, not built before the sixth century, cuts across it. However it may have been in earlier times, it is certain that when the walled area of Carthage occupied most of the isthmus [Fig 3], the tombs were all inside the walls: there was indeed nowhere else for them to go. The earlier cemeteries, too, were forgotten and desecrated by the growth of the commercial quarter. The Motyans, on the other hand, had moved their cemetery to the mainland by the sixth century.

Coffins were used by some, both in east and west, during the whole period we are dealing with. No doubt it was a rich man's habit. Some were plain rectangular monoliths with gabled or flat lids, the gabled type being frequent in the east, the flat more usual in the west, though gables occur on late coffins at Carthage. Monolithic coffins occur in the sixth century at Utica and Carthage, giving way, at Utica at least, to slab-built coffins in the fourth century. Brick-built tombs also have been found at Utica. At Motya monolithic coffins were used for inhumations until the latest period, though cremation cists were often slab-built. Wooden coffins also occurred at times both in the east and in the west. Traces of some were found by Delattre in the cemetery at Ste Monique.

But plain coffins, though common, are of little interest. Richer Phoenicians favoured decorated ones. The earliest with which we need concern ourselves is that of Ahiram [Plates 15, 38], a thirteenth-century coffin reused by him in the tenth century (pp. 107 f., 173). This shows no Egyptian influence in its shape. Anthropoid clay coffins were popular in the Lebanon and Palestinian coastlands at this time and just before, and may have been a Philistine, i.e. Aegean, importation. This type also continued to be used, at times, during the first millennium, even in colonies such as Malta.[126]

After Ahiram there is a gap in our series of decorated coffins in the east until we come to those of Tabnit and his son Eshmunazar II [Plate 16]. These were two kings of a Sidonian dynasty which has been ascribed by scholars either to the sixth century, or to the middle of the fifth, or to 332–280.[127] Both coffins are of black basalt and are wholly Egyptian in style. Tabnit's was reused and still carries the hieroglyphic inscription of its first occupant, as well as Tabnit's own Phoenician inscription. Eshmunazar's was new, perhaps bought in Egypt. Now, Tabnit's coffin was found in a hypogeum which also contained four well-known coffins in Greek style dating from the second half of the fifth century to the last quarter of the fourth (p. 183 f.). We must surely place the two Egyptian coffins earlier than these, i.e., in the second of the above periods at latest, but most probably in the first, and assume that Tabnit and Eshmunazar both ruled in the sixth century BC.[128] The importance of these coffins is that they, or others like them, appear to have set the fashion for a series of anthropoid limestone or marble coffins [Plates 17, 18] that were used in Phoenicia proper and in some of the western colonies, and cover the greater part of the fifth and fourth centuries, to judge from their style (pp. 183, 195). They have been found in considerable numbers at Sidon; others, but fewer, come from Cyprus, Sicily, and Gades. None, curiously enough, is known from Carthage, perhaps because the vogue had gone out before Greek artists were able to ply their trade there after the Sicilian wars. These coffins of Graeco-Egyptian style were in use at the same time as the wholly Greek types from Tabnit's hypogeum.

Though it produced none of these, Carthage has yielded four anthropomorphic coffins of the early third century BC from the Ste Monique cemetery (p. 195). Two show bearded priests in long tunics holding *paterae*; another, even more interesting, shows a female figure, probably a priestess, scarf on head, clad in a flowing *peplos*, flanked by wings of birds (vultures?) which fold over in front of the body. She holds a dove in her right hand and a bowl in her left. Above her head-scarf is a hawk's head, showing Egyptian influence, though the costume and general style is Hellenistic. The meaning of the figure is doubtful. Most see in her a priestess. Picard believes she is a goddess. If she was meant as a representation of the defunct within the coffin, it was wholly idealized, for the bones were those of a toothless old crone with a big, broad nose and jutting jaws, of African, even negroid blood, perhaps. This bird priestess and one of the bearded priests were in the same grave, forming a pair. The fourth of this group is a lady clad like a normal Greek funerary statue of the time. All must be Greek work. To see what native sculpture of the time was like, we look to another coffin from the same Ste Monique cemetery, roughly carved in local limestone with a flat-fronted image of a noble Carthaginian *rab*, Baalshillek, looking for all the world like a medieval monumental brass effigy [Plates 21, 22].

Phoenician interments, like most ancient pagan ones, usually had objects deposited with them. These could be pottery or metal vessels to hold food and drink, small wooden, ivory, or glass containers for perfume, cosmetics and the like, combs, spoons, razors and other implements for toilet or other use, and lamps. There would also have been articles of clothing, or wrappings on the body (though these rarely survive, even in fragments), together with jewellery, hairpins, amulets, beads and other things which the defunct may have been wearing, coins (once minting had begun) and masks and figurines of ritual import. Even the cremation-urns in the Tanit precinct often yielded amulets and small articles of jewellery, as well as the occasional small lamp or pot, and beside the urns were sometimes drinking vessels and other items. The Atlit cremations had numerous objects of these kinds with them, and so had the earlier burials elsewhere, e.g. at Byblos. But the Sidonian coffin burials yielded few accessory objects so far as is recorded, except an occasional ointment vase. At Carthage and other western sites grave-goods were far more frequent. Indeed, almost all the Punic objects in our museums have come from interments and, were it not for the burials, we should know little of the pottery and other things which the Phoenicians used in their day-to-day existence. It is noteworthy that on all Phoenician sites the earlier graves produce more grave-goods than the later ones. At Carthage graves of the seventh and sixth centuries are, in general, richer than those of the fifth and fourth, and when the last years of the Punic city are reached, both the tombs and the Tanit precinct show a comparative barrenness, and almost a lack of interest, it would seem, in spending much money on the dead.

8 Language, Script, Texts

The Phoenicians, wherever they went, held firm to their own language and script, though changes in dialect grew up as time went on in the different regions they occupied. Minor variations in letter forms also arose; though it is perhaps rash to dogmatize too much about the 'newness' of certain forms of letters in monumental inscriptions, since there is so little material to base a judgement on and, in particular, no manuscripts except a few cursive scribbles, chiefly on potsherds. The forms may have existed long before in the written texts. It is plausibly suggested[129] that the forms of neo-punic letters in north Africa from the first century BC onwards are, in part at least, derived from long-established cursive writing, and this may have happened in other instances also.

Curiously enough, the Phoenician language died out sooner in the homeland, where it gave place to Aramaic and Greek during Hellenistic times, than in the western colonies. Neopunic inscriptions occur up to the third century AD and the early fathers, especially St Augustine (p. 20,) indicate that the language survived in their day in north Africa, at least as a patois, beside the official language, Latin, and the inhabitants still thought of themselves as Canaanites.[130] In Sardinia, too, always a backward country, it may have lasted equally long and perhaps also in Malta. In the Acts of the Apostles the people of Malta are called *barbaroi*, that is, they spoke a language which was neither Greek nor Latin and must, therefore, have been a Phoenician dialect; some would, indeed, recognize certain Phoenician elements even in modern Maltese, though that language is usually believed to be based most strongly on Arabic. For business and commerce, however, and for written documents Latin became all-powerful in

Hebrew letter	Hebrew	Phonetic value	Ahiram	Elibaal (Osorkon bust)	Shipitbaal	Mesha	Kara Tepe bilingual	Punic	Neo-punic	Early Greek	Modern Greek	Modern Roman	Greek letter
aleph	א	ʾ	ԟԟ	𐤀	ԟԟ	𐤀	𐤀	𐤀	አ	𐌀	A	A	alpha
beth	ב	b	99	9	ℓ	9	9	9	9	ᗷ	B	B	beta
gimel	ג	g	1	ʌ	ʌ	1	ʌ	ʌ	Λ	Γ	Γ	G	gamma
daleth	ד	d	◁	Δ	◁	Δ	◁	Δ	Δ	Δ	Δ	D	delta
he	ה	h	ヨヨ			ヨ	ヨ	ヨ	Ꙗ	ヨ	E	E	epsilon
waw	ו	w	YY	Y	YY	Y	Y	Y	y	F		V	digamma
zayin	ז	z	I		I	II	I	ᒪ	𐤆	I	Z	Z	zeta
heth	ח	ḥ	𐤇		𐤇	H	𐤇	𐤇	𐤇	𐤇	H	H	eta
teth	ט	ṭ	⊕		Θ	⊗		⊙	⊗	⊗	Θ		theta
yodh	י	y	2	2	2	2	ʒ	ᴧ	ᴧ	𐤉	I	I	iota
kaph	כ	k	Ѡ	Ѡ	ѠѠ	⅄	⅄	⅄	⅄	K	K	K	kappa
lamedh	ל	l	L	L	L	6	C	ᒪ	ᒋ	Λ	Λ	L	lambda
mem	מ	m	𝄞𝄞	ᶘ	𝄞𝄞	⺌	4	4	X	Ɱ	M	M	mu
nun	נ	n	ᔎ	4	4	⅄	ᒕ	ᒕ	𐤍	ᴎ	N	N	nu
samekh	ס	s	∓			𐤎		⅄	ɤ	∓	Ξ		xi
ayin	ע	ʿ	O	O	O	O	O	O	ᴜ	O	O	O	omicron
pe	פ	p	))	)	))	?	?	?	?	ᒋ	Π	P	pi
tsade	צ	ṣ				ᴖ	⅄	𐤑	𐤑	M			
qoph	ק	q			ᑟ	ᑟ	ᑟ	𐤒	𐤒	ᑟ		Q	
resh	ר	r	ᑫ	9	99	ᑫ	ᑫ	ᑫ	ᑫ	ᑭ	P	R	rho
shin	ש	š	W	W	WW	W	W	Ӌ	ᒉ	ⴹ	Σ	S	sigma
tau	ת	t	+x	✗	+x	X	X	𐤕	ᒉ	Τ	Τ	T	tau
Probable dates of inscriptions			early 10th cent.	c.915	end of 10th cent.	c.830	8th cent. B.C.	5th cent. & later	2nd cent. & later	8th cent. B.C.			

Fig 33 *The development of the alphabet from the tenth century* BC

the west in the wake of Rome's political conquests in that area.

What, then, was this Phoenician tongue which had such a long life? It was derived from the old Semitic speech of the Canaanite stock to which the Phoenicians belonged and was very closely allied to the Hebrew spoken by the Israelites and to Moabite, as seen on the Mesha stone (p. 111). The Phoenician and Hebrew scripts, both monumental and cursive, were closely akin and developed along parallel lines [Fig 33]. This family, with Aramaic or Syrian, form the north Semitic group of dialects, as distinct from the east Semitic (Akkadian, i.e. Assyrian and Babylonian) and the south Semitic (Arabian). Between them these Semitic tongues long held a dominant position in nearer Asia. Even when foreign tongues, such as Hittite or Hurrian, arrived before or during the second millennium BC they never ousted Semitic, and the area has retained Semitic speech till today, first in Aramaic and cognate dialects, and later in Arabic.

In the late Bronze Age in the Levant, as the finds at Ras Shamra (Ugarit) have shown, there existed a great variety of languages and scripts. Besides the non-Semitic Egyptian, Hittite, Hurrian and others, there was Aramaic (spoken in the Syrian area) as well as the Canaanite and Akkadian groups. The late Bronze Age levels at Ugarit have yielded tablets written in six different combinations of script and dialect.

The most important and best known of these is Ugaritic, written in alphabetic cuneiform [Fig 16]. It is of great interest to find this Canaanitic dialect being written thus, at a time when the Phoenicians were developing their own alphabetic script,[131] which many scholars now believe was derived from an earlier alphabetic one showing affinities with the Egyptian hieroglyph script used in Sinai in the first half of the second millennium BC for inscriptions in a Canaanite dialect. This script was written vertically. There are some inscriptions found in middle and late Bronze Age levels at Byblos and elsewhere which are possibly intermediate between it and the developed Phoenician alphabet, the earliest example of which may still be the text on Ahiram's coffin [Plates 15, 38; Fig 34]. This Ahiram inscription is now generally agreed to belong to the early tenth century BC, because its letter forms are akin to, but earlier than, those of the Abibaal and Elibaal [Plate 39] inscriptions on statues of Sheshonq I (950–29 BC) and Osorkon I (929–893 BC) of Egypt, both found at Byblos, which belong to the last half of that century; and its archaeological context is now recognized to be compatible with such a date (p. 173).[132] It is true that Dunand and others have dated the Shipitbaal, Azarbaal and Abda inscriptions from Byblos several centuries

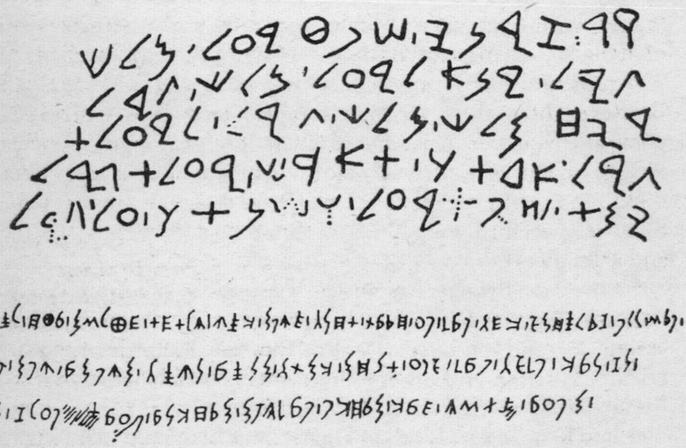

Fig 34 *The Phoenician inscriptions of Shipitbaal (end of tenth century* BC) *and Ahiram (early tenth century* BC)

before this, but Albright has shown that this dating is untenable and that none but the Azarbaal inscription (on a *spatula*) can be earlier than Ahiram, and then only by a few years. The Shipitbaal and Abda texts fall at the end of the tenth century, after Elibaal's.[133]

The Phoenician script in the Ahiram text [Fig 34] shows an alphabet of twenty-two consonants, which, as Contenau says, 'admirably render the sounds of that language'. Vowel letters were never used by the Phoenicians, though the Hebrew language much later developed a system of indicating its vowel sounds, partly by giving a double use to three of its consonants and partly by adding vocal points. The forms of the Phoenician letters were standardized by the ninth century at latest and this standardized form was carried westward by the colonists, thus ensuring that there was virtually no difference in the classic script wherever it occurred.

It was, too, this standardized script which the Greeks adopted and greatly improved, notably by using some of the letter forms for vowel sounds. The earliest extant Greek inscriptions belong to the eighth century and it seems pretty certain that the borrowing took place not long, if at all, after 800, i.e. at the very time when Greece was expanding her commerce eastward and renewing her Levantine contacts. Not long after that the same script was being used in Italy for the Etruscan language and Italic dialects. It is generally held that this arose from re-borrowing from the Cumaean Greeks, and not from direct Phoenician contacts, though objects inscribed in Phoenician, such as the famous silver bowl from Praeneste [Fig 54] inscribed 'Eshmu-

Fig 35 *Gold pendant from Douimes, Carthage, dedicated by Yadamilk, son of Padai. H. 0·015 m. Eighth(?) century* BC

nazar, ben Asto' (p. 180), must have reached Italy not long, if at all, afterwards.

In Cyprus, until recently, the earliest Phoenician inscription was on a bronze bowl which, it says, was dedicated to Baal of Lebanon by a governor of Qartihadashti, servant of Hiram king of the Sidonians. This belongs to the second half of the eighth century (p. 49). But we now have a tomb inscription from the island which is placed in the first half of the ninth century by Honeyman.[134]

The earliest Punic text at Carthage of any consequence – perhaps the earliest of all – is the gold pendant in the Carthage Museum [Fig 35] from a tomb in the Douimes cemetery (p. 204), inscribed 'to Astarte, to Pygmalion, Yadamilk son of Padai. Whom Pygmalion saves is saved.' This is usually ascribed to the seventh or early sixth century BC, but the script suggests that it may be no later than the eighth century.[135] Few inscriptions from that city, however, antedate the later fifth century and most belong to the last two centuries of its existence. At Carthage, through cursive influence, the letters have greater suppleness of form than those in the east, their tails grow longer and they develop thick and thin strokes [Plate 23]. But these are perhaps idiosyncrasies of the monumental letterers rather than of Carthaginian writing in general.

In Sardinia the earliest inscriptions are the Nora stone and two fragments from Bosa. Some ascribe these to the ninth century (pp. 57, 59) and link the script with the ninth-century inscription from Cyprus; and even Rhys Carpenter, who adopts a very short chronology for all the westward expansion, accepts a late eighth-century date.

Modern decipherment of Phoenician took place in the eighteenth century. Some inscriptions from Kition (Larnaka) in Cyprus, brought back to Oxford in the seventeenth century by Canon Pococke, were translated by John Swinton, Keeper of the University Archives, in 1750, in his *Inscriptiones Citieae*. Shortly afterwards the Abbé Barthélemy in Paris published his own results based on coin legends and a bilingual Greek and Punic *cippus* from Malta, which had reached Paris and is now in the Louvre (two were found, the second [Plate 36] being now in the National Museum, Valletta). Were it not for the close connection with Hebrew, so well known from the Bible, decipherment could not have proceeded so fast, for the amount of material available even today is comparatively small.

Most inscriptions, whether eastern or western, are lifeless and stereotyped dedications giving the names of the dedicator and the deity and the reason for the offering, but rarely any other useful details. One example, from Carthage, runs: 'To the Lady Tanit Face of Baal and the Lord Baal Hammon, offering made by Bodashtart son of Hamilcar, son of Abdmelqart, son of Bodashtart, because he heard his prayer.' Another, from Byblos (on the statue of Sheshonq I already mentioned), is no more informative: 'Abibaal, king of Byblos and the Egyptian overlord of Byblos have offered this to the goddess (Baalat) of Byblos and the god (Baal) of Byblos.' We have also the stereotyped sacrificial tariffs (p. 95f.).

In the east, but not as yet in the west, some longer texts occur. Until recently the longest monumental inscription in any North Semitic dialect was Mesha's famous stele in Moabite of *c.* 830, which has been of such help in the study of all these documents.[136] It is in thirty-four lines telling of the wars between Moab and Israel in the time of Omri and Ahab, and is highly reminiscent of the Biblical turn of phrase, thus (ll. 14–18): 'And Chemosh said to me "Go take Nebo from Israel". I went by night and attacked it from daybreak to noon. I took it and killed all: 7,000 men, boys, women, girls and maidservants, because I had devoted it to destruction for Astarte-Chemosh. I carried off thence the [vases?] of Yahweh and dragged them before Chemosh.' The Phoenician inscription on Tabnit's coffin from Sidon is wholly an adjuration not to desecrate his tomb, because it contains no treasure. 'Open not my tomb,' it ends, 'and trouble me not, because to do so is an abomination to Astarte and if you dare to open it and disturb me may you have neither offspring under the sun among the living nor a bed of repose with the shades.' The text on Eshmunazar's coffin [Plate 16] is more interesting. After an even more detailed adjuration against disturbance, he says he was an orphan, son of a widow, and died young, and then tells of his dynasty and of the temples they built to Astarte and others in Sidon, and adds: 'So the lord of kings gave us Dor and Joppa, mighty lands of Dagon which are in the plain of Sharon because of the fine works I accomplished and we added them to the frontiers of the state so that they may belong to Sidon for ever.' This claim to have expanded Sidonian influence southward in the sixth century is very interesting as a contemporary historical document.[137]

In recent years there have been many additions to our Phoenician corpus. Two of the most important are the inscriptions [Plate 37] found in the years 1947 and 1948 at Kara Tepe in the Taurus (p. 54). Apart from their own intrinsic interest they have the added value of being translations of a companion text in Hittite hieroglyphs, towards the decipherment of which they will give great aid. These inscriptions, which are generally believed to belong to the late eighth century,[138] were set up by Asitawandas, king of the Danunians (of Adana), telling of his achievements and execrating his enemies. They are each in three columns of about twenty lines.

Other very important new finds are the three inscriptions on gold plates found at Pyrgi (mod. Santa Severa), one of the harbours of the Etruscan city of Caere (mod. Cervetri), in 1964, one of which is Punic, the other two Etruscan. These record the dedication of a temple or shrine at Pyrgi to the Phoenician goddess Astarte by Tiberie Velianas, the chief magistrate, or ruler, of Pyrgi in the early years of the fifth century BC (p. 155). The text of one of the Etruscan inscriptions, though not an exact 'bilingual', is clearly based on, but a shorter version of, the Punic one. The other Etruscan text stands alone.[139]

But all in all our Phoenician epigraphic material is far from impressive. For the east, we may still hope that when an appropriate site is excavated an archive of clay tablets comparable with those of Canaanitic Ugarit will be found. But in the west we can have scant hope of finding clay tablets or documents or other materials to supplement our meagre inscriptions. We yearn for such things as the original Punic text of Hanno's report of his journey, or of the inscription giving the cost of constructing the temple of Melqart at Gades, which Strabo says was placed on two bronze stelae eight cubits high. There must have been many others, too, and we are fortunate that Hanno's text, at least, has survived in Greek translation (pp. 163 ff.), however garbled.

Yet these 600 Greek words of Hanno, important as they are, form a poor substitute not only for the lost inscriptions, but also for the great library of Punic literature known to have existed at Carthage in 146.[140] The loss of such eastern Phoenician books as existed (and apparently there were at least historical and poetical works, if not other kinds)[141] is remedied in part, now, by Ugarit texts, as well as by Hebrew literature, but there is nothing comparable in the west. All we have from these Punic books are about forty citations from the Latin translation of the twenty-eight books of Mago's agricultural treatise which the Roman Senate had made after the sack of Carthage. These occur in Varro, Columella, Pliny and other writers and deal with agriculture, vines, olives, animal

husbandry and bee-keeping, some at quite considerable
length.

This loss of Phoenician literature means that the Phoenicians
appear before us in a less favourable light than might otherwise
have fallen on them. Were there a Phoenician epic of their
western adventures we might see the Phoenician traffickers to
better advantage than they appear in from the two Homeric
epics and the tradition Herodotus refers to (p. 151 f.). Were
there, equally, a comedy of manners written by a Carthaginian
playwright, the picture of the Punic merchant in the *Poenulus*
of Plautus (pp. 135, 152 f.) would be shown up as the caricature
it undoubtedly is, with nasty jibes at Punic character and
habits:

> Et is omnis linguas scit, sed dissimulat sciens
> Se scire: Poenus plane est: quid uerbis opust?[142]

Such jibes, of course, need not surprise us, whether they be
taken from the Greek original of the late fourth century, or be
Plautine additions dating from the period just after the second
Punic war.

9 Warfare

Circumstances and geography made the Phoenicians sailors rather than soldiers. This may seem a strange statement about the countrymen of Hannibal, but the exception proves the rule, and in any case even Hannibal's armies were not wholly Punic; many Iberians and Libyans served in them, as well as Gauls and Italians.

Eastern Phoenicia lay on the land route between Egypt and the best lands of western Asia [Fig 9], a constant route for conquerors moving in either direction. Thus their cities, as we have noted (pp. 49 ff.), often had to withstand siege, unless they opened their gates without resistance to the conquering general. The cities were fortified, as we see from many Assyrian reliefs, including the pictures of Tyre's battlements on the Balawat gates and on Luli's relief (p. 122) and from coins of Sidon of the early fourth century BC [Plates 48, 51, 110,a; Fig 37]. We get a picture of what a siege of such a place would be like in Ezekiel's [143] prophecy about Nebuchadnezzar's siege of Tyre:

Thus saith the Lord God: Behold I will bring upon Tyre Nebuchadrezzar king of Babylon. . . . He shall slay with the sword thy daughters in the field: and he shall make forts against thee and cast up a mount against thee, and raise up the buckler against thee. And he shall set his battering engines against thy walls, and with his axes he shall break down thy towers. . . . With the hoofs of his horses shall he tread down all thy streets: he shall slay thy people with the sword and the pillars of thy strength shall go down to the ground. And they shall make a spoil of thy riches, and make a prey of thy merchandise: and they shall break down thy walls, and destroy thy pleasant houses: and they shall lay thy stones and thy timber and thy dust in the midst of the waters.

We hear little of any land warfare in which the east Phoenicians were involved or of their organization for such fighting, though there was, for example, the occasion when Shalmaneser III defeated the king of Aradus in a pitched battle (p. 49). We know far more about their fleets. All the major powers with which they had to deal were land powers, and so, when these required fleets of sea-going ships, they were apt to call on the Phoenicians to provide and man a contingent. When Sargon II attacked Cyprus he used them, and Phoenician navies also helped the Persians. Darius had them for his war with the Ionian Greeks and in Xerxes' fleet at Salamis (480 BC) there were 300 Phoenician triremes out of a total of 1,207 (p. 69). The crews wore helmets and linen corslets and carried light shields and javelins. The Phoenician squadron, which was considered the best part of the fleet, fought on the left wing, opposite the Athenians, and as usual acquitted themselves well.

The trireme, used then, was not a new type of warship at the time. It had replaced the older variety of warship, as seen on Luli's relief (pp. 122, 159 f.), which had only two banks of oars, sometime during the seventh century BC. Clement of Alexandria[144] cites a tradition that the Sidonians invented it, and this may well be true: good and telling arguments for its being a Phoenician rather than a Greek invention have recently been put forward by Basch.[145] Pharaoh Necho II was having triremes built in Egypt for his fleet *c.* 600, according to Herodotus,[146] and he must have adopted the type from Phoenicia. It reached Greece sometime during the sixth century.[147] From then onwards the trireme was the normal ship-of-the-line, both of the Greeks and of the Phoenicians, for about 150 years, though the Greek type differed from the Phoenician in shape and many other characteristics, as Basch shows. Then, *c.* 400 BC, the quadrireme, and very shortly afterwards the quinquereme, were invented (p. 160), the first perhaps at Carthage and the second by Dionysius of Syracuse, to outdo his rival Carthage, with whom he was then at war.[148] Thereafter from the later fourth century, the quinquereme remained the crack ship in the navies of the Phoenicians, Greeks and Romans during the whole of the Hellenistic period.

A feature of all warships during the centuries we are speaking of was the beaked prow, for ramming the enemy or breaking his oar-blades by driving past him at close quarters [Plates 51, 110,b]. Some have said that this was a Phoenician invention, but it occurs on ships on Attic geometric vases, and is now generally thought to have descended, both in Phoenicia and in Greece, from Mycenaean models.[149]

East Phoenician harbours were mainly, it would appear, roadsteads. Hiram the Great of Tyre saw that the site of his city on two offshore islands [Fig 2] gave a fine chance to arrange northern and southern roadsteads between them and the mainland to give protection in whatever direction the wind lay – a system which later became the normal Phoenician usage. Only the northern one of these roadsteads still remains to shelter local barques, the southern being silted up by the effect of Alexander's mole. East Phoenicia does not seem to have adopted the 'cothon' or internal dock.

From the detailed accounts of Sicilian and Roman wars in Polybius, Livy and other writers, we know a great deal more about the fighting habits of the western Phoenicians than about those of the eastern cities. Carthage, having a large hinterland, found, as time went on, that her African subjects made good conscript soldiers and she used them to the full, but this also made it necessary for the Carthaginians to adapt themselves to land fighting at times of native unrest. By the time of the sixth-century wars of Malchus and his Magonid successors, Carthage must already have had a potential army both of citizens and subjects that was not untrained in warfare. This, when joined with troops supplied by allied cities in Sicily and by mercenaries (p. 117), made up a formidable force. From the last years of the fifth century until her final defeat Carthage was engaged in frequent fighting; yet she never developed a standing army. Neither was this the practice of the Greeks or Romans at that time, for the Roman permanent legionary forces did not exist before the first century BC.

It is not certain whether Carthage had a cadre of professional officers. Her generals, however, were specifically appointed for the business in hand, and were not, as at Rome normally, the chief magistrates for the year. When they were successful and powerful, as the Barcids were before and during the second Punic war, they retained their commands for many years at a time. This must have given Carthage a great pull over her opponents, and it was usually when those opponents took a leaf out of Carthage's book, and their successful generals remained in command for long periods – as Dionysius of Syracuse, Timoleon and Scipio Africanus did – that they were able to win the day against her.

The use of mercenaries had also come into prominence by the time of Carthage's major wars. It was not a new idea, for they are mentioned in the east long before, and it may be that Ezekiel's words about Tyre in the sixth century, 'Persia and Lud [Lydia] and Put [part of Africa] were in thine army, thy men of war',[150] perhaps indicate mercenary service. But it grew rapidly as a general practice in the fifth century, and Diodorus[151] tells us that Hamilcar had mercenaries from Italy, Gaul and Spain in his army at Himera (480). Later, Greeks themselves fought as mercenaries for Carthage against Greeks, and at times, as, for example, after the capture of Motya, they received short shrift from their Greek captors. Yet the main fighting strength in Punic armies was Carthage's own citizenry and her subject peoples – mainly Libyans and Spaniards; and this is what we might expect. The cost of mercenaries must have been a strong deterrent, and up to the end of the second Punic war, while Carthage had a wide empire to recruit from, she needed them only for major wars. Nor were such men always docile, as she discovered during the Mercenary war (p. 64).

For their main forces in pitched battles the Punic armies used heavy-armed foot-soldiers. In this they followed the fashion of the day – we may compare the Greek hoplite – and the use of mercenaries, many of them Greek, on opposing sides, must have encouraged such uniformity. These troops were armed with the normal sword and spear and carried at first a round shield, later a long one, such as was also adopted by Romans and Gauls about the same time. They wore defensive armour besides. A finely decorated bronze breast- and back-plate found in a wooden chest (p. 131 f.) in a late third-century BC tomb at Ksour-es-Saf in Tunisia[152] is Campanian work and probably belonged to a mercenary from Italy or a Punic veteran of Hannibal's army who acquired it in Campania.

Armies of the time also employed cavalry, slingers, archers and light-armed troops, and in this the Carthaginians were no exception. The Macedonian conquerors, Philip and Alexander, developed the use of Macedonian and Thessalian cavalry, and Carthage, who could draw on the fine Numidian horsemen and, later, on Spanish and Gallic, followed suit. Hannibal's cavalry force when he entered Italy was about one-quarter of his whole army. Up to, but not apparently including, the Punic wars, Carthage used many chariots, and even sent chariot forces overseas to Sicily and elsewhere with her armies. Diodorus[153] tells of up to 2,000 two-horse chariots being used at times, and even if these figures are exaggerated they at least signify that the chariot was a main arm of the Carthaginian forces. They must have brought the practice with them from the east, where chariot fighting was normal. Eastern chariots even down to Seleucid times were sometimes scythed, and it is possible that the Carthaginian ones were so also.[154]

The disuse of the chariot by Carthage seems to correspond in time with the adoption of the elephant as a beast of combat, though it may be that we should not see a direct connection between the introduction of the one and the disuse of the other. Elephants were introduced into Mediterranean warfare after the Greeks met them during Alexander's campaigns in India; and Carthage, having a supply of them ready to hand in north Africa, made them a normal component of her armies from the early third century onwards. She used them in Sicily and Spain, and Hannibal performed the difficult feat of bringing more than thirty of them over the Alps in 218, though all except one died of the winter cold thereafter. Between fifty and a hundred was the usual number for a general to have at his command in a major engagement. That they were a successful arm is certain, and one of the clauses in the peace treaty (201) after Zama was that Carthage must cease even to hunt and capture the north African elephants. In the east, elephants carried fighters in a turreted howdah; in the west, there was only a driver with goad [Plate 110,m]. The elephant carried some body armour and was used to rush and confound the

enemy's ranks. Scipio counteracted this by opening paths
between his ranks, through which the elephants rushed and
did no harm. The beasts were not an unmixed blessing: at
times they panicked and attacked their own side.

In the Mediterranean the art of siege warfare was greatly
developed during the fourth century BC and much of this
development took place in Sicily. But many of the stratagems
which then seemed new in the Mediterranean must have been
long known farther east, where it would have been difficult to
teach the Assyrians much about the normal methods of siege-
warfare – the ram, the attacking mound and tower, and sapping
up to and even under the walls. One weapon, however, the
catapult, may have been invented by or for Dionysius, for
Diodorus says that it was first used by him at Motya in 398. It
discharged bolts or balls a distance of several hundred metres
and its effect was revolutionary. Towns could no longer feel
safe with only one line of wall, but had to have further lines as
well to keep the attackers at *ballista*-length away. Motya with
its single wall hugging the shore was badly caught once
Dionysius had rebuilt the mole joining Motya to the mainland,
so that he could get his siege-engines and *ballistae* within
range, and no doubt other towns were soon in the same trouble.
Carthage in the third century BC profited by this lesson when
she constructed her famous defences across the narrow part of
the isthmus [Fig 3], for these consisted of three parts: a thick
wall with towers at intervals and with casemates for men,
elephants and horses in two stages, an intermediate rampart
(perhaps an earthen bank), and, farther out, a ditch with a
palisade behind. The line of this defence, long sought by
archaeologists, was found on air-photographs in 1949 by
Général Duval (p. 31),[155] whose subsequent excavations
revealed an outer ditch, 20 m. wide, and an inner ditch, 5·3 m.
wide, with lines of post-holes and sleeper gullies for a palisade
in between [Plate 7]. There were also connecting corridors
from front to back at intervals, and some bastions. This
corresponds well with Polybius' description of the outer
works. The line of the main wall, which would have been on
the inside of all this, was not discovered.

Though her navy must have been Carthage's first line of

defence and her shipbuilding was pre-eminent, her fleets in wartime do not seem to have been so all-powerful as we might expect. They were frequently defeated not only by the Greeks, but even by the Romans, who, the story goes, were so unused to sea warfare at the time of the first Punic war that they had to use a captured Punic quinquereme as a model on which to build their new fleet! Knowing that in seamanship they could not match their foes, they also invented the device of a grappling-plank to enable them to seize and board the Punic ships. With its aid they succeeded in winning the battle of Mylae (260), the first major sea engagement in the war, and three others, including the last, that of the Aegates Islands (241). The Carthaginians still relied on the old method of ramming the opposing ship or, by passing at close quarters, shattering the oars on one side. Their rowers were mainly Carthaginian citizens and their prowess is vouched for many times by ancient writers. In the Sicilian wars the fleets were usually between 100 and 200 strong, in the first Punic war they tended to run to over 200, but there would always have been smaller ships also, as well as triremes or quinqueremes.

The circular port at Carthage had 220 docks of which 160–70 would take quinqueremes. It is difficult to see how, on the basis of the present topography [Plate 5] around the circular lagoon (p. 29), an emplacement large enough to take so many could be constructed, even if some of the berths were dry. But the ancient testimony is not to be lightly discarded, and it may be that reconstruction of the area in Roman times has obliterated the topographical indications which would explain the mystery. At Motya, west of the south gate, Whitaker excavated a rectangular basin which he identified as a cothon. It is a small basin, 51 by 35·5 m., with a channel, 7 m. wide at its narrowest point, leading to the sea [Fig 36]. Whatever this basin was in its present form, it cannot have been a cothon, for recent excavations by Isserlin[156] have revealed that it is a secondary feature; its south wall is, indeed, continuous, providing no access from the sea. Its date is still uncertain, but it probably existed before the fall of the city in 398. However, there is evidence that some, at least, of the walling of this basin, especially in the S.W. corner, is founded on earlier masonry. Besides, clearance of the southern part of the channel leading from the sea revealed that it possessed side walls and paving of fine ashlar dating from the late sixth century BC, the paving having a wide groove down the middle, which would

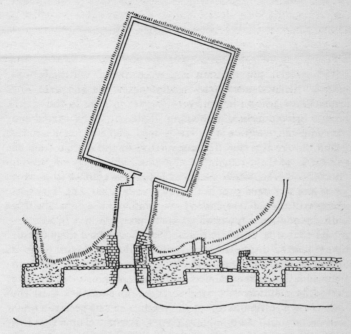

Fig 36 *The rectangular basin and south gateway, Motya, after Whitaker, 1921. L. of basin 0·51 m.*

take a ship's keel; and since the channel continues northward, but without side walls of stone, and splays out on the east side, there may well have been an early cothon on the site of the basin. If so, it was abandoned later, since the paved part of the channel was found to have been effectively blocked against the passage of ships by a secondary cross wall resting on a layer of silted mud.[157]

All Phoenician towns of any size were walled. On the bronze
gates of Balawat set up by Shalmaneser III (859–24) one
scene shows tribute-bearers crossing from Tyre to the mainland to bring offerings to the king [Plate 48]. The turreted and
battlemented enceinte of Tyre is well depicted on its rocky
island. There is a slightly later picture of the Tyrian walls in
the scene of Luli's flight in the Nineveh reliefs of Sennacherib (705–681), where Luli and his family embark from what
looks like a postern gate in the town wall [Plate 51]. The per-
spective of the artist seems to have conflated the houses within
with the one-story town wall, which has what look like battlements at that level, while the houses above show their double
doors flanked by pilasters. Another illustration of what is
almost certainly a Phoenician city on one of the same series of
Sennacherib's reliefs depicts independent houses of various
designs, usually of two stories, the upper smaller than the
lower [Fig 37]. At the top of the picture can be seen the town
wall or the wall of a temple precinct. Barnett claims that this
depicts one of the Phoenician cities taken by Sennacherib in his
third campaign, and he rightly sees in these upper stories with
their small square window-openings with balustrades supported on miniature palm columns the typical Phoenician
'upper window'. Such are often mentioned in the Bible, as
when Sisera's mother looks out for Sisera or Jezebel watches
Jehu,[158] and they are also depicted in the 'woman at the
window' ivories (p. 176) from Calah (Nimrud) and Arslan
Tash, which represent a cult-scene of Astarte worship, the
woman being a prostitute votaress [Plate 62]. Evidence for
another type of multi-story building is to be seen in a fragmentary model tower from Carthage [Plate 24], the extant

part of which shows three stories, and there may originally have been more. Whether this model represents a light-house or a watch-tower who can now say? The walls of Sidon with towers and battlements that are only, it seems, one story high occur [Plate 110,a] on early fourth-century coins of that city (p. 157).

Normally Phoenician towns were not large, and their houses, therefore, tended to be crowded together and of more than one story. Strabo[159] says that those at Tyre and Aradus had many stories and the Tyrian ones were higher than houses in Rome itself. Appian[160] gives no fewer than six stories to the houses in the narrow streets between the forum and Byrsa at Carthage. But elsewhere the two-story house survived in the west, as we can see from the most interesting tomb-painting of the fourth century discovered at Djebel Mlezza on the peninsula of Cape Bon. Apart from shrines or tombs (p. 101) the painting depicts a town with battlemented walls and within it seventeen two-storied houses of different sizes [Fig 31,b]. Allowing for the roughness of the drawing as compared with the fine carving of Sennacherib's artist, there is a remarkable similarity between the architecture they each depict, and we may accept the style as that of a normal Phoenician town house.

Excavations have not as yet been very helpful in supplementing the monumental evidence. The house which Whitaker excavated at Motya (p. 34) was well built and well laid-out with workshops and storerooms attached, but it had pebble mosaics of Greek style and workmanship, and the building was probably more Greek than Phoenician in outlook. The designs of the mosaics, however, with their animals in combat, show oriental influence, and the house probably belonged to a Phoenician.

On the peninsula of Cape Bon some houses have been found in a small town of the third to the second century BC at Dar Essafi (Kerkouane), near the cape,[161] where the inhabitants were clearly fishermen and purple dyers (p. 135). One had a small bathroom with a tub containing a seat [Plate 10]. Elsewhere on the site there was a well-preserved bath with a carefully planned drainage system. The rooms had pavements of pink cement set with little marble cubes, a type which occurs

Fig 37 *Relief from the palace of Sennacherib (705–681 BC) at Nineveh depicting the sack of a Phoenician town*

in many places in the Mediterranean at this period and preceded the normal mosaic floor which developed in the late Hellenistic period [162] and has remained in currency ever since. These houses had blank exterior walls and looked inward towards a small courtyard – a type which was well suited for the Tunisian countryside and did not die out with the Punic period.

Some late Punic houses have recently been found at Carthage itself, especially on the south slope of Byrsa [Plate 9], where remains of a number built in square *insulae* with straight, well-drained streets turned up, 3 or 4 m. below Roman levels. [163] The plans are simple with groups of rectangular

rooms without architectural pretensions. The walls, which still stand at times a metre or more high, were of brick or clay on a substructure of stone and were coated with pitch for weather-proofing. Sometimes stone orthostats were set among the bricks or clay for strength, and elsewhere rubble was used in place of brick. Walls were often covered with stucco, as Punic constructions frequently were.

Phoenician water-supply was based almost wholly on cisterns, though we have seen (p. 31) that Carthage had at least one major spring, the 'Fountain of a thousand amphorae' [Plate 8]. In the Canaanite east at the beginning of the Early Iron Age a new system of lining storage cisterns with impermeable lime-plaster was developed which at last made it possible to store good rainwater for long periods, so that settlers were no longer obliged to seek sites near springs or streams. This system was no doubt brought westward by the colonists. Later, perhaps by borrowing from the Greeks, an even better material, a true cement, was evolved, and many cisterns with such lining exist from the later years of Punic Carthage.

The Bible and archaeology combine to show that the Canaanites, like all the Semites, were basically tillers of the soil and
herdsmen. The Ugaritic religious texts, with their emphasis
on the seasonal cycle, confirm this. When, however, these
Canaanites settled on the sea-coast they naturally took to
fishing, and the proximity of the Lebanon forests, whose wood
made such fine ships, led to the initiation of trade between
Byblos and Egypt in Giblite bottoms. The narrowness of the
coastal strip of cultivable land made it necessary to supplement
native resources by imports, such as livestock and corn, which
they could get from Egypt and perhaps from Mesopotamia
also. Even in Palestine, where the cultivable land was much
wider in extent, such imports were needed, as we see from the
patriarchal stories.

The Phoenicians, energetic as they were, and with a good
bent for money-making, soon learnt to develop industries of
their own, based at first on the raw materials which their land
and coastal waters provided, but later on imported raw
materials as well. In this way they fostered their joinery and
their skill at building in wood and stone, of which, for example,
the Hebrew monarchy made such good use. They became
renowned, too, for textile working, using the products of their
own flocks and crops, helped out by further supplies of flax
and cotton from Egypt and wool from the Mesopotamian
uplands. These textiles they coloured with their far-famed
purple dyes, derived from murex shell-fish (p. 135 f.). Among
imported raw materials they used ivory, metals and semi-
precious stones for the jewellery, trinkets and works of art
which they traded far and wide.

They brought this mixed economy of industry and trading

with them overseas and developed it in their western settlements as the years passed. It is, however, only in north Africa
that we can judge of its success, for we know little as yet of the
economic background of the other western settlements.

The Tunisian hinterland near Carthage possesses some of
the richest agricultural land in the Mediterranean, which
became one of the chief granaries of Rome in imperial days. It
is not surprising, therefore, that, as Carthage's dominance over
these rich areas grew, the inherited agricultural and stock-
breeding skill of her people should have blossomed forth once
more, so that her farming was outstanding and she produced
experts, such as Mago,[164] whose handbook on husbandry and
agriculture was used and cited in translation by Roman writers
such as Varro and Columella (p. 112 f.).

Industries must have grown up rapidly at Carthage. Shipbuilding was essential to provide ships to control her empire
and keep trade moving. So, too, for such a large city, was
building in wood and stone, and of smaller industries there
were potting, metal-working, and no doubt much textile-
making as well, though on this we are less well informed.

Even the Punic wars will not have affected their industrial
activities overmuch. Ancient historians indicate more than once
that the Punic bent was peaceful, and that they were only too
happy to apply themselves to industry and trade. Though good
fighters when pressed, they made (p. 117 f.) much use of sub-
ject-peoples, allies and mercenaries to fight their battles for
them.

AGRICULTURE

The earliest and most widespread Phoenician industry was,
as we have seen, agriculture and husbandry. In the east their
agricultural practice differed little, if at all, from that eastern
norm which scarcely changed in that part of the world until
mechanization arrived in quite recent times. Sources indicate
that they not only raised stock and grew edible crops and fruit,
but also cultivated flax for linen, so far as their exiguous
terrain permitted.

For Carthage the forty or so extracts we have from Mago's

lost treatise (p. 112) cover all types of husbandry and agriculture – cereals, vines, olives, stock-raising, apiculture. His
treatise could not have been written if Punic farming had not
been carefully systematized. Diodorus [165] shows that it was so
by the late fourth century, when he records that Agathocles'
troops, landing on the Cape Bon peninsula, found the countryside full of fine rural dwellings and largely given over to stock-
raising and the cultivation of vines and olives. The main
regions where cereals were grown were the Bagradas valley and
central Tunisia. The scope of their production is seen when we
recall that Scipio, campaigning in that very region, demanded,
as part of a proposed peace treaty between Rome and Carthage
in 203, a contribution of half a million bushels of corn and
300,000 of barley, [166] and that similar figures are cited as
Carthaginian contributions at other times.

Punic stelae show the type of plough that was in fashion
[Fig 25,l], which was ox-drawn, according to Mago, and closely
resembled the modern Berber plough, and also, from what
we know of it, the ancient plough in Israel. The grain, when
harvested, was stored in sealed silos, usually underground for
safety and to keep it in good condition. Such underground
silos still exist in Mediterranean countries like Malta.

Second only to cereals in the Phoenician agricultural
economy were the vine, the olive, the fig and the date-palm.
We have seen already that the date-palm, φοῖνιξ, bore the
same Greek name as the Phoenicians themselves. Carthage and
other towns used it as a badge on their coins [Plate 110,f, h, l],
and it appears, too, on many Carthage stelae, one of which
depicts two men perched at the top of the trunk of a date-palm
and another shows a monkey (or a man, but note the long tail)
similarly placed [Fig 25,o,p]: on both the palms are in fruit
and the scenes may therefore represent the date harvest,
though Gsell believes they represent the process of polleniz-
ing. [167] A similar scene occurs in miniature on a scarab from
Douimes [Fig 38]. Mago had much to say about vine and olive
culture and Columella cites a recipe of his for a wine, called in
Latin *passum*, of a type still used in Morocco. There is no
doubt that wine was a staple of Punic economy. We should
note also that the pomegranate, which was very much beloved

Fig 38 *Faience scarab with monkeys climbing a palm-tree, Douimes, Carthage. L. 0·018 m. Seventh or sixth century* BC

in the east and became an attribute of Aphrodite of Paphos, etc., was also very popular at Carthage. In fact the Romans called it *malum punicum* and it appears frequently on stelae.

The main stock, both in the east and west, was cattle, but the ass (for traction and burden) and the sheep and goat were common too. Mago, cited by Columella, gives an interesting description of a good Punic cow:

It should be young, thickset, with big limbs, long horns, blackish and strong, a broad wrinkled brow, shaggy ears, black eyes and lips, open, curled-back nostrils, long muscular nape, ample dewlap reaching almost to the knees, broad breast, huge shoulders, large belly like that of a beast with young, long flanks, large loins, straight back (flat or a little depressed), round rump, thick, straight legs, short rather than long, well-shaped knees, large hooves, very long and bristly tail, close and short body-hair, red or brown in colour and soft to the touch.[168]

The horse, as is well known, reached the Levant from central Asia during the second millennium BC, but the ancients kept it for hunting and war and did not employ it as a draught animal on the farm. Fowls and even ostriches were cultivated, the latter partly for their eggs, the shells of which were made into bowls, etc., and decorated (p. 201 f.) and are commonly found on Punic sites [Plate 52; Fig 77]. Bee-keeping was of necessity a prominent activity in ancient countries, for the honey was the main ancient source of sugar and the wax was needed for many things, including medicine. The Punic variety of wax, *cera punica*, was specially famous, as is indicated by Pliny and other ancient writers.

FORESTRY AND WOODWORKING

The world-wide fame of the cedars of Lebanon in antiquity is well known [Plate 1]. It is less frequently realized, though there is plenty of ancient evidence for it, that other trees, such as the fir, which would provide a better wood for many purposes, also abounded there. The possession of these at their doorstep naturally led the eastern Phoenicians to be experts in every kind of woodwork. The western colonists, wherever they had forests available, were no doubt equally ready to utilize them, but Carthage itself was not too well placed in this respect, for, though parts of her hinterland were wooded, her nearest large forests were in the Aures mountains and farther south, in regions over which she had no direct control, even at the height of her power.

Timber was much used in architecture, though the Phoenicians did not usually build their large buildings wholly in wood. The later houses, as we have seen (p. 124 f.), were normally of brick, stone or clay, though those of several stories, such as the ones the Roman troops encountered in Carthage in 146 BC, may have had upper stories of wood. There is, however, no doubt that wood was much used for internal furnishing of buildings. The inner sanctuary, for example, of Solomon's temple was panelled with cedars from floor to ceiling and its ceiling was of cedar beams and planks forming recessed panels.

It is unfortunate that remains of Phoenician cabinet-making are of necessity so rarely preserved. In east Phoenicia wooden coffins were used at times from the twelfth dynasty onwards, and when, as so often, bronze handles affixed to repoussé lion's-head plates are found in Hellenistic tombs in that area, they indicate that a wooden coffin has perished. It is also clear that many of the stone coffins were modelled on wooden originals.

It may be that some of the wooden coffins found in Egypt, especially in lower Egypt, where Phoenician settlements existed in several towns, were made by Phoenician woodworkers, and there are several chests from north African sites which must illustrate the work of a Punic craftsman. One was found in the tomb of the late third century BC at Ksour-es-Saf near Mahdia,

Fig 39 *Limestone models of furniture from tombs, Douimes, Carthage. H. (a) 0·049, (b) 0·022, (c) 0·09, (d) 0·074 m. Seventh and sixth centuries* BC

which also contained the bronze cuirass of Campanian work-manship (p. 117 f.).[169] The wood is said to be cedar or cypress and the coffer is made of planks fitted together with wooden dowels, as normally in Egypt. Other such wooden chests were found at Thapsus and Gighti. Wooden furniture existed in plenty in Phoenicia and much of it was decorated with ivory finials and panels.[170] We may note the chairs or couches which

Assyrian soldiers are removing from a Phoenician city in one
of the sculptured panels found at Nineveh [Fig 37]. Punic
wooden furniture is illustrated occasionally on stelae and also
by stone models of chairs, tables and stools found in tombs
of the seventh and sixth centuries at Carthage [Fig 39].
Some of these are exactly comparable with stools or seats on the
Nimrud ivories,[171] so the types seem to have been brought
from the east. Sculpture in wood, too, was practised, but little
remains, though Picard mentions a fine, unpublished head of
Demeter in the National Museum, Tunis, which was found
under the temple of Demeter on Ste Monique hill, Carthage.[172]

Among the tools that appear on stelae at Carthage some, at
least, may be woodworkers' tools, though Gsell and others[173]
seem too quick to ascribe tools to woodworking which could
belong to another trade, e.g. that of the smith or mason.

STONE-WORKING AND QUARRYING

The Phoenicians, everywhere, were practised stonemasons,
adept at shaping and finishing their building stones for erecting
fine ashlar walls; indeed, in planting new settlements, they
always sought the proximity of good stone outcrops for quarrying. Mostly the stone used was coarse shelly limestone or
sandstone. Earlier buildings and walls, even when made of
squared ashlar work, tended to consist of large blocks of uneven
sizes [Plate 14]: later, perhaps under Greek influence, especially in the west, they developed a much more even walling of
squared blocks, sometimes plain, sometimes chamfered and
rusticated [Plate 13]. Such blocks, however, were often, as in
the sea-wall at Carthage, only the facing for a rubble core.
Stones for ashlar work were well fashioned and jointing was
careful, so that the stones bedded well together and mortar was
unnecessary, but occasional use of a lime mortar in thin layers,
or, at Carthage, of a clay filling, occurred. Building as they did
in coarse stone, they usually faced it with white stucco, capable
at need of taking a painted decoration. Coarse limestone stelae
in the Tanit precinct were also sometimes stuccoed.

Stone coffins, which occur on most Phoenician sites (for the various types, see pp. 102 ff.), show the Phoenicians' skill as masons. At Utica, for example, plain monolithic lidded coffins, fashioned with the utmost regularity and accuracy, so filled the tomb that the lids had to be lowered on ropes for which the necessary grooves were left at two corners and along one side of the lid. Decorated sarcophagi, which were also frequent, are discussed below (pp. 173, 183 f., 195 f.).

Stone was quarried wherever it occurred. The Phoenician habit of using rock-cut tombs no doubt provided the masons with much of the stone they needed, but large quarries unconnected with any cemetery also exist. Picard says that one at Cape Bon may be compared with the well-known *latomiae* at Syracuse. It was underground with entrances on the seashore to facilitate shipment of the blocks across the bay to Carthage.

TEXTILES AND DYEING

We cannot be very precise about the textiles the Phoenicians made, for no fragments of any consequence have survived on any Phoenician site, nor is there anything surely Phoenician even from Egypt, where textiles have been found in quantity. But Egyptian tomb-paintings and faience tiles depict Asiatics of Semitic type (not necessarily Phoenicians, of course) wearing long, flowing or closely wrapped woollen robes of many colours, often with sashes [Plates 59, 60], and, since sculptured representations show that the Phoenician normal garb was just this, it is not out of place to recall these representations here. The Balawat gates, however [Plate 48], depict Phoenicians wearing long, close-fitting garments and pointed caps, while in the Luli relief the figure in front of the city gate is clad in a knee-length tunic [Plate 51]. All appear to wear short, trimmed beards. No doubt, as so often in ancient and modern times, people discarded long robes, or held them up with a girdle, if intending to indulge in something specially active.

The polychrome robes 'of the Sidonians' are noticed more than once in Homer, and we may point, too, to Joseph's coat of many colours, though that belonged to an earlier epoch. Indeed, as Contenau remarks,[174] an Egyptian crowd, with its light, pleated and starched white garments, looks very different from a group of Phoenicians, who preferred elaborate garb, with much colour and embroidery, more like that of the Assyrians. The priestly dress of Phoenicia, however, was often more Egyptian in style.

. At Carthage the eastern fashion in dress seems to have survived with little change, although, if we can believe the later sculptures and terracottas, some Greek fashions appeared there in Hellenistic times. But the Carthaginians' devotion to the traditional dress was strong enough to cause remark amongst the Greeks and Romans, as in Plautus (pp. 113, 152 f.), where Milphio says of the Carthaginian Hanno:

> Sed quae illaec auis est quae huc cum tunicis aduenit?
> Numnam in balineis circumductust pallio?[175]

and later addresses him as 'tu qui zonam non habes'.[176] What is certain, from the few illustrations we possess, is that the normal Carthaginian dress was plain and simple and, though the women took to the Greek peplos and girdle, the men were on the whole not inclined to copy Greek modes.

Spinning and weaving implements are found occasionally in tombs and there are stray references in ancient authors to textile-making, as when Diodorus[177] mentions the linen cloths (ὀθόνια) of Malta, which were used for garments, caps and cushions of special fineness and softness. Mostly, the spinning and weaving will have been a home industry, not openly commercialized, though some householders must have used slaves to do it on an organized scale.

The dyeing industry was diffused far and wide throughout Phoenician lands. Tyre and Sidon themselves were noted centres, and it seems that the Phoenicians had the monopoly of it in the east and that the murex from which the dye was made [Fig 40] is now virtually extinct there because they exploited it so much. Heaps of the shells exist in the west, too, to testify to the existence of the industry. Some of them, at least, date from Phoenician times, being found at sites such as Dar Essafi (p. 123), which ceased to be occupied in the second century BC. The shell heaps and rock-cut vats and the general situation indicate that the town was devoted to fishing and dye-extraction. The murex, when it is dead and putrefied, secretes a yellowish liquid which provides – according to the strength used – tones ranging from rose to dark violet; for the darker tones exposure to the sun is necessary. The method was to break the shell, extract the fish and deposit it in the vats, where the dye liquefied out. Shell heaps and vats exist also near Tyre and Sidon. It was best to have the 'factory' on the lee side of the town, as the odour was not pleasant.[178]

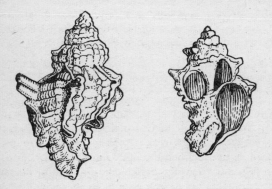

Fig 40 Murex trunculus, *one of the two common forms of murex in the Mediterranean*

METAL-WORKING

Regular use of iron began in the Levant about 1200, just when the Phoenicians were developing their independence. In Saul's time the Philistines had iron, the Israelites had none,[179] and we may be sure that if the Philistines had it, so had the Phoenicians. It was, however, for their work in copper and bronze and the precious metals that the Phoenicians were renowned. Copper they could obtain from Cyprus, which produced it prolifically in antiquity, and whence copper ingots shaped like hides were widely exported in the Bronze Age;[180] they also got it from Asiatic sources. Silver and gold came from Ethiopia and maybe from Asia Minor. But the demand for all these metals and for tin, to make bronze, was great, and so, when supplies were known to be available in the far west and also east of the

Red Sea, Phoenician mariners were encouraged to seek them. The Wadi Arabah, between the Dead Sea and the Gulf of Aqabah, also contains deposits of copper, which were exploited from time to time from the Chalcolithic period onwards. Rothenberg's recent excavations at 'Solomon's Pillars' (site no. 200) in the Timna valley, 20–30 km. north of Eilat, have revealed Egyptian temples of Sethos I (1318–04 BC) and Ramesses III (1198–66 BC), one over the other, with Chalcolithic structures underneath and a Byzantine casting installation above them. Previously he had explored, and partly excavated, numerous copper-mining and smelting sites in the Timna area, which, in 1962, he confidently believed were Solomonic.[181] Following his discovery of the Egyptian temples he now equally firmly believes that it was the Egyptian founders of the temples who were responsible for the copper installations and that there is no longer any evidence for copper-working in the area in Solomon's time or for some centuries thereafter.[182]

No remains of metal-working seem to be recorded from any Phoenician site,[182a] but this is clearly due to chance, for smelters of iron and copper are mentioned on funerary stelae and hammers and tongs and other metal-working tools are depicted [Fig 25,j]. Many ancient texts tell of the skill of these workers. Apart from Homer's mention of silver bowls of Sidonian work (p. 151), we may recall the Tyrian workman called Hiram whom Solomon fetched to make metal fittings for his temple: 'His father was . . . a worker in brass; and he was filled with wisdom and understanding and cunning, to work all works in brass.'[183] This man made lavers, pots, shovels and basons, and also the two pillars of brass, Jachin and Boaz, set up in the porch of the temple, both of which had brazen capitals five cubits high 'of lily work' (i.e. they were lotus capitals of Egyptian style) with 200 pomegranates in rows round about and nets of checker work and wreaths of chain work. 'In the Plain of Jordan did the king cast them, in the clay ground [A. V. margin 'in the thickness of the ground', i.e. in a pit] between Succoth and Zarethan.'

Metal objects, too, survive. Outstanding, both as fine metal-work and as fine art, are the decorated bowls of the seventh century that occur in Cyprus and Etruria [Plate 47; Figs 53–55], as well as at Nimrud and in Greece (pp. 177 ff.). Metal statuettes of deities and worshippers are sometimes finely cast in solid form, though the majority are cheaper types of summary execution, mass-produced for dedication in sanctuaries [Plates 80–82, 84–87, 94]. Among metal vessels there is one form which is purely Phoenician and very distinctive [Plate 54]. This is a jug with oval body and neck tapering upward to a circular or trefoil mouth and with a widely swung handle from rim to shoulder, ending in a palmette. The shape, which is graceful, is common in pottery of the eighth to the sixth century on many Phoenician sites [Plate 113] and also occurs in glass [Plate 53] in the 'Aliseda treasure' (p. 145), and in alabaster.[184] Metal examples are frequent in Spain (usually in bronze) and Etruria (usually in silver) and have recently been discussed fully by Blanco Freijeiro and Garcia y Bellido, who cite Cypriote prototypes, but none from the homeland.[185] Pottery examples are as frequent at Carthage as elsewhere, but that site has yielded no metal one of just this type, though a bronze jug with trefoil mouth and ovoid body, found by Delattre at Douimes, must fall into the same general class, and the same cemetery also produced a similar one in ivory.[186]

The Phoenicians also excelled (pp. 202 ff.) in the manufacture and design of metal jewellery, mainly of gold and silver. They made much use of repoussé work and granulation, but rarely, if ever, used filigree, which was so beloved by the Greeks. Necklaces, bracelets, ear-rings and pendants of all kinds are found [Plates 104–108; Figs 35, 78, 79], not only in Phoenicia and Cyprus, but also at Carthage and in Sardinia, and examples also reached Etruria. As for Spain, however, much of its gold jewellery [Plates 97–99; Fig 81], once thought of as Phoenician, is now ascribed to local craftsmen, perhaps influenced in part by Phoenician work (p. 207).

It is not known how much of all this fine metal-work was made in the west. At least some of the better jewellery probably was, but most western metallurgy would be of a utilitarian sort, making arms and armour, tools and implements, and plain containers for everyday use. There is, however, one metal type, at least, namely the copper razor (pp. 197 ff.), which is wholly western in distribution and was undoubtedly produced in Punic workshops.

POTTING

Pottery vessels and objects have been found in abundance on many Phoenician sites, and we know, now, their general chronological pattern. We are hindered, however, in studying the Phoenician pottery development as a whole by the paucity of well-dated pottery sequences from the main homeland sites during the first millennium BC. Cypriote sequences of the Iron Age are comparatively well understood, and so are the contemporary Israelite ones. The fullest sequence of all, however, is at Carthage.

There is a certain type of red-slipped and burnished ware which is found on many Syrian and Lebanese sites, such as Al Mina and Khaldé (near Beirut), and also in Palestine at Ecdippa, Bethpelet, Dor and Atlit, for example.[187] It occurs also at er-Retabeh in the Egyptian Delta [Plate 111,b], and seems to be closely related in style and shape to examples [Fig 41] from as far west as Spain (p. 59). Presumably this ware would be found at Tyre and Sidon also, were the appropriate levels excavated. Alongside this red-slip burnished ware, coastal sites from Al Mina southwards also

Fig 41 Red-burnished jug with 'mushroom' lip, Torre del Mar (near Malaga). H. 0·20 m. Eighth or seventh century BC

yield plain red or buff (varying towards orange) wares [Plate 112,c], and these, too, seem to have been carried westward by the colonists: the red ware often has a buff or cream wet-smoothed wash. Some Iron Age pottery from inland sites such as Hazor and Samaria also resembles early west Phoenician pottery both in shape and in ware.

In Cyprus the great bulk of Iron Age pottery falls into two groups: white ware in which the design is painted in one or more colours on a pale ground and red ware with painted design in black, and occasionally other colours as well, on a red ground. These two varieties lasted with no technical change from *c.* 1000 until 400 or thereabouts, and though the shapes show distinct connections with mainland and western Phoenician forms they cannot be called direct parents or off-spring of them. The designs are either linear only or floral, figural or pictorial. Although designs such as the palmette, the guilloche and the Egyptian lotus might be derived from Phoenicia, the figural motifs seem to lean rather towards the Aegean in style. Some pottery vessels from Cyprus, however, all early, show a much greater affinity with the normal early Phoenician wares noted above. The excavations at Larnaka (p. 53) have yielded quantities of this ware and perhaps, there-fore, it was made *in situ*, though some of it is so like mainland pieces that import is not out of the question. The shapes are usually jugs of the well-known type with neck-carination, either with a polished red surface over all and red clay as well [Plate 111,a], or with a lighter clay base, some parts being red-painted and burnished and some left in light colour and tricked out with simple linear decoration [Plate 112, a, b].[187]

The western Phoenician pottery sequences [Plate 58] have been fully discussed by Cintas, who shows that the pottery from Sicily, Sardinia and Ibiza fits well with that from Carthage.[188] Decoration, except at first, is minimal and the shapes are utilitarian in the extreme. The earliest pots at Carthage often have linear bands and a triglyph pattern on the shoulder. After the seventh century, some pots show simple linear bands, but most are plain until Greek influence (princi-pally, perhaps, from vessels like the Egyptian Hadra vases of Hellenistic date) led to the occasional use in the fourth century and later, with the horizontal bands, of simple vegetable motifs and, in one instance only, of a design of ostriches drinking at a fountain [Fig 42]. In the earlier tombs at Carthage the attrac-tive jugs with mushroom or trefoil lips abounded [Plate 113]. In later tombs the common pottery is dull and generally poorly made.

All the high-class pottery found in Punic tombs was im-ported – first protocorinthian, Corinthian, Etruscan and a little Attic black-figured ware (p. 154), and then, from the fourth century, the red-figured and black-glazed wares of south Italy. At Motya the story follows closely that of Carthage, though there are, of course, far more Greek imports, including fine Attic vases. A few very early pots in Sardinia, from Sulcis, resemble east Phoenician ware of the red-burnished sort, but the bulk of the pottery from that island is later and plainer, and is closely akin to contemporary north African wares. In Malta we

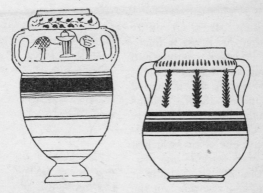

Fig 42 *Painted urns from Carthage. Sc.* c. ½. *Fourth century* BC

again get a similar sequence, though at the start there are some crude early shapes which seem to show little resemblance to anything elsewhere and may be more native than Phoenician. Occasionally, in later Maltese tombs, we find vessels that are clearly made by Greek potters, but under Punic influence. One such piece is the fine jug of the late fourth or early third century BC from Tal Liedna, near Pawla [Fig 43],[189] which not only has an ivy spray on the shoulder, but also a plastic serpent's head at the top and a Medusa mask at the base of its typically Punic double-round handle. But the ordinary Maltese pottery of the fifth century and later is thoroughly plain and dull [Plate 115]. Pottery from Spain and other sites in the far west is plentiful from at least the eighth century BC onwards (pp. 59, 139). The sequence fits well into the general Phoenician pattern, but there was also some contamination by native Iberian styles.[190]

It is surprising that the Phoenicians should not more frequently have imitated, as the Etruscans and Italic peoples did, the finely decorated foreign wares which came to them from time to time. In Spain, too, the native Iberians, with their fine pottery elaborately decorated with red linear patterns, could surpass the Phoenicians. The truth is that the Semites were never interested in fine pottery, but contented themselves with the purely utilitarian.

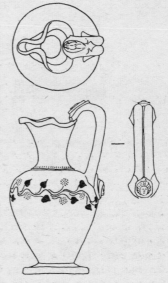

The same stress on utility rather than prettiness is manifest in Phoenician lamps and amphorae and terracotta figurines. Figurines are discussed below (pp. 186, 188 ff.). Lamps [Plate 114; Figs 44, 45] were simply clay saucers, undecorated, with one or two pinched beaks for the wicks – one usually in the east, two usually at Carthage and elsewhere in the west.[191] These remained in fashion even after Hellenistic trade introduced first the Italiote black-glazed lamp and then the so-called Rhodian and other far more serviceable closed Greek types.

Fig 43 *Jug from tomb 3, Tal Liedna, Malta. H. 0·225 m. Late fourth or early third century* BC

Phoenician amphorae for wine, oil and other products are equally distinct and recognizable. In the east they were more or less biconical, their lower half having straight tapering sides ending in a point. The type occurs in late New Kingdom Egypt (*c.* fourteenth century BC) and may have been derived thence, unless the borrowing went the other way. It occurs also at Nimrud in the ninth century. In the west the biconical form [Fig 47] was usual down to the fourth century, but in the later fourth century another type was evolved [Fig 48] where the bottom ended in a peg which could be stuck in the ground or in a hole in a shelf or other support. These types are characteristic of all Punic sites in the Carthaginian sphere of influence except, curiously enough, Sicily, where Greek types seem to have been predominant, and Malta, where a round-based jar with only a slightly excrescent point was the norm [Fig 46].

Occasionally, but not as often as we might expect, seeing

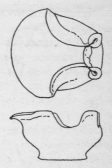

Fig 44 *Phoenician lamp, Atlit, Israel. L. 0.152 m. Seventh century* BC

Fig 45 *Punic lamp, Ste Monique, Carthage. L. 0·09 m. Third century* BC

that at least the common types of pottery must have been made in many different centres, potters' ovens and other traces of manufacture have been found. There seem to be no published records of any in the Phoenician homeland, but Carton records evidence for potters' workshops at the Belvedere near Tunis, and Delattre found remains of some at Douimes.[192] But the best-known instance is Gauckler's[193] discovery of a potters' quarter at Dermech, where, among other debris, he found one complete oven, still stacked with its pots. The pots were late types, but even so it is straining the evidence to assume, as some have, that they belong to the year 146 BC and that failure to clear the oven was due to the approach of the conquering troops! The oven was of the up-draught type with a pot-chamber in two stages above a firing-chamber. Moulds for figurines (p. 82) were also found on this site at Dermech [Fig

17], but no major figurine-factory has yet turned up at
Carthage. Between the two lagoons at Salammbo slighter
traces of pottery-working occurred,[194] including a crude
potter's wheel formed of two sandstone blocks, the upper one
with a pivot for turning in the socket of the lower. It is a
primitive type which needed two workers – one to turn the
wheel, the other to fashion the pots. Some late potters' ovens

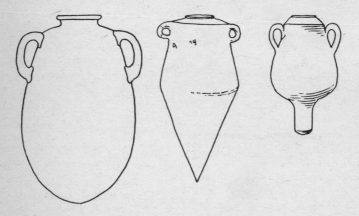

Fig 46 *Punic amphora from tomb 10, Ghajn Dwieli, Malta. H.
0·054 m. Late fourth or early third century* BC
Fig 47 *Biconical Punic amphora. H. c. 0·40 m. Fourth century* BC
Fig 48 *Punic amphora with peg bottom. H. c. 0·20 m. Third or second
century* BC

have also been found at Utica,[195] where amphorae and other
coarse pottery were made. They were of the same general type
as those at Dermech. Good clay for pottery exists in various
places on the Carthage peninsula, notably near Sidi Bou Said,
and at Cape Gamart. An inscription mentioning a potter called
Matar comes from Motya.[196]

GLASS-MAKING AND GLAZING[197]

From the seventh to the third century core-made fabrics [Plate
57] made up the bulk of the glass vessels which were produced,

1
2

3

4

5

6

7

8

9

10

11

12

13

14

15

16

17   18

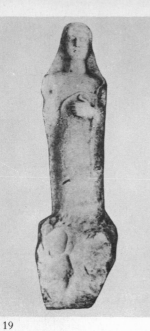

19

20

21

22

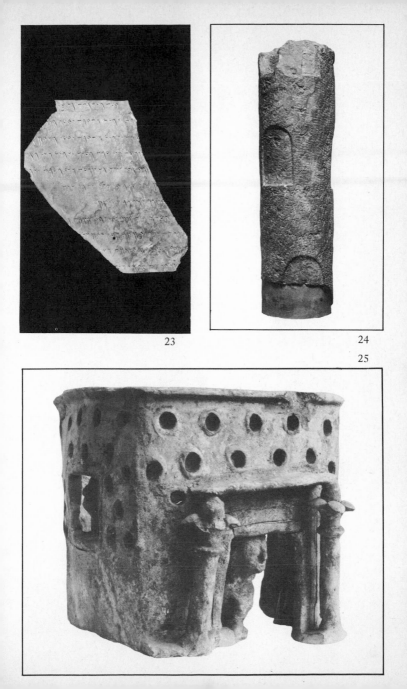

23

24

25

26

27

30

31

32

33

34

35

36

37

38

39

40

41

42

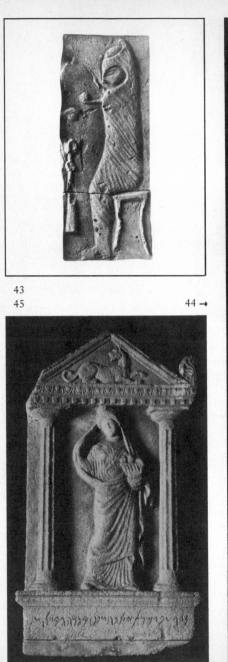

43

45

44 →

46

47

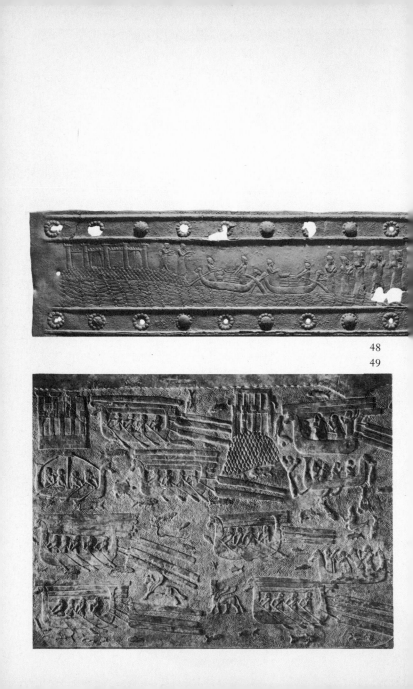

48
49

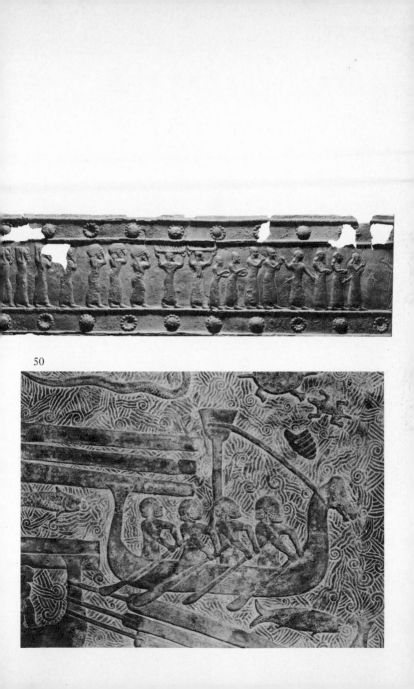

50

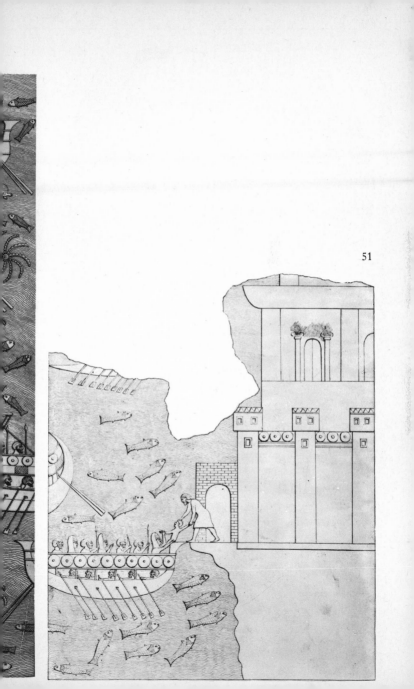

52

53

54

55   56
57

a   b   c

58

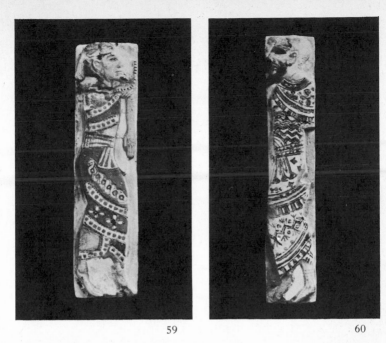

59   60

61

62

63

64

65

66

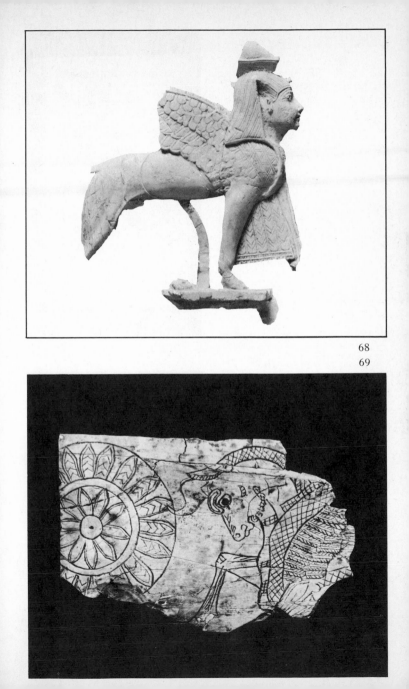

70

71

72

73

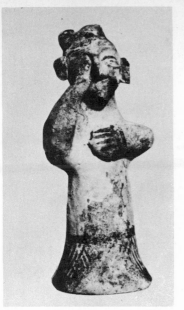

74

75
76

77

78   79 →

80

81

82

83

84

85

86

87

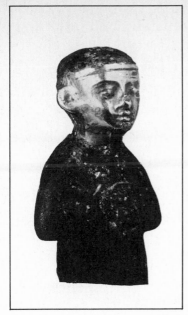

88

89

90

91

92

93

94 a

94 b

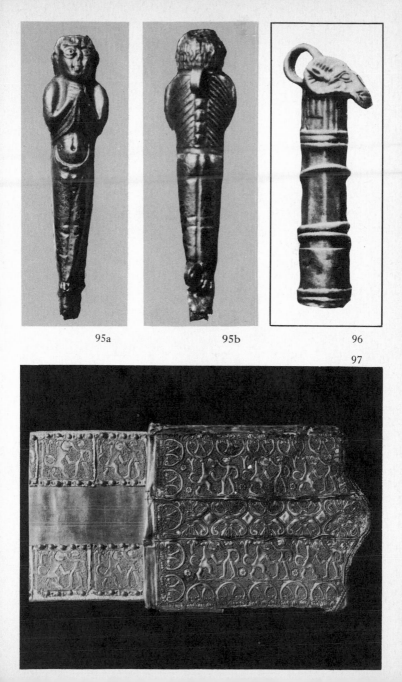

95a   95b   96
                                              97

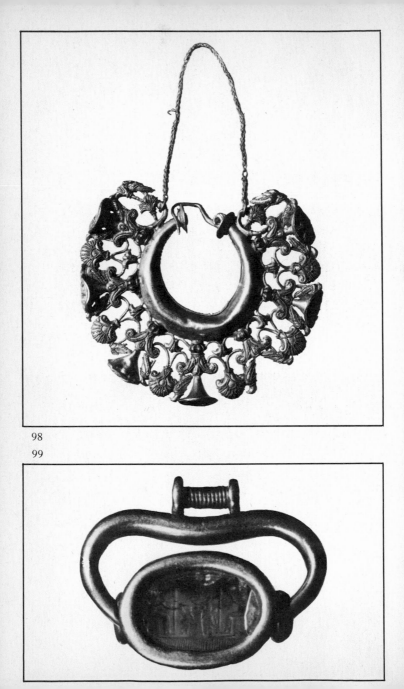

98

99

100

101

102

103

104

105 106

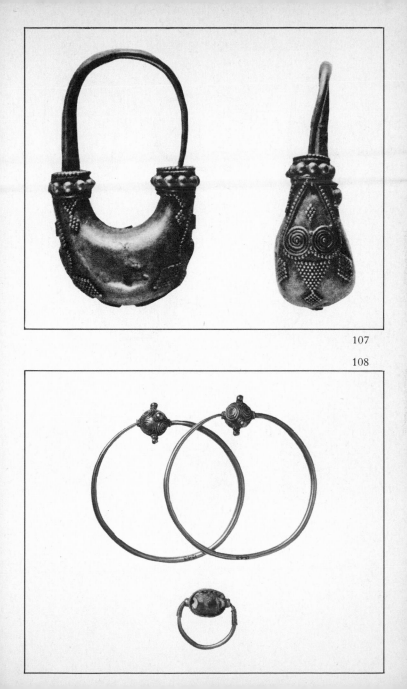

107

108

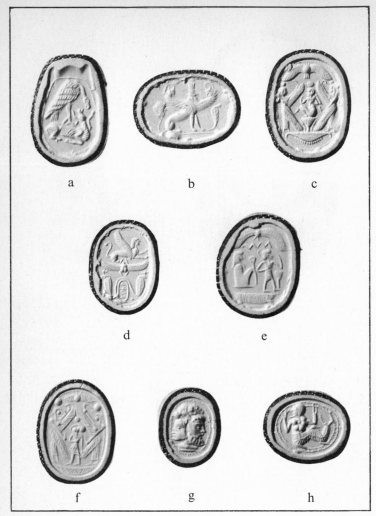

a   b   c

d   e

f   g   h

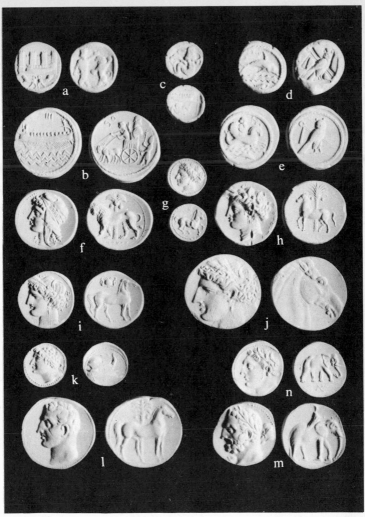

111

112
113

116

but a number of monochrome, often nearly colourless, cold-cut glasses of the period are known [Plate 53], as well as beads, pendants (especially small mask-pendants [Plates 55, 56], also modelled on a core), scarabs and amulets. It is traditionally thought that all this glass was made by Phoenicians and it is very likely that tradition is in this instance correct. In the middle of the second millennium BC workshops for core-made glass existed both in Egypt and in Mesopotamia. Core-made vessels of the middle of the first millennium are also frequent in Mesopotamia, but they differ in form and detail from those which occur throughout the Mediterranean. In Egypt, on the other hand, core-made ware was practically unknown in the first millennium BC, except occasionally in the Delta. We must, therefore, ascribe this Mediterranean core-made glass either to the Syrian coast, i.e. Phoenicia, or to somewhere farther west, perhaps Rhodes. At present we cannot decide, though the Plinian tradition that glass was invented in Phoenicia, if it can claim any basis of fact, must refer either to this core-made glass or to a much later development, namely, the invention of blown glass during the first century BC (and that seems too close to Pliny's own day).

The cold-cut glass was most likely, to start with, a Mesopotamian speciality, and it was certainly in use both at the Assyrian court from at least the eighth century (the Sargon II vase from Nimrud) and at the Persian three centuries later, where the use of ὑάλινα ἐκπώματα – colourless crystal cups – is mentioned by Aristophanes in the fifth century.[198] But many of the shapes are not typically Mesopotamian and some, such as a seventh-century jug from La Aliseda in Spain [Plate 53], are purely Phoenician, being frequently found in metal and pottery (p. 138). This piece, of green translucent glass, is engraved with Phoenician copies of Egyptian hieroglyphs, including cartouches, one of which bears royal titles and the others the formula regularly used to introduce a divine spell. Glasses like this and the Sargon vase may have been made by Phoenicians working at the Assyrian court.

However it may have been with the vessels, glass trinkets (beads, particularly, and scarabs) were certainly made in Phoenicia, though factories for such products may also have existed in the Egyptian Delta, seeing that fine glass sands abound in the western desert near by.

There is evidence at Carthage, too, for the manufacture of either vessels or trinkets, for Gauckler describes a glass-maker's furnace he found at Dermech 'under the sanctuary of Jupiter Ammon'.[199] This must date from the fourth century or later, when Carthage and other western cities were becoming more industry-minded.

Glazing of pottery was current in Mesopotamia, but not in Egypt, so far as is known. Some small glazed pottery vessels, perhaps Mesopotamian, reached the Syrian area and the Greek islands in the seventh and sixth centuries, but we need not connect them with the Phoenicians. What concerns us more is faience, i.e. glaze on an almost pure silica base. Unlike glass-making, the manufacture of faience was continuously prevalent in Egypt from predynastic times onwards and was specially common in Saite times for figurines and amulets and small vessels, particularly New Year bottles. Certain types of faience flasks in the form of men and animals spread widely through the Mediterranean in the seventh and sixth centuries and are found at Carthage. Their style shows Egyptian affinities, and since many other faience types of the period are even more Egyptian, there is no reason to look outside Egypt, presumably the Delta, for their place of manufacture. So, too, with the amulets and scarabs. The seventh- and sixth-century ones are strongly Egyptian in style. After the end of the twenty-sixth dynasty (525 BC) the manufacture of scarabs is said to have ceased in Egypt.[200] The later Phoenician ones, therefore, diverge from the traditional pattern and some, at least, were made in the west.

CARVING IN IVORY AND BONE

Much ivory was worked in Phoenicia and Syria: much was also worked at Carthage. Elephant tusks, which the eastern Phoenicians had to fetch from India or from Punt, via the Red Sea (once their supply from Syrian elephants died out in the early first millennium BC), could be acquired overland by their Carthaginian cousins from the Garamantes and others.

Carthage also had her own elephant farms in north Africa, especially later, when she used elephants so much for warfare.

The carved ivories [Plates 61–65, 67–69, 71; Figs 52, 73–76] were used either to embellish architecture or furniture, or to make statuettes or small articles such as combs, boxes, hairpins and ornaments. Assyrian records reveal how flourishing the trade was in the Levant in the ninth century and later, for they show that the Assyrian monarchs of the period received, by gift or tribute, great quantities of ivory furniture, boxes and the like from Carchemish, Damascus, Sidon and other places.[201] These eastern ivories were traded far – to Greece, for example, and Etruria. They had become usual in Carthage in the seventh century and some even found their way to Spain. We do not know when a western ivory-carving industry grew up, but it certainly flourished at Carthage by the sixth century at the latest (pp. 199 ff.).

Though ivory produced the more finished product and was more sought after, the commoner material, bone, was also used, especially for decorative panels and strips for wooden boxes, for toilet articles, such as unguent-vases [Plate 66], cosmetic spoons and hairpins, and for amulets, seals, game-pieces, counters, dice and the like. It is often not easy to distinguish ivory from bone with the naked eye.

The near eastern caravan trade, which brought African gold
and ivory, slaves, corn and cattle to Asia and Asiatic metals,
metal goods and textiles to Egypt, began early and is well
illustrated by the patriarchal narrative in the Bible. While
the lighter, smaller goods could go by animal transport overland, the coastal sea route and navigable rivers were used, so
far as possible, for the heavier and bulkier cargoes, such as
timber.

Assyrian reliefs (p. 161) depict some of this traffic [Plates
49, 50]. We see smallish river-boats manned by Phoenicians
carrying logs (or perhaps whole trunks of fir trees) either
stretched out on what must have been some sort of upper deck,
or tied to the stern of the boat (or perhaps raft,[202] since the
propulsion is by paddling) and trailing behind in the water.
One boat [Plate 49, top right] seems to be finishing loading;
another part of the same relief shows the unloading process.
How this traffic went from Lebanon to the Mesopotamian
rivers is unknown. It may have gone overland from the lower
reaches of the Orontes, or else by ship to Tarsus to join the
main traffic highway from Asia Minor [Fig 9].

Canaanite traders from Byblos are mentioned in Egyptian
texts from the Old Kingdom onwards, but, although we recognize these men as ancestors of our Phoenicians, their activities
do not concern us directly. Yet in shipping and commerce, at
least, the tradition from the Old Kingdom Giblites to the
Phoenician thalassocrats of the Solomonic era was unbroken.
The mighty empires of Egypt and Mesopotamia fostered it, for
it was useful to them, and however much the coastal cities may

have been in vassalage politically, they were no doubt left to pursue their commerce reasonably freely.

Phoenician ventures farther afield did not, however, begin until the power of the Minoan and Mycenaean merchant venturers, who had dominated the eastern Mediterranean sea routes for many centuries, was smashed by northern invaders about 1200 BC, at the very time when the Canaanites of the coastal Phoenician cities, reinforced by Mycenaean settlers within their gates, were well placed, as Elisha, to take on the mantle of the Aegean Elijah. We may picture their Mycenaean trading friends telling them of the great riches that lay before them if they would but organize themselves for long-distance trading to the west; for it is now known that the Aegeans had already strong contacts with south Italy and Sicily and the islands of the Tyrrhenian sea, and some knowledge of the rich metal deposits in Spain, Brittany and Britain may have been current, even if the Mycenaeans themselves had not actually penetrated so far.[203]

It is probable that to start with the Phoenicians travelled westward not as true colonists but as traders. Although the Hebrew incursion into the Promised Land brought on some overcrowding and drove at least some of the Canaanites to take refuge with their coastal cousins, the surplus population so created cannot have been enough to people the numerous early colonies which ancient sources postulate. We may believe, rather, that, apart from a few key sites like Utica, Carthage and Gades, most of the early settlements, especially in the west, were little more than charted anchorages where ships could pull in after a day's sailing, the sites being chosen basically as being an appropriate distance from one another. That is why early material is so rarely found on these sites. Those in the west mostly did not develop into real colonial towns until many centuries later; those in the east mostly lost their Phoenician character when Greek trading revived in the eighth century.

We get echoes of early Phoenician trading in the Bible, in Hiram the Great's dealings with David and Solomon. In the second quarter of the tenth century, during David's reign, we read:[204] 'And Hiram king of Tyre sent messengers to David, and cedar trees, and carpenters, and masons: and they built

David an house.' Later in the century Hiram was providing similar services for Solomon:[205]

> Solomon sent to Hiram, saying . . . command thou that they hew me cedar trees out of Lebanon . . . and I will give thee hire for thy servants according to all that thou shalt say: for thou knowest that there is not among us any that can skill to hew timber like unto the Zidonians. . . . And Hiram sent to Solomon, saying . . . I will do all thy desire concerning timber of cedar, and concerning timber of fir. My servants shall bring them down from Lebanon unto the sea: and I will make them into rafts to go by sea unto the place that thou shalt appoint me, and will cause them to be broken up there, and thou shalt receive them: and thou shalt accomplish my desire, in giving food for my household. . . . And Solomon gave Hiram twenty thousand measures of wheat for food to his household, and twenty measures of pure oil: thus gave Solomon to Hiram year by year.

Later, Hiram helped Solomon in the Red Sea trade:[206] 'Then went Solomon to Ezion-geber, and to Eloth, on the sea shore in the land of Edom [Fig 50]. And Huram sent him by the hands of his servants ships, and servants that had knowledge of the sea; and they came with the servants of Solomon to Ophir, and fetched from thence four hundred and fifty talents of gold.' The equivalent account in the book of Kings[207] begins rather differently: 'King Solomon made a navy of ships in Ezion-geber', but then adds in the next chapter, 'and the navy also of Hiram, that brought gold from Ophir, brought in from Ophir great plenty of almug trees and precious stones'. Later[208] we read of Jehoshaphat, king of Judah, making 'ships of Tarshish to go to Ophir for gold: but they went not; for the ships were broken at Ezion-geber'. The position of Ophir is disputed. It is often placed in south Arabia, but some seek it in India. Ophir's reality as a source of gold is vouched for, now, by a potsherd recently found at Tel Qasile near Jaffa [Plate 41], inscribed 'gold of Ophir to Beth-horon 30 shekels', which the excavator, Maisler, ascribed to the eighth century B.C.[209]

Wherever Ophir was it seems wrong to strain the Biblical narrative and connect it with the account in the first book of

Kings[210] of the navy of Tarshish which the king had at sea bringing once every three years gold, silver, ivory, apes and peacocks; or with its variant in the second book of Chronicles,[211] which says that this navy of Tarshish plied to Tarshish for these goods.

The situation of Tarshish is a well-known crux. Some would identify it with Tarsus in Cilicia, especially in connection with Jonah, who in his flight boarded a ship at Joppa for Tarshish:[212] but there is no reason to abandon the traditional equation of Tarshish with the far west, whatever we may feel about its identification with the historical Tartessos of king Arganthonios. Ezekiel[213] refers to silver, iron, tin and lead coming to Tyre from Tarshish and these four metals, with gold, make Tarshish sound very like Spain, while ivory, apes, peacocks, and gold again, could all have been hinterland products shipped from north African ports. North Africa was more tropical in climate in antiquity, so that apes and even lions existed there.

The same prophet Ezekiel, inveighing against Tyre when Nebuchadnezzar was planning its capture, describes the merchant power of the city and the wide distribution of its commerce: 'Thy riches and thy wares, thy merchandise, thy mariners, and thy pilots, thy calkers, and the occupiers of thy merchandise, and all thy men of war, that are in thee, with all thy company which is in the midst of thee, shall fall into the heart of the seas in the days of thy ruin.'[214]

We hear of the Phoenician trading reputation – both its good and its bad points – in Greek sources also, from the *Iliad* and *Odyssey* downwards. At the funeral games of Patroclos in the *Iliad* one of the prizes was a chased silver bowl of Sidonian make brought oversea by Phoenicians.[215] This reference must belong at latest to the eighth century BC, when the *Iliad* is thought to have been written down. In the *Odyssey*, which may be up to a century later, Odysseus pretends that he had during his wanderings been carried off to Phoenicia by a Phoenician 'practised in deceit, a greedy knave who had already done much mischief among men'.[216] There he was kept a year and then carried off again on another cargo ship bound for Libya. Elsewhere[217] Eumaeus describes how when he was a child

Phoenician traders came to his father's home and suborned his nurse (a Sidonian herself) to come back to Phoenicia with them and bring the child with her, to be sold into slavery. These Phoenicians, as so often, were in no hurry: 'they dwelt with us a whole year', Eumaeus says, 'and got together much wealth' before they carried him off captive. Herodotus, in attempting to give an explanation of the origin of the quarrel between Greece and Persia, recounts similar stories about Phoenician woman-stealing in early times from Greece.[218]

This Phoenician traffic with Greece proper and the Greek islands must have died out soon after the renascence of Greek commerce in the eighth century led to rivalry between the two colonizing movements. In Sicily they may have continued to traffic direct with the Greeks, at least until the early fifth century, when the enmity arose which culminated in Carthage's defeat at Himera in 480. In Spain they were in rivalry with the Greeks, especially the Phocaeans, who planted a colony at Mainake in the late seventh century BC, and perhaps other colonies also, and the Samians, who traded with Tartessos, until, in the sixth century, Phoenician hegemony was strong enough to drive the Greeks from the south-eastern Spanish coast.[219]

This Asiatic–European rivalry, which split the Mediterranean seaways into two opposing preserves, lasted until Alexander's conquests finally brought the whole eastern Mediterranean, including Phoenicia, under Greek sway and created a commercial, at least, if not a political *pax hellenica* throughout the ancient world. Alexander, we are told, had in mind to attack Carthage, but his death saved her politically; commercially and socially she was already becoming hellenized, and was therefore ready, as her eastern cousins were, to profit by the new peace and send her merchants and seamen once more into Greek waters for commerce. The conditions at this time are well exemplified in Plautus' *Poenulus*, which was copied from a Greek comedy – probably the Καρχηδόνιος of Alexis.[220] Plautus wrote his play in the early years of the second century BC, just after the end of the second Punic war: Alexis' original will have been a little over a century earlier. The general thread of the play is probably taken from the

Greek original, and, though the Punic passages in the Latin version (the text of which is unfortunately very corrupt in the manuscripts) may be a Plautine addition, we should no doubt accept the Punic merchant, Hanno, as a type familiar in late fourth-century Greece as well as in Rome of the second century BC. We note, too, that traffic in children, which Homer ascribed to the Phoenicians, and on which the plot of this later play hinges, was not entirely out of the question, even in Hellenistic days. Inscriptions of the fourth century and later found in Greece, set up by or mentioning Phoenicians and Carthaginians, also indicate trade relations.

Apart from raw materials such as timber from Lebanon, the metals of the far west and the purple dye for which they were so famous, the Phoenicians also traded in finished goods which they produced, e.g. fine cloths, metal-work and agricultural products, besides acting as middlemen, at certain times at least, in carrying Egyptian and Greek manufactures. The finds at Carthage indicate that genuine Egyptian amulets and trinkets reached there in some quantities during the period of the twenty-sixth dynasty, but far fewer of them arrived after the end of the sixth century, the mass of goods of Egyptian type that are current in the western Mediterranean from then on being made either in Phoenician factories in the east or at Carthage itself.

Greek goods provide a different problem. We have seen that Phoenician commerce with Greece and the Aegean must have ceased (p. 152) soon after the eighth century. On the other hand Greek trade (especially Corinthian) with Greek colonies in Italy brought a constant stream of Greek goods to that peninsula, where, as tomb finds show, they were greedily acquired by Etruscans. Some things normally labelled Phoenician, such as core-made glasses, repoussé and engraved metal bowls, ivories and trinkets, also reached Etruria from at least the seventh century onwards, if not the eighth, and some Phoenician influence on certain mainland pottery forms and decorative techniques has also been noticed. Thus it seems probable that both Greeks and Phoenicians were trading with Italy. The Phoenician objects were certainly not carried by Greek ships, nor is it likely that they were carried by the

Etruscans, who do not seem to have frequented the eastern Mediterranean as traders, and we must therefore assume that it was Phoenicians themselves who brought them.

Now, from the late eighth century onwards, both Greek pottery and bronzes and Etruscan *bucchero* and Etrusco-corinthian vases were reaching Phoenician settlements in the western Mediterranean, including Carthage, where large numbers of them have turned up in Punic tombs.[221] Doubtless, too, Etruscan control of the important metalliferous region of Italy led to metal ores and products being part of this trade. We cannot say whether it was Etruscan or Punic traders who were responsible: it is most unlikely to have been the Greeks. Both Etruria and Carthage were strong maritime nations, who made common cause to prevent the spread of Greek colonies within their joint spheres. The Etruscans controlled what is still aptly called the Tyrrhenian sea and dominated parts of Corsica, Sardinia and the Balearics. They were even (according to one ancient tradition) active on parts of the Spanish coast, but the Carthaginians, allied to the Etruscans though they were, were not pleased that they should take an interest in Spain. Diodorus, as we shall see (p. 170), tells a story about the Carthaginians dissuading the Etruscans from founding a colony on a certain Atlantic island, and this, he says, once for all stopped the Etruscans from attempting any advance into the far west.

On the other hand, it is known from the text of her first treaty with Rome in 509, the year after Rome threw off the Tarquin yoke, that Carthage had by then some interest in central Italy. By this treaty, which defined commercial and political spheres of influence, Carthage agreed not to harm a number of named Latin towns, whether dependent on Rome or not, and not to build a fort in Latium. We may infer, despite the doubts of many scholars, that such language means what it says, and that these provisions would not have been included if Carthaginians were not in the habit of going to central Italy. Indeed suggestions have recently been put forward that Phoenicians, whether western or eastern, were active at Rome from the seventh century onwards. Van Berchem and Rebuffat[222] have both argued recently for the presence of a 'colony' of Phoenician traders at Rome at this early date under the protection of Melqart, whose cult, as they believe, was practised in the Forum Boarium. And whatever may be the truth of this, it is at least now certain from the Pyrgi inscriptions (p. 112)[223] that a temple or shrine of Astarte and a Punic merchants' colony existed at Pyrgi in Etruria, some thirty miles north of Rome, a few decades at most after the date of this first treaty between Rome and Carthage. It may be, therefore, that both Etruscan and Punic ships took part in bringing these Greek and Etruscan things to Carthage and other western settlements, and that this was the main, if not the only, route by which Carthage acquired her Greek imports. This would help to explain why, when Etruria was in decline and Carthage was hostile to the Greeks during the fifth and fourth centuries, the Attic and other mainland Greek imports, which still flooded into Italy, are virtually absent at Carthage. It seems, indeed, clear that during all this time political rivalry prevented direct trade between Greeks and Carthaginians.

COMMERCE AND TRADE WITH LESS-CIVILIZED
PEOPLES

But the Phoenicians did not trade only with their civilized neighbours in the Mediterranean and nearer Asia. We have already noted one instance, the Ophir trade (p. 150 f.), where they went farther afield, and the eastern Phoenicians also trafficked with Africa via the Red Sea. Moreover the Phoenicians on the north African coast, benefiting from the work of explorers (p. 169), had trade relations by land, as well as by sea through marts on the west coast of Africa, with the far interior of the Sahara and perhaps even Nigeria and elsewhere to the south [Fig 50]. The Sahara was then less dry than it is today and was peopled by a white, Libyan race, akin to the Numidians and others. No black population would be encountered until the Sahara had been crossed. Regular caravan routes existed between the north coast and Nigeria and between Egypt and Mauretania. There is no doubt that it was the Phoenicians and not the Greeks, whose African colonies were never powerful, nor the Egyptians, whose trade was confined to the Nile basin and its immediate hinterland, who passed on the products of this huge area – gold, ivory, wild beasts, and above all perhaps slaves – to the civilized Mediterranean world. The Carthaginians may even have used an inland route to Egypt via Siwa oasis, by-passing Greek Cyrenaica, for some of their trade with that country.

Coastal traffic is also attested by ancient authors. Herodotus[224] says that he learnt from the Carthaginians that, in trading with the Libyans living beyond the Pillars of Heracles, they adopted methods of barter. Leaving their goods on the beach they returned to their ships and raised a smoke. The natives then laid gold beside the goods as a barter price and retired to a distance. This coming and going continued until the Carthaginians were satisfied with the price offered. 'Neither side', adds Herodotus, 'cheats: the Carthaginians don't touch the gold till they are satisfied and the natives don't touch the goods till the others have accepted the gold.'

There is an even more interesting and circumstantial story in a Greek *Periplus* of *c.* 350.[225] This describes the west African coast down to an island called Cerne (also, as we shall see, mentioned earlier by Hanno, pp. 166 ff.) where Phoenician merchants traffic with the Ethiopians. They bring their goods to the mainland in boats, where they exchange unguents, Egyptian stone (probably glass, one of the ancient names for which was λίθος χυτή, 'poured stone' [Plate 57]), Attic juglets (χόες) and another unidentified item for animal skins (domestic and wild), elephant tusks and wine. Now that Phoenician pottery of the seventh and early sixth centuries BC has been found as far south as Mogador (pp. 33, 59) I find no difficulty in accepting what the author of this *Periplus* says at its geographical face value. Phoenician remains in Morocco have been found in increasing quantities recently. We can expect that further field-work will yield even more widespread evidence of Phoenician and, later, Punic trade and settlement on this part of the Atlantic coast.

COINAGE

Though the use of coinage began in Greek lands during the seventh century BC and it had become normal there by the early years of the sixth, the Phoenicians did not adopt it so early, despite their flair for commerce and trade. The age-old nature of their commercial traditions and their frequent contacts with more primitive peoples made them (as we have seen, p. 156) proficient in the use of barter.

In Persia coinage began under Darius towards the end of the sixth century, and for a while the Phoenicians, who were a part of his great empire, made no attempt to strike coins on their own, no doubt partly because it was injudicious, but partly also because they felt little need of it, since their trade with Greek lands, where alone coinage flourished, had virtually ceased. The Persians themselves, indeed, minted their darics and *sigloi* primarily for use in their Greek dominions in Asia Minor, and we can guess that Asiatic trade nearer home was so well organized on the old system that there was little urge to alter it, until Greek business men came to the east in greater numbers after the Persian wars.

The earliest eastern Phoenician coinage was struck by Tyre about the middle of the fifth century BC [Plate 110,d].[226] Sidon, Aradus and Byblos followed during the late fifth or early fourth century, and the initiation of these coinages probably indicates both the growing weakness of the Persian empire and a rebirth of Phoenician trade with Greek lands. The other towns did not strike until Hellenistic times. The types these early issues bear are interesting. At Aradus [Plate 110,c] the coins depict either a fish-tailed deity or a bearded male head (perhaps Melqart) on the obverse and a galley and hippocamp (or waves) on the reverse; at Byblos, a galley and hippocamp on the obverse and a vulture or a lion attacking a bull on the reverse; at Tyre [Plate 110,d, e], a dolphin and murex shell or Melqart on hippocamp on the obverse and an owl on the reverse. The Sidonian types [Plate 110,a, b] are more varied; some of the early obverses show a war galley lying before a fortress with battlements and towers, no doubt Sidon itself, others show the same galley, often very finely drawn with interesting details, riding over the waves; smaller denominations have other types, such as the head of a bearded king with low cap of oriental type. On larger coins one reverse has been held to show the king of Persia riding in a trap drawn by four horses [Plate 110,b], with an attendant behind, on foot, who may represent the king of Egypt or of Sidon. But Seyrig has recently, and very plausibly, suggested that the figure in the trap is the statue of the local Baal, and that the attendant, on foot, is the king of Sidon, acting as priest in a religious procession.[227] Other reverses show what is certainly the king of Persia shooting a bow or slaying a lion [Plate 110,a]. With these we may compare a scaraboid gem from Sardinia [Fig 82] showing a similar scene, which may, of course, be a locally manufactured piece, copied from the Sidonian coin-type. That the Persian king occurs at Sidon only is perhaps because she was then the chief city and possessed a palace of the Persian king (p. 50). These Phoenician coins are all silver or bronze. For gold, the Persian daric held the field. It is interesting, too, that the most northerly city, Aradus, used the Persian standard; the others all used the native Phoenician.

The western cities began striking even later. The first coins for which Carthage was responsible were gold on the Phoenician standard and silver tetradrachms on the Attic [Plate 110, f–h,j], struck in Sicily from the end of the fifth century onwards, when she needed coins to pay her mercenaries there. Legends are in Phoenician characters with the names of Motya, Panormus and other Siculo-punic towns, of Carthage and of 'the Camp' – an indication that the coins were headquarters' money. On the obverse side was a head of Tanit in the guise of the Sicilian Persephone and on the reverse a horse, a lion or a palm tree, all of which, except the lion, were adopted for Carthage's metropolitan coinage from the later fourth century BC [Plate 110,i]. This metropolitan series was struck on the Phoenician standard, mainly in gold, electrum and bronze, silver issues being rare until the late years of the century when Hamilcar had obtained control of the Spanish mines. From the end of the third century, though precious metals continued to be used, bronze was the main medium of coinage at Carthage, and these bronze coins spread far and wide – in a few instances even to Britain and the Azores (pp. 163, 170).

The only other Phoenician towns in the west who had their own coinages before the third century BC were those in Sicily, all of whom began minting in the fifth century. Coinage at Gades and Ibiza began in the third century and Carthage herself had a mint in Spain at Carthago Nova while her Spanish empire lasted. There is a series of issues ascribed to that mint, mainly silver [Plate 110,k–m], with Punic types such as the horse and palm tree, or the elephant, on the reverse, and various heads which are clearly portraits on the obverse. These have recently been identified by E. S. G. Robinson as portraits of the three Carthaginian generals, Hamilcar, Hasdrubal and Hannibal, and of the Roman general Scipio, who took Carthago Nova in 209 BC. That such portraits may exist is a matter of great interest and this identification, if it wins acceptance, will bring us in a happy fashion more closely face to face with these famous soldiers.[228] A coin of Gades (obverse, Melqart: reverse, elephant) which is contemporary in style, probably belongs to this Barcid series [Plate 110,n]. There are no coins of Sardinia or Malta which certainly antedate their annexation by Rome.

We know nothing of the organization of Phoenician mints. Their system will have been copied from the Greeks, and it may be that even Greek workmen were employed, just as Greek artists were largely responsible for the designs on the coins.

SHIPS

Two main types of seagoing ship existed in the ancient Mediterranean during the period of Phoenician independence: the 'long' ship for war and at times for long-distance trade and exploration; and the 'round' ship, for normal commerce. The Phoenicians used both, as we can see on the Nineveh relief depicting Luli's flight from Tyre in 701 BC [Plate 51].[229]

The 'long' ships on that relief may have developed from the penteconter, a 'long' ship of fifty oars in one bank, which is depicted on early geometric Greek vases, but of which no Phoenician illustration is available. It was, clearly, current in

the Mediterranean at the beginning of the first millennium
BC, and was used both for war and for long journeys of a more
peaceful kind. It may, indeed, have continued in use for long
journeys down to the fifth century BC, or longer, if we can
believe the Greek text of Hanno's *Periplus*, which names this
as the kind of ship Hanno used (p. 166).

Luli's 'long' ships, as can be clearly seen on the relief, have
two banks of oars, each oar manned by one rower; and there
is a deck above, along which warriors' shields are hung, as
normally on Phoenician warships (we see them again on many
of the galleys on fourth-century coins, p. 157). The ships have
a pointed ram at the prow, a feature now believed to be of
Mycenaean origin (p. 116), and a high, convex stern on either
side of which is a steering-oar [cf. Fig 49,c]. There is, as well,
a central mast with sail, but the normal propulsion was by
rowing. These were probably used as the 'ships of Tarshish'
which went on long-distance voyages, whether to Tarshish
itself or elsewhere – to Ophir, for example (p. 150). Such ships
would need to be armed, and faster than the ordinary merchantman.

During the seventh century the trireme with three banks of
oars, each oar still manned by one rower, was developed in
Phoenicia from this earlier type, to serve as the normal ship
of war. The Greeks copied the general principle of this development in the sixth century, but their triremes were much
narrower, and not fully decked, as the Phoenician ones were,
and in order to fit in three banks of oarsmen they had to invent
the *apostis*, or outrigger, above the gunwale to carry the top-
most bank of oars.

Later still, about 400 BC, two quite new types of warship,
first the quadrireme and then the quinquereme, were invented
(p. 115). These worked on a completely different principle,
with single banks of long oars each manned by four, or five,
oarsmen. The quadrireme soon gave way to the quinquereme,
which was adopted by all the navies of Hellenistic times and
is the type which is delineated on many Phoenician coins of
the fourth century and later [Plate 110,b].

Luli's 'round' ships are smaller than the 'long' ships and
have convex prows and sterns in symmetrical arrangement.

They, too, have two banks of oars below a raised deck with shields outside the gunwale, but they have no sails. It has been suggested that these are the vessels which were called *gauloi* in Greek (*gôlah* in Phoenician). [230] They are descended, as Basch shows, from the typical Levantine merchantman of the late Bronze Age, such as is illustrated by a terracotta model of that period found at Byblos. [231] This model shows the same

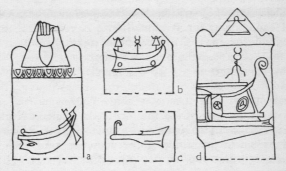

Fig 49 *Punic stelae with boats and a steering-oar, precinct of Tanit, Carthage. Fourth or third century* BC. *Various scales*

round shape with high prow and stern in fore-and-aft symmetry. Indeed the type may have been much older and may have functioned as the traditional coastal craft of the Byblos trade from the third millennium BC, or even earlier. It probably changed little, if at all, down to Hellenistic times, when a different style of heavier and larger merchantman was developed, such as the fine one [232] depicted on a well-known Sidonian coffin of the second century AD.

A much smaller boat used by the Phoenicians, perhaps mainly for fishing or as river-craft, was the *hippos* mentioned by Strabo and others, that is a boat with horse-head prow, such as we see carrying logs on the Assyrian reliefs from Khorsabad [Plates 49, 50]. Sometimes these boats had horse-head sterns as well, as, for instance, on the Balawat gates [Plate 48], and, perhaps, on a ring from the 'Aliseda treasure' (cf. p. 206). [233] Normally this type appears to have been paddled, not rowed.

Some of the boats illustrated on Carthage stelae [Fig 49,a,b] seem to be small harbour-craft rather than ocean-going vessels. This type did not change much between Punic and Roman times, as we can see from the existence of similar shapes of craft on north African mosaics of imperial age.

EXPLORATION

Phoenician voyages within the Mediterranean cannot be called exploration, for by the Bronze Age, at least, if not earlier, all the main Mediterranean routes had been well charted. For real exploration we must look farther afield, and by good fortune we have a number of stories to help us.[234]

Herodotus[235] describes how some Phoenicians sailed in ships down the Red Sea at the bidding of Pharaoh Necho II (609–593) to circumnavigate Africa [Fig 50], a feat which they accomplished in just under three years, stopping each year between seed-time and harvest to provision themselves before continuing their journey. Most modern commentators accept this story as genuine on the basis of their statement – which Herodotus says he did not believe – that, as they sailed round Libya they had the sun on their right hand (as would occur during such a journey).

The next two voyages are those of Hanno, who went to west Africa, and Himilco, who sailed northward round Iberia. That Herodotus, writing in the middle of the fifth century, does not mention these, but records Necho's circumnavigators, suggests that they had not yet taken place, and we should probably ascribe them to *c.* 425 or a bit later. We know more of Hanno's than of Himilco's, because Hanno's own short account of it, which was set up in the temple of Saturn (Baal Hammon) at Carthage, has been preserved for us in a Greek translation, whereas Himilco's voyage is only known from details about it that are incorporated in the *Ora Maritima* of Avienus, a Roman geographical text-book in verse compiled in the fourth century AD. Both journeys are also mentioned by the elder Pliny, who took a poor view of Hanno's veracity. They were undertaken, as we have seen, when Carthage

(p. 63) was attempting to strengthen her interests in the west because the Greeks blocked her progress nearer home.

Himilco's journey was doubtless intended to open up the western tin route, perhaps at a time when the Spanish mines were not yielding enough. With no source other than Avienus' copying of a 800-year-old story to guide us we must not try to press the details too closely. Mention, however, of both the *gens Hiernorum* and the *insula Albionum*[236] suggests that Himilco did not stop at Brittany – the Oestrymnian promontory as he calls it[237] – but passed on across the channel, and in effect led the way for Carthage to take part in the Cornish tin trade, which, we may assume, Mediterranean traders were already exploiting via the overland route across Gaul. There is, unfortunately, no direct archaeological evidence of Phoenician contacts with Britain at this period to support the Himilco story,[238] although a number of Iron Age finds in Cornwall indicate Iberian contacts. The few Carthaginian coins found in Britain are later, and in any case do not necessarily imply direct contact.[239]

If there is little we can say about Himilco, the situation is far different for Hanno.[240] The only extant manuscript is no earlier than the tenth century AD and has been garbled by much scribal copying, yet the story is so interesting and circumstantial that it has been widely commented on in modern times. Most scholars accept the basic story, but when it comes to identifying the places Hanno mentions and deciding how far Hanno penetrated, opinions differ. One modern writer[241] considers the text largely, if not entirely, forged. While we should not follow him in that, we must admit that the tale as we have it is full of inaccuracies and inconsistencies. It has been suggested, however, that these could have been intentional in the publicized version, so as to put Carthage's rivals off the scent and frighten them off.

The text runs as follows:

This is the story of the long voyage of Hanno 'king' of the Carthaginians into Libyan lands beyond the Pillars of Heracles, which he dedicated on a tablet in the temple of Kronos:

I. The Carthaginians decided that Hanno should sail beyond the

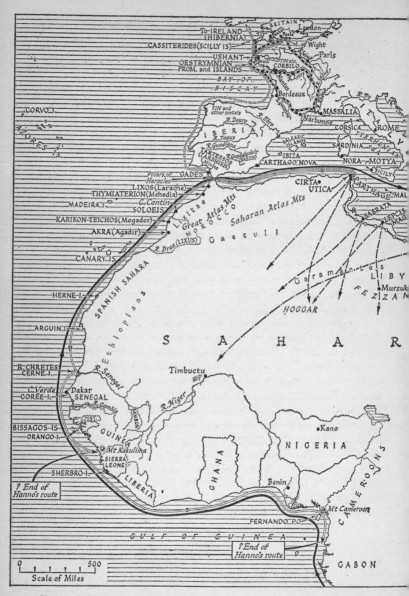

Fig 50 *The spread of Phoenician trade and exploration*

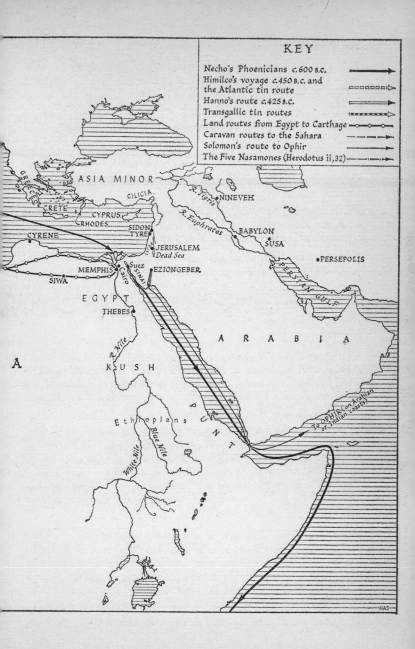

KEY

Necho's Phoenicians *c.*600 B.C.	
Himilco's voyage *c.*450 B.C. and the Atlantic tin route	
Hanno's route *c.*425 B.C.	
Transgallic tin routes	
Land routes from Egypt to Carthage	
Caravan routes to the Sahara	
Solomon's route to Ophir	
The Five Nasamones (Herodotus ii, 32)	

ASIA MINOR

R. Tigris   NINEVEH

GREECE   CILICIA

CRETE   CYPRUS

RHODES   R. Euphrates   BABYLON

CYRENE   SIDON   SUSA
TYRE

JERUSALEM   • PERSEPOLIS
Dead Sea

MEMPHIS   Suez   EZIONGEBER
Cairo
SIWA

EGYPT   A R A B I A

THEBES

A

K U S H

R. Nile

Ethiopians   To OPHIR (on Arabian or Indian coasts)

Blue Nile

White Nile

HAS

Pillars of Heracles and found cities of Libyphoenicians. He set sail with 60 penteconters and about 30,000 men and women, and provisions and other necessaries.

II. After sailing beyond the Pillars for two days we founded the first city which we called Thymiaterion. Below it was a large plain.

III. Sailing thence westward we came to Soloeis, a Libyan promontory covered with trees. There we founded a temple to Poseidon.

IV. Journeying eastward for half a day we reached a lake not far from the sea, covered with a great growth of tall reeds, where elephants and many other wild animals fed.

V. A day's sea journey beyond this lake we founded cities on the coast called Karikon Teichos, Gytte, Akra, Melitta and Arambys.

VI. Passing on from there we came to the large river Lixos, flowing from Libya, beside which nomads called Lixitae pastured their flocks. We stayed some time with them and became friends.

VII. Inland from there dwelt inhospitable Ethiopians in a land ridden with wild beasts and hemmed in by great mountains. They say that the Lixos flows down from there and that among these mountains Troglodytes of strange appearance dwell, who according to the Lixitae can run more swiftly than horses.

VIII. Taking interpreters from the Lixitae we sailed south along the desert shore for two days and then for one day eastward and found a small island 5 stades (*c.* 1 km.) in circumference at the farther end of a gulf. We made a settlement there and called it Cerne. We judged from our journey that it was directly opposite Carthage, for the voyage from Carthage to the Pillars and from there to Cerne seemed alike.

IX. From here sailing up a big river called Chretes we reached a lake, in which were three islands bigger than Cerne. Completing a day's sail from here we came to the end of the lake, overhung by some very high mountains crowded with savages clad in skins of wild beasts, who stoned us and beat us off and prevented us from disembarking.

X. Sailing from there we came to another big wide river, teeming with crocodiles and hippopotamuses. We turned again from there and came back to Cerne.

XI. We sailed south for twelve days from there, clinging to the coast, which was all along occupied by Ethiopians who did not stay their ground, but fled from us. Their speech was unintelligible, even to our Lixitae.

XII. On the last day we came to anchor by some high mountains clad with trees whose wood was sweet-smelling and mottled.

XIII. Sailing round these for two days we reached an immense gulf, on either shore of which was a plain where by night we saw big and little fires flaming up at intervals everywhere.

XIV. Taking on water here, we sailed on for five days along the coast until we came to a great bay which our interpreters called the Horn of the West. In it was a large island and in the island a salt-water lake, within which was another island where we disembarked. By day we could see nothing but a forest, but by night we saw many fires burning and we heard the sound of flutes and of beating of cymbals and drums and a great din of voices. Fear came upon us and the soothsayers bade us leave the island.

XV. We sailed thence in haste and skirted a fiery coast replete with burning incense. Great streams of fire and lava poured down into the sea and the land was unapproachable because of the heat.

XVI. We left there hurriedly in fear and sailing for four days we saw the land by night full of flames. In the middle was a high flame taller than the rest, reaching, as it seemed, the stars. By day it was seen to be a very high mountain called the Chariot of the Gods.

XVII. Thence sailing for three days past fiery lava we reached a gulf called the Horn of the South.

XVIII. At the farther end of this bay was an island, like the first, with a lake, within which was another island full of savages. By far the greater number were women with shaggy bodies, whom our interpreters called Gorillas. Chasing them we were unable to catch any of the men, all of whom, being used to climbing precipices, got away, defending themselves by throwing stones. But we caught three women, who bit and mangled those who carried them off, being unwilling to follow them. We killed them, however, and flayed them and brought their skins back to Carthage. For we did not sail farther as our supplies gave out.

There is general agreement on the identification of the places Hanno mentions up to and including the river Lixos, which is taken to be the river Draa on the boundary between Morocco and Spanish Sahara. The Lixitae, with whom he stayed for a time, would be Berbers and the inhospitable Ethiopians black men, the normal meaning of the word in Greek. That the Lixitae provided interpreters for the rest of the journey is important, for it shows that they were partly, at least, familiar with the regions farther south. Three days' sail from here Hanno founded Cerne on an island. Its position is crucial, for it is the farthest permanent settlement of the Phoenicians on the west African coast mentioned by any ancient writer. Three main identifications have been propounded for Cerne:

1. Herne Island, off Spanish Sahara;
2. Arguin Island, some 200 miles south of that;
3. An island, not exactly identified, near the Senegal delta.

Modern commentators, almost without exception, agree that the big river Chretes must be the Senegal. Admittedly Herne Island would conform with Hanno's text by being about three days' sail from the river Draa and also by being about the same number of miles from the straits as Carthage is. But it seems most unlikely that Hanno having reached the Senegal would go back as far as Herne. It looks as if we must abandon the distances given in the text, and place Cerne at or near the mouth of the Senegal. Some corroboration of this comes from the description of Cerne traffic in pseudo-Scylax (p. 156) who speaks of 'a big city up to which the Phoenicians sail'.[242] This can only indicate a riverine city, and there is no navigable river near Herne or Arguin. Besides, these places on the Saharan desert coast are unlikely sites for a mart which traded with a populous hinterland. Placing Cerne at or near the Senegal, both Hanno's story and that of pseudo-Scylax fall into place. What Hanno did was to sail up one branch of the Senegal to a lake and down another branch, the river swarming with crocodiles and hippopotamuses. This secondary trip was not in fact a coasting voyage at all.

The mountainous wooded promontory mentioned in the next paragraph will have been Cape Verde, and the large gulf, which came next, the mouth of the Gambia. From here on differences in identification become acute, some taking Hanno to the Cameroons, or even Gabon, while others say he stopped at Sierra Leone. The main arguments for the short view are that there is little or no sailing wind in the gulf of Guinea and the torrid heat and adverse currents would make rowing too difficult; also that the times Hanno gives are inconsistent with any longer journey. Those who adopt the longer view (and it certainly seems preferable, though it means abandoning the figures of distance cited in Hanno's text) maintain that the Cameroon mountain, 13,370 ft high and a volcano, more nearly resembles the Chariot of the Gods, as described, than does Kakulima (2,910 ft) in Guinea. However important the debate is for the story of Phoenician exploration, it has no bearing on that of Phoenician colonization, for this part of the journey had no lasting effects. We may note, however, that the Lixite interpreters must have made the journey before and been in contact with the natives.

The only ancient reference to Phoenician land exploration across the Sahara is a very unlikely story in Athenaeus,[243] a Greek gossip writer of *c.* AD 200, who mentions that a Carthaginian called Mago crossed the desert three times on a diet of dry meal without water! But, even if we discard this tale, as we must, it is certain that the riches of Africa were a powerful incitement to Phoenician merchants, and it would be surprising if some of them did not organize themselves for such a journey from time to time, even if they normally left this to middlemen, like the Garamantes, who lived inland of modern Tripoli, and the Gaetulians to the west of them. We have in this connection Herodotus' tale of five Nasamones[244] who made a long Saharan journey to a town inhabited by negro dwarfs and a crocodile-infested river flowing east–west, perhaps the Niger.

Passing to the Atlantic we may, in the first place, set on one side the famous Atlantis myth, for there is no evidence that the Phoenicians were ever directly concerned with it. Plato, who used the myth for his own philosophical purposes, derived it through Solon from Egyptian sources. It has indeed recently been suggested that the myth should be divorced from any connection with the Atlantic and thought of as an Egyptian folk-memory of the great Minoan empire, ruined physically and politically by the widespread destruction which followed the violent eruption of the volcano on Thera (mod. Santorin) in the Aegean towards the beginning of the fifteenth century BC.[245]

There is very little evidence about Phoenician activities in and around the Atlantic islands. Since Phoenician colonies existed for many centuries on the Atlantic coast of Africa (p. 59) there can be little doubt that at least Madeira and the Canaries, if not the Azores, would have been well known to Phoenician mariners. The only ancient reference worth citing is Diodorus' account[246] of a Gaditan ship, blown off its course into the Atlantic, which discovered a large island with a good climate, perhaps Madeira. Diodorus, perhaps copying Timaeus of the fourth century BC (as he often did), adds that the Etruscans, who were strong on the sea at the time (so that it should have been before their defeat at Cumae in 474), wanted to found a colony there but the Carthaginians put them off; yet no evidence of Phoenician settlement at Madeira has been found. The Canaries are certainly too close to the African coast to have been unknown to the Phoenicians, but there can have been no colony there either, for the primitive Guanche culture of the islands is believed to have lasted untainted until the fifteenth century AD. The Phoenicians may also have reached the Azores at some stage, for eight Punic and one Cyrenaecan coin of the fourth and third centuries BC were found as part of a hoard on Corvo Island in 1749, although unfortunately they are now lost.[247] Whatever emphasis we feel like placing on this single find it must at best imply no more than exploration, for if there were no Phoenician settlements in Madeira and the Canaries, such can hardly have existed as far west as the Azores.

1. ORIGINS

The Phoenicians are never more elusive than in their art. It is undeniable that artists of Phoenician birth and culture existed and flourished, but when we seek to distinguish their artistic creations and, still more, to define the general characteristics of Phoenician art, we run into many difficulties.

Towards the end of the Bronze Age a great mixture of artistic forces existed on the Levant coast and in its immediate hinterland. Since the time of the twelfth dynasty, if not before, Egyptian *chefs-d'oeuvre* were well known (p. 40 f.) to the Canaanite inhabitants and Egyptian forms and motifs were also imitated on objects made locally. These Egyptian influences continued to permeate Levantine art under the powerful kings of the eighteenth dynasty, and we cannot be surprised that the trend remained strong even after the decline of Egyptian power under the later Ramessid rulers.

The influences from the other great artistic area of the time, Mesopotamia, were not so widespread in the second millennium BC as those of Egypt. They are specially noticeable in glyptic art – in those cylinder-seals and stamp-seals often termed Syro-Hittite, whose motifs and style are so obviously derived from those of Assyria and Babylonia, with, however, clear differences and some admixture of Egyptian motifs that show them to be peripheral copies. It was not until the Assyrian hegemony during the early part of the first millennium that there was any strong Mesopotamian influence on major arts in the Levant coastlands. Before that, Levantine sculptural designs and types leant more towards those of Anatolia and the Hittites. Finds at Ugarit, such as the well-known stele of the thunder-god, show many traces of Hittite influence in costume and attributes, but the stance and attitude veer more towards the Egyptian. In the fifteenth and fourteenth centuries the Hurrian (Mitannian) power [248] might have brought different cultural influences to bear, but these people had no distinctive art of their own, and except for some cylinder-seals and the Hurrian white-on-dark painted pottery, we can ascribe no artistic products to them.

There were also influences from the Aegean. Much Middle Minoan polychrome pottery of the early second millennium BC was found at Ugarit and a Minoan colony was settled there; there are also, for example, spiral designs of Cretan style on a fragment of a silver bowl [249] from Byblos. Later, in the second half of the second millennium, Mycenaeans spread Aegean contacts and settlements eastward.

What, then, may reasonably be called Phoenician in this mixture of styles at the end of the Bronze Age and the beginning of the Iron Age? It is unfortunate that the only town site in Phoenicia proper which has yielded certain remains of that time is Byblos, and the material in question is still largely unpublished. Apart from a little early pottery, found in *sondages* at Tyre, [250] nothing that has been found in controlled excavations in the habitation areas of other major Phoenician towns can be dated earlier than the sixth century BC. That is not to say that such towns do not, or will not, yield earlier things. Already tombs at Khirbet Selm, Qrayé and Khaldé in the Lebanon have provided pottery of the early Iron Age [251] and further digging may produce even better results. Moreover, small bronzes and other minor objects of early Phoenician style have been bought in Phoenicia and must come from one or other of its cities, and we may also derive evidence from objects made in Phoenician style and probably by Phoenician craftsmen that come from Palestinian sites of the early Hebrew monarchy, such as Hazor, Megiddo and Samaria, as well as from sites in Syria and Assyria.

It is often hard to distinguish the true Phoenician style from the similarly mixed style of the north Syrian coast and its hinterland. The art of Phoenicia proper reveals a stronger Egyptian influence than we can discern in that of the Syrian

naked [Plates 80–82]. They sometimes are made in pairs, or even in groups of four. Attributes tend to be missing, but may at times have existed as separate attachments, and the figures adopt a stark frontal pose which is dull and uninteresting. A better type of figurine [Fig 51], fully fashioned in the round, also occurs on late Bronze Age sites, examples from Ugarit and elsewhere being frequently illustrated: this is the variety to which the Melqart figurine, found in the sea near Sciacca (p. 56), belongs [Plate 93].

3. THE NINTH CENTURY AND ONWARDS IN THE HOMELAND

There is a wide gap in date between these late Bronze Age types and the next group we can cite, none of which is earlier than the ninth century. There should not be such a hiatus in the evidence, for whatever happened at Ugarit, there was no long break in continuity in the Phoenician cities themselves, so far as we know, after the Sea Raiders had worked their will. Moreover the two groups are closely akin in style and little or no gap in artistic tradition can be recognized.

IVORY CARVING

The well-known series of ivories from Samaria, Arslan Tash and the Assyrian palaces at Nimrud and Khorsabad, which are not, however, all in one style, are usually thought to cover a period of over a hundred years from the later ninth to the earlier seventh century B C. Scholars have long debated which, if any, can reasonably be called Phoenician, and which should be ascribed to Syrian (that is, by now, Aramaean and not Canaanite) or perhaps Assyrian schools.

Some recognize two basic groups, a Phoenician and a Syrian. The former, which is well represented by finds at Arslan Tash and in the N.W. Palace at Nimrud, shows a strong mixture of Egyptian and Asiatic motifs in a typical Phoenician manner.[253] We may consider, for example, a panel from Arslan Tash depicting the 'woman at the window' – the votaress of Astarte (p. 122) – in which the subject is wholly Canaanite, but the woman wears an Egyptian wig and the window is supported by little columns with lotus capitals [Plate 62]. Another panel, also from Arslan Tash, is even more Egyptian in style, for it shows a female figure with costume and attributes that are basically those of the Egyptian goddess Isis, winged and holding lotus flowers, but facing an Asiatic tree-of-life [Plate 71]. There could be no better example of Phoenician adaptation of Egyptian motifs. A winged sphinx of blatantly Asiatic style, but once again having many Egyptian features, such as the double crown and head-dress, is also from Arslan Tash and provides a good illustration of the open-work type of ivory carving, so common in this group [Plate 68]. The stiff, frontal pose makes a strange contrast with the sleek body of the sphinx, which seems as if poised for action. On the other hand a fragmentary panel from the N.W. Palace at Nimrud, which showed a pair of male figures, clad wholly in Asiatic style, plucking fruits from a winged disk, seems mainly Assyrian in outlook, though certain details betray its Phoenician origin [Plate 67]. Equally Assyrian in aspect are many incised panels from boxes, such as a fine piece showing a winged bull butting (it would appear) a large rosette [Plate 69]. The drawing here is excellent, and the bull shows an almost Cretan liveliness.

All these ivories were probably used to decorate pieces of furniture made by Phoenician craftsmen either in the Levant or in Assyria itself.

The Syrian group, which is represented by the finds in the S.E. Palace at Nimrud and by stray examples from elsewhere in the near east and the Aegean, consists mainly of fragments of small boxes, fly-whisks, combs and the like. A piece of a round box shows part of a scene of two female sphinxes with long hair on either side of a sacred tree [Plate 63]: the face is wholly Syrian in style and countenance. An unguent vase in the form of a hollow female figure in long-sleeved dress, whose features seem more Asiatic than Egyptian, despite an Egyptian wig, comes from Sidon and is of bone, not ivory [Plate 66]. A woman's head, on the other hand, of ivory, with low, circular crown and well-modelled hair in long locks, is again wholly Syrian, well illustrating the features of a Semitic lady of the time [Plate 65,a]. The cavity for a tenon shows that it is part of a larger object. Another ivory figure [Plate 64], also an unguent vase, which is clothed in a long girdled tunic which leaves the breasts uncovered for the hands to hold in Asiatic fashion, from Beirut, forms a good pendant to the one from Sidon. Heads of purely Egyptian style, however, also occur among this group [Plate 65,b].

From these it will be clear that the Phoenician artist (and indeed the Syrian artist too, if he was not actually a Phoenician working in a Syrian style) had a good command of his material and a thorough sense of composition, by which he was able to fit a complicated scene into a small and confined space without appearing to cram it in. His modelling, too, of figures in the round is excellent, especially considering the intractability of ivory. Whether his apparently religious designs were meant to be merely decorative, and without religious intent, is a question which is difficult to answer. It applies not only to the ivories, but to other Phoenician art as well, including the repoussé or incised metal bowls to which we must now turn.

DECORATED METAL BOWLS

These, like the ivories, are found almost anywhere but in Phoenicia. They come from the Assyrian palaces, from Cyprus (in quantity), from Greece and from Etruria. Many are even more Egyptian in outlook than the ivories, others are more strictly Levantine or even Assyrian, though there are few, if any, that show no Egyptian traits. Their absence in Phoenicia has led some to believe they may be Cypriote, but it would seem that the mixed Egypto-Assyrian styles of their decoration prove their mainland origin, for had they been Cypriote they would have been less affected by the Egyptian and more by the sub-Mycenaean geometric Greek styles. They are a bit later in date than the ivories, belonging, it seems, mainly to the seventh century.

A fragment of a silver bowl from Amathus in Cyprus shows a complete mixture of styles [Fig 53]. In the outermost frieze Assyrian archers and Greek soldiery attack a city from the right, while Egyptian-looking soldiers climb ladders up the

Fig 54 *Phoenician silver bowl, mainly Egyptian in style, from the Bernardini tomb, Praeneste, Italy, inscribed with the owner's name, Eshmunazar, at the top of the central design. D. 0·195 m. Later seventh century* BC

walls on the left and other Egyptians cut down trees with Aegean double-axes! In the second frieze Egyptian deities and a winged scarab are placed on pedestals or altars of Egyptian design and, near by, two Phoenicians holding Egyptian ankh-amulets flank a typical stylized Phoenician palmette.

At Praeneste in Italy the Bernardini tomb of the later

Fig 53 *Fragmentary Phoenician silver bowl of mixed style from L. P. di Cesnola's excavations at Amathus, Cyprus (see di Cesnola, Cyprus: its Ancient Cities, Tombs and Temples, pl. 19). British Museum: formerly John Ruskin collection. D. 0·205 m. Seventh century* BC

seventh century contained two of these bowls that are wholly dissimilar. One, of silver [Fig 54], is almost completely Egyptian in style, with a central design showing a pharaoh slaying his enemies and round it four papyrus boats carrying deities or winged scarabs. Yet there is an Asiatic-looking lion under the pharaoh and a crouching, bearded Levantine in the exergue.

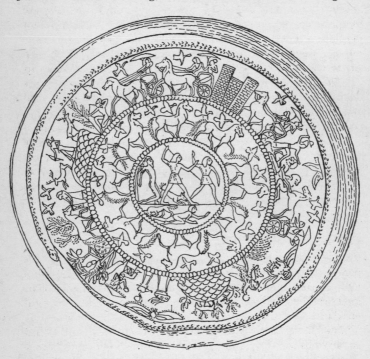

Fig 55 *Phoenician silver-gilt bowl, mainly Asiatic in style, Bernardini tomb, Praeneste, Italy. D. 0·19 m. Later seventh century* BC

A long inscription in hieroglyphic characters makes no sense, but there is also an inscription in Phoenician (added afterwards) giving the name of the owner, 'Eshmunazar, ben [son of] Asto'. This is the most Egyptian-looking of all these bowls, yet it is certainly not of Egyptian manufacture. The other Bernardini bowl [Fig 55], which is silver-gilt, is basically Asiatic in flavour. The outer frieze contains chariots and archers, and a very Assyrian-looking building with turrets, yet there is also a winged scarab. The inner frieze shows eight prancing horses and some birds; and the central medallion has a mixture of figures of Egyptian and Asiatic types. A particularly curious feature of this bowl is the serpent which encircles the whole design. Assuming that these two bowls, found together, are roughly contemporary, we may marvel that such different designs could come from Phoenician workshops at the same time. A similar mixture of Asiatic and Egyptian can be seen on the well-known silver-gilt bowl from Idalion in Cyprus [Plate 47]. Concentric friezes show scenes of combat – humans with lions and winged gryphons and sphinxes. The central medallion resembles that on the bowl from Praeneste with a scene of pharaoh slaying his enemies.

The Phoenician artist's sense of composition, especially when he tackled a frieze, comes out very clearly in all these bowls. Though there is a great amount of detail, it fits in very easily without overcrowding. With these as examples we need not wonder at the Homeric fame of the Sidonian artificers.

METAL STATUETTES AND STONE SCULPTURE

The homeland has produced fewer metal statuettes of this period than of earlier styles. A bronze figurine of a lady in a long, close-fitting tunic held by a tasselled girdle has her hair in three plaits and wears a low, circular head-dress and a tight necklace, no doubt of beads [Plates 84, 85]. The general style reminds us of the bone and ivory vases from Sidon and Beirut already discussed (p. 176 f.). Another female figure of bronze [Plate 93,a,b] is clad in a triple-flounced skirt to the knees, perhaps of Aegean origin. Both have a stiff, frontal pose and can claim no real artistry. A third figurine, seated and wearing an ankle-length close-fitting plain garment, has a very typical Levantine round face (compare again the bone vase from Sidon): her hair, probably not a wig, falls in curls on her shoulders [Plate 86].

Male figures of the period are very difficult to distinguish from their precursors of the late second millennium. One example must suffice, a figure in a short conical cap, holding a *patera* and seated on a throne flanked by lions [Plate 87]. Such poor, crudely modelled productions were clearly mass-produced for dedication in a sanctuary. We need spend little time on them.

Fig 56 *Limestone stele with Baal on a lion, Marathus. H. 1·70 m. c. eighth century* BC

Fig 57 *Alabaster relief with a carpet design of palmettes above a winged sphinx, Aradus. H. 0·61 m. Eighth to seventh century* BC

Let us pass on, rather, to stone sculpture, in which there are some better things to record. A limestone stele [Fig 56], 1·7 m. high, from Marathus, carved in relief, shows an egyptianizing winged disk and a Phoenician disk and crescent surmounting Baal in Egyptian dress with crown and *uraeus*, holding, however, a lion cub and standing on a lion which itself stands on a conventional mountain – all motifs which can readily be paralleled in Assyrian art. This piece is clearly in the same line of descent as the well-known thunder-god stele from Ugarit of the very end of the Bronze Age. Its style, however, recalls many of the ivories, and from this and its find-spot we may ascribe it to the eighth century or thereabouts. A fine alabaster relief from Aradus again resembles the ivories in many of its details and is presumably roughly contemporary with them [Fig 57]. On it a carpet panel of Phoenician palmettes between guilloche borders surmounts a squatting winged sphinx with double crown. In the lowest panel is a low altar or table. Another fragmentary relief,[254] probably from the same monument, shows a similar palmette carpet with guilloche borders, but this time surmounting a pair of winged gryphons just like those on the Malta fragment described below (p. 203 f.). None of these is likely to be later than the seventh century.

The Sidonian and western anthropoid stone coffins (pp. 103, 195) belong to the fifth and fourth centuries[255] and are, therefore, later than anything we have hitherto been discussing. Though the example illustrated [Plates 17, 18] is male, they are mainly female. A few show considerable Egyptian influence in their heads and head-dresses, though very soon the artists turned over to the new fashion of depicting Greek physiognomy and hair styles. Eastern ones rarely depict more of the person than the head, the rest of the body tapering mummy-like to a flattened ledge representing the feet. Some of the western examples show more of the human form and dress, as we shall see (p. 195).

These coffins illustrate how Greek art was invading the Phoenician homeland at this time. In the very tomb which contained Tabnit's Egyptian coffin were later burials in coffins of wholly Greek aspect (p. 103) dating from the late fifth to the end of the fourth century.[256] The earliest, called that of 'the satrap', is in Parian marble. It has a gabled lid with acroteria, and the two long sides depict, respectively, a seated man with servants, horse and chariot; and a panther hunt. The short sides have four armed youths in conversation, and a banquet scene. The latest is the 'Alexander' sarcophagus in Pentelic marble, on one side of which is a battle of Greeks and Persians with Alexander in lion's-skin head-dress in the thick of the fray. There is nothing Phoenician in the style, and these coffins are plain signs of the coming extinction of Phoenician art and culture as it had existed for well over half a millennium.

The end indeed came very soon. There are some monuments of true Phoenician style which are probably roughly contemporary with the coffins. The finest is perhaps the well-known memorial stele of Baalyaton (p. 94) from Umm el Amad, now in Copenhagen, depicting Baalyaton himself (the face is clearly a portrait) standing to right in long tunic and wearing a low circular cap [Plate 44]. At the top of the stele is a winged disk with *uraei*. This is the best of several similar stelae from Tyre or Umm el Amad, all of comparable date – probably the fourth century or a bit later. The portraiture shows Greek influence. Another contemporary piece is the stele of Yehawmilk from Byblos, showing a bearded man in long robe with cloak and low, round cap holding up a *patera* towards a seated Hathor in horned disk head-dress. His garb has a Persian look, but is clearly Phoenician, for it resembles that of some earlier eastern Phoenician priestly figures, as well as western examples. Such pieces [257] had few successors. The conquest of Alexander effectively killed Phoenician art in these regions.

4. PHOENICIAN ART IN CYPRUS

Difficult as it is to distinguish Phoenician styles in the homeland, it is even harder to do so in Cyprus. Cypriote art seems to have developed more or less uniformly during the early part of the first millennium in a style no doubt in part descended from the Mycenaean (there is no evidence that the Mycenaeans were ever driven out of Cyprus) and in part revivified, if that is a fair term, by influences from the Phoenician and Syrian mainland and from Greece itself. Egyptian motifs and styles that can be seen on Cypriote objects do not necessarily imply direct contacts with Egyptian artists' products, for they could come via Levantine art, as no doubt the Assyrian influences did. During the eighth century new Aegean influences came eastward in the train of commerce from Ionia and Greece proper (p. 21), and these strengthened the earlier Aegean elements in Cypriote art and led to what has been termed the Graeco-Phoenician styles of the seventh century onward. Yet, as Myres long ago pointed out,[258] the art of Iron Age Cyprus was developed *in situ*; it is neither Greek nor Phoenician essentially, and both its Phoenician and its Hellenic elements are secondary and late.

From the point of view of Phoenician art, therefore, Cyprus provides many problems and few clear-cut illustrations. Some things, such as proto-Aeolic capitals [Plate 46], objects bearing the Phoenician palmette, some types of jewellery, and votive figurines, can readily be picked out as Phoenician, while the figured metal bowls (pp. 177 ff.) and some of the normal bric-a-brac – amulets, scarabs and pendants – indicate here, as elsewhere, Phoenician commerce. But it is striking that, though some early pottery [Plates 111,a, 112,a, b] shows resemblances in form and finish to pottery from Phoenicia and Palestine, and from western sites (p. 139 f.), most Cypriote pottery of the time shows strong local characteristics descended from the Cypro-Mycenaean, and must have grown up on the spot without any major influx of Phoenician types. And so it is with sculpture and figurines also. In short, though Cypriote art shows some Phoenician influences, it is only comparatively rarely that objects from Cyprus can be called truly Phoenician.

To illustrate Phoenician – or at least nearer Asiatic – influences in Cypriote art we look first at a copper or bronze pot-stand or incense-brazier from Curium [Plate 83] of a class usually assigned to the closing years of the second millennium. Each of its four sides forms an open-work panel in which is a male figure and a stylized tree with branches formed by spiral coils. One panel shows a harpist seated; the other three depict men carrying objects that are probably (a) two fish, (b) a cup and two rolls of cloth, and (c) a copper ingot in the form of a hide. The figures are in Asiatic garb and wear shoes with turned-up toes that suggest Hittite prototypes and occur frequently on north Syrian sculptures down to the ninth century BC, if not later. This piece was probably made in Cyprus, but is linked artistically with north Syria rather than Phoenicia.

We can discern occasional Phoenician elements in Cypriote sculptures and terracotta figurines of the early Iron Age. A most interesting little limestone figure of a woman [Plate 72] which is extraordinarily modern-looking – one thinks instinctively of a Meissen or Chelsea genre figure – is not easy to parallel in its present context. There can be no doubt about its Asiatic (Myres calls it Assyrian) affinity. The figure, in the round, stands on a square bracket, with four other figures below, and is probably the handle of a large stone vessel. The hair, which is confined by a broad frontlet, falls on the shoulders in plaits and behind in a dense mass; we may compare the little bronze figurine [Plates 84, 85] from the mainland (p. 181). The figure wears a long tunic over which is a heavy cloak, its end held up in the left hand. She wears necklaces and armlets, and her feet are sandalled. There is a little Greek influence here, perhaps, but no Egyptian, and once again it is best to think of the Levant coast as its spiritual home, though its material, limestone, indicates local manufacture. We can hardly follow Perrot in calling it an image of 'la grande déesse phénicienne'; it must represent a human lady of noble rank.[259]

There are male statues also which show mainland influence. Some, such as one from the sanctuary at Ayia Irini [Plate 70], are clad in the plain short-sleeved, long tunic of priestly type which is typically Phoenician (p. 93 f.), and wear the pointed cap that occurs, as we have seen, on many bronze statuettes of the late second millennium and later from Phoenicia and Syria. The snow-man type of small terracotta figurine [Plate 74], found in hundreds in sanctuaries at Kition and elsewhere, can be paralleled at Al Mina and also farther south, for example at Tell Beit Mirsim in south Palestine.[260] The tubular body with splayed base is typical. Heads and faces are at times well delineated in Levantine style and at others roughly made in childish fashion. Large terracotta heads in similar childish style are found, and remind us of early western pieces [Plates 75, 76] from Carthage and Ibiza (p. 188).

Architectural details also reveal many Levantine traits. Most noteworthy and obvious are the volute capitals of the seventh century and later in a style termed proto-Aeolic, which were used purely decoratively on stelae, as well as on architectural columns and pilasters. Sometimes the volutes are combined with other Phoenician motifs, such as curled palmettes and sphinxes, as on a stele [Plate 46] from Golgoi (Athienou), or curled palmettes and lotus plants, as on the capital of another stele from the same site [Fig 58]. Similar capitals have been found in Palestine at Samaria, Megiddo and elsewhere in levels of the tenth to the seventh centuries BC, but not yet in Phoenicia itself. Devolved examples, considerably later in date, are found in north Africa, and even in Spain.[261]

Another type of Cypriote capital was based on the lotus and was certainly derived from Egypt. We see it on the little terracotta shrine from Idalion in the Louvre, which is usually ascribed to the seventh century or thereabouts [Plate 23]. The columns are roughly made, but their lotus form is unmistakable.

Fig 58 *Limestone capital of 'proto-Aeolic' type with curled palmettes and lotuses, from Golgoi, Cyprus. H. 1·05 m. Sixth century* BC

All in all it is not in Cyprus that we should look for pure Phoenician art styles. Too many other influences were current in that island to permit Phoenician art to manifest itself there in an unsullied form.

5. ART IN WESTERN PHOENICIA

Western Phoenician art in part imitates eastern styles and in part is influenced by the art forms of the colonists' western neighbours, especially those of the Sicilian Greeks and the Etruscans, and of certain Iberian peoples. In general, before the fifth century eastern influences are in the ascendant; thereafter these are replaced by others, mainly Hellenic.

The term western Phoenician art means, of course, primarily the art of Carthage; for the predominance of Carthage in the political sphere led to her predominance in the artistic also. Whether the other colonies were founded by her, or were independent settlements which later fell under her dominion, does not make any difference. We can trace Carthaginian, i.e. Punic, influences everywhere, even in things which are clearly products of the locality and could not be imports from Carthage. Once again it is better to discuss the objects by categories according to the material they are made of than to attempt a single chronological treatment.

TERRACOTTAS

Common things such as terracottas are inherently more likely to be of local manufacture than imported from far afield. Yet some clearly did travel and we have to try to distinguish the truly Punic from those which belong to the main stream of mixed Graeco-Asiatic Mediterranean styles of the earlier first millennium BC.

In the precinct of Tanit at Carthage (pp. 86-8), in the earliest stratum, an occasional terracotta figurine was placed alongside an urn. Thus a bottle of red ware in the form of a cow [Fig 22], the body painted with red stripes, was found above an amphora of similar ware. Such animal figurines are typically Phoenician, occurring on many sites in the east and west, and derive from Mycenaean prototypes. We may compare the imported (probably Cypriote) example [Fig 27] found in Cintas's early shrine-deposit (p. 89). In the same stratum very primitive and crudely fashioned figurines occurred [Plate 75], of a type found also in early graves at Ibiza [Plate 76], and we have already seen something very similar in Cyprus. Such crude things must have been made locally.

Other figurines of a somewhat later date (perhaps late seventh or early sixth century), that may be local, show considerable foreign influence. A peculiar multiple vase for offerings [Fig 59] has seven separate containers in the form of 'tulip' vases such as occurred in the lowest Tanit stratum and in contemporary Punic tombs [Plate 58,f], and it has, besides, a Hathoresque head above a long-horned cow's head. The art, though mixed, is basically Punic. On the other hand, figurines

of seated and standing deities of the sixth century are either so
Greek or so Egyptian in aspect that they cannot have been
made locally, for there is no evidence that Greek or Egyptian
artists worked at Carthage at this early date.

Fig 59 *Sevenfold vase of pottery, Douimes, Carthage. L. 0·30 m.
Seventh or sixth century* BC

Fig 60 *Terracotta mask
of Egyptian style,
Douimes, Carthage. H.
0·175 m. Sixth century* BC

Fig 61 *Terracotta mask
of Greek style, Douimes,
Carthage. H. 0·165 m.
Sixth century* BC

With figurines we may consider the masks that occur often
at Carthage and in Sicily, Sardinia and Ibiza. There are two
main varieties, the normal face and the grimacing.[262] The first

group are based on Egyptian or Greek prototypes and represent smiling females, occasionally with added jewellery, such as one from Dermech which still retains a nose-ring and once had ornaments on the ears as well [Plate 78; Figs 60, 61]. The others, which are wholly mask-like, with large holes for the eyes and usually for the mouth as well, have distorted faces which resemble an African tribal mask more than anything normally found in a Mediterranean context, especially as they

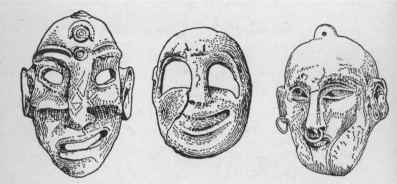

Fig 62 *Terracotta grimacing masks, Dermech (Carthage), and Ibiza. H. c. 0·20 and 0·16 m. Seventh century* BC

Fig 63 *Terracotta mask, Douimes, Carthage. H.0·195m. Sixth century* BC

are often tattooed [Fig 62]. They have been compared, it is true, with masks from the Artemis Orthia sanctuary at Sparta in Greece.[263] Recently, however, similar masks with eye-sockets, but not so distorted in countenance, have been found at Hazor in late Bronze Age contexts, one [Plate 77] being from in a potter's workshop. This shows that the western ones have at least distant eastern prototypes and can be considered wholly Phoenician.[264]

The western examples belong to the seventh and sixth centuries BC, as do the Spartan ones. But if the two groups are connected (and this seems extremely unlikely), the borrowing was surely by, and not from, Sparta. A third type, which seems to be wholly Punic and without parallels in the east, is repre-

sented by the famous Douimes male mask with nose-ring and
ear-ring(s) [Fig 63]. There is nothing of a grimace here and the
eyes and other features are properly sculpted.

In the fifth century and later Greek styles of statuette
predominate at Carthage. Many are indistinguishable from
contemporary ones in Greek Sicily and elsewhere; but some,

Fig 64 *Small terra-
cotta head of deity.
Third century* BC

Fig 65 *Terracotta
head of Demeter in
the form of an
incense burner; the
eyes are painted
black. Ste Monique,
Carthage. H. c.
0·30 m. Third
century* BC

Fig 66 *Terracotta
figurine from a
child's tomb, Ste
Monique,
Carthage. H.
0·09 m. Third
century* BC

if not all, were made in Carthage by immigrant Greek workers,
as is shown by their very number, by their clay, and by the
discovery of moulds for figurines among debris of potters'
ovens at Dermech (p. 143). The statuettes represent deities of
both sexes, such as a head of a deity, perhaps Baal Hammon
[Fig 64], in a high cap like a Persian tiara (compare Sardinian
gems (p. 209) with god or king in similar head-dress), or
heads of Demeter in the form of incense-burners, such as were
found in great quantities on a sanctuary site at Ste Monique

[Fig 65], or (this one more Punic than Greek in style) a male votary standing stiffly to the front with right hand outstretched [Fig 66]. All along the north African coast figurines of these graecizing types have been found in Punic cemeteries.

Passing to Ibiza and Spain we find, on the one hand, numerous statuettes wholly or basically Greek, such as could have come from Greek towns in north-east Spain, or have been made locally by Greek artists. Others are by no means Greek in style, being rather a mixture of Phoenician and Iberian. They are either nude or dressed in elaborately decorated tunics, and they often wear flashy head-dresses and jewellery [Plate 79], not unlike those of the Lady of Elche, who is now accepted as Iberian. A specially interesting discovery at Ibiza was a deposit of votive half-length figures of a deity identified by Spanish archaeologists as Tanit, found on the site of the sanctuary at Cueva d'es Cuyram (p. 39), which seems to have lasted from the fifth century to Roman times.[265] The figures are not only Punic in dress and attributes, but basically so in physiognomy as well.

STONE SCULPTURE

The earliest of the Punic stelae in the sanctuaries at Carthage, Nora and Motya (p. 88)[266] belong to the seventh and sixth centuries BC. Some are in the shape of thrones,[267] either alone or on a tall pedestal [Fig 24,d], others are of rude shape and embryonic design and cannot claim to illustrate any special artistic tradition [Plate 33], but they are interesting in that they seem to be in direct descent from similar stelae found in the much earlier eastern sanctuaries at Hazor (p. 86) and elsewhere (Plate 29).

The later aedicule-stelae (p. 88) with Egyptian mouldings and stepped tops and sometimes with disk, diamond, or crude human figure in a *naos* [Plate 30; Fig 24,a,c,f], were carved, no doubt, by stone masons rather than sculptors, but are, none the less, of good form and some minor artistic pretension. They lasted from the later sixth to the fourth century. Similar stelae, certainly later than the fourth century, are in true Greek style and carved by Greeks, including the fine one in Turin (p. 82), dedicated to Persephone by Milkyaton the suffete [Plate

45]. Equally elaborate types, but a little earlier and usually Phoenico-Egyptian in style, occurred in Sardinia, such as the fine example from Sulcis depicting a female figure in an Aeolic *naos* below a winged disk and a band of *uraei* [Plate 34]. A few of Greek type also occurred at Sulcis.[268]

Two very important reliefs in coarse limestone, which are wholly Punic, and correspond in date with these *naos*-type stelae, were found by Cintas in level II (late fifth to early third century BC) in the sacrificial precinct at Hadrumetum (p. 86). One, a somewhat incomplete panel, 17 cm. high, from a stele, shows Baal on a throne flanked by sphinxes and confronted by a standing worshipper [Plate 42]. Baal wears a conical cap and is bearded; the worshipper wears the typical Semitic long robe, and in composition the piece is redolent of the Phoenician ivory style. Cintas drew a very true comparison between it and a gold ring with a similar scene, though without the worshipper, from a fifth-century tomb at Utica.[269] The figure on a Sardinian gem (p. 209), seated before an altar [Fig 82,b], is better interpreted, perhaps, as a king. The other relief, which is part of a larger panel, 45 cm. high, from a similar stele, forms an interesting parallel to this Baal [Plate 43]. It represents a cloaked and hooded goddess, a parallel to which does not readily come to mind among Phoenician objects, though the face greatly resembles that of the female mask with nose-ring from Carthage [Plate 78].

The numerous series of sculptured stelae in hard limestone (p. 88) begins about 400 BC [Plates 32, 35; Figs 25, 28, 67]. These, which occur in thousands at Carthage, but are not, like the coarse limestone stelae, found normally on sites outside north Africa (though Perrot[270] illustrates a fine one from Lilybaeum in Sicily depicting a worshipper before an altar), have at times much greater artistic pretensions. Those from the Dermech area, coarsely carved, and once covered with stucco, retain little of any artistry that may once have been present on their stucco facing, yet their designs are often interesting as illustrations of Carthaginian life. But many stelae from the Tanit precinct, made in a stone of very fine grain and not stuccoed, often show incised figural and other patterns comparable with those on the copper razors (pp. 197-9) with which they are contemporary. These were no doubt produced by Greek artists or artists trained by Greeks.

Stelae also occur in the cemeteries at Carthage. At Ste Monique Delattre found a number with adorant figures in a

Fig 67 *Limestone stele with stylized floral pattern, precinct of Tanit, Carthage. W. 0·16 m. Third century* BC

Fig 68 *Limestone funerary stele with a female figure in a* naos, *Ste Monique, Carthage. H.* c. *0·75 m. Third century* BC

plain rectangle or a columnar *naos* of Greek or Graeco-Punic form [Fig 68]. These were clearly cut to a pattern and make no pretence of individual treatment for each interment. Though now anepigraphic, they may once have had painted inscriptions to identify the owner. Also from Ste Monique, and much more interesting, is a statue in the round on a tall rough-hewn base that clearly was set up over a tomb [Plates 19, 20].[271] It is interesting for its style, which is Graeco-Punic, for the dress of the lady, which is certainly not Greek and must reflect local usage, and for its careful execution, which extends to delineating individual hairs in the coiffure. But it is even more interesting because of its close similarity to statues from the cult-deposits of Cyprus, showing that a stylistic connection between eastern and western Phoenician art had not died out even by the third century BC.

The same phenomenon seems to be illustrated by the anthropoid coffins from Soloeis and Gades.[272] These are most unlikely to have been imported from the east, yet they resemble very closely their eastern fellows (pp. 103, 183), though they show, usually, more of the human form. Thus one Soloeis example depicts a lady clad in a Doric chiton and holding an unguent vase, while the figure on the Gades coffin has both arms and feet.

No anthropoid coffin has yet been found at Carthage, but we have instead the well-known coffins of the early third century BC from the Ste Monique cemetery, the lids of which depict human figures in high relief (p. 103).[273] The three finest represent a priestess and two priests, one priest's coffin and that of the priestess being from the same tomb. The priestess, who retained much of her original colour when first found, wears a Greek chiton overlaid from the waist down by the wings of a bird (probably a vulture, copying the Egyptian Isis-Nephthys figures) but she carries a dove in her right hand, an attribute which seems to connect her with Aphrodite or Demeter/Persephone. Her head-dress is surmounted by a hawk's head and its tassels on the shoulders end in bird's claws. Whatever we think of the attributes and other characteristics, the face of the lady is pure Greek. The two priests' coffins are closely akin, except that the figure on one has no head-dress and the other wears the bandeau or short stole referred to (p. 94) as part of the Punic priestly garb. Both are bearded and are wholly Greek in physiognomy and in the *himation* which they wear. A fourth coffin in this series represents a lady – not a priestess – wearing the *peplos* with head-fold that is so frequent on Hellenistic statues and figurines. Nine other coffins in this cemetery now seem almost plain, but they once had elaborate painted decoration. All thirteen are in the form of Greek

temples with *acroteria*. As a group they must be the work of
Greeks who settled at Carthage and graecized its artistic
culture, just as other Greeks changed that of the Etruscans;
but they retain many more Phoenician characteristics than do
the contemporary eastern ones of the 'satrap' series (p. 183 f.).
It is interesting to compare these hellenized coffins with the
contemporary ossuary of Baalshillek (p. 104), which is wholly
Phoenician in aspect [Plates 21, 22].

METALWORK

Most bronze art objects found at Carthage and in its neighbourhood are of foreign make, like the Corinthian gilt-bronze jug
from a tomb on the hill of St Louis, the Egyptian figurine
of a bearded man from Douimes [Fig 69], the cuirass of third-

Fig 69 *Small bronze figurine of Egyptian style, Douimes, Carthage. H.
0·05 m. Sixth century* BC

century south Italian fabric from a tomb at Ksour-es-Saf, and the
mirror-cover of Hellenistic type from Ste Monique. It is particularly strange that Carthage seems to have produced no
bronze figurines in the eastern Phoenician style (pp. 174 f.,
181 f.). Nor are we much better off if we look to other western
sites. A bearded male figurine with a high *calathos* head-dress
from Gesturi (or Genoni), Sardinia, often called 'Sardus Pater',

which is late and under strong Greek influence, closely resembles an even later, neo-punic, terracotta figure of Baal Hammon from the sanctuary near Siagu (Tunisia). This Sardinian piece is perhaps Punic work of the third or second century BC.[274]

In Spain there is one important bronze from Gades, portraying a priest with a gold face-mask [Plates 88–90]. There is nothing Greek or Iberian here. Stance and general lines remind one of Egyptian statuettes – even of *ushabtis* – and the gold

Fig 70 *Copper razor with designs in Greek style, Ste Monique, Carthage. H. 0·18 m. Third century* BC

mask is a frequent Egyptian trait. But the dress is Phoenician and the features Semitic, and it must be Phoenician work of the fifth century at latest.[275]

The copper razors,[276] which are so well known at Carthage and in Sardinia and Ibiza, are perhaps more Punic than any other product of western Phoenician art. Though some come from tombs of the sixth century and earlier, the vast majority

of extant pieces comes from fourth-century or later tombs at
Ste Monique and elsewhere.

Those of the earlier group are not decorated, except, on
occasion, with simple pointillé designs. The later ones are
often elaborately engraved with figures of deities or sacred

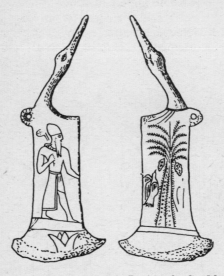

Fig 71 *Copper razor with designs in Punic style, Ste Monique,
Carthage. H. 0·145 m. Third century* BC

symbols, some Egyptian, others Punic, and some a mixture of
both these. Greek types are rarer, but one from Ste Monique
shows Heracles seated on a rock and, on the other side, a
youthful figure, possibly Asklepios [Fig 70]. At times a Greek
type will be on one face and an Egyptian or Egypto-Punic one
on the other. As all the types, whatever their artistic parentage,
seem to be religious in content, these razors as a whole provide
some of our best illustrations of the divine types and symbols
current at Carthage. One, with a date-palm on one side, shows
a Baal of wholly Phoenician aspect on the other, carrying an
axe on his right shoulder, and bearded, with a conical cap [Fig
71]. Others carry dedicatory inscriptions. But the predomin-

ance of Egyptian motifs [Fig 72], especially those connected
with the Isis-Horus cycle, indicates that, despite the helleniz-
ing influences that were then current at Carthage and despite
the invasion of Greek cults, Punic religious iconography
remained in some degree tied to the Egyptian.

Fig 72 *Copper razor with design in
Egyptian style, Ste Monique,
Carthage. H. c. 0·12 m. Third
century* B C

Fig 73 *Ivory mirror-
handle from a tomb on
the hill of Juno,
Carthage. H. 0·16 m.
Seventh century* B C

IVORIES

The ivory carvings that were so prominent among eastern
works of art have their counterparts made in the west, but these
are not normally of the same artistic merit. We note first a
mirror-handle of the seventh century, which may be of eastern
or western manufacture [Fig 73]. It comes from a tomb on the
hill of Juno and takes the form of a standing goddess in a long,
decorated girdled robe which reaches to the feet. The head is

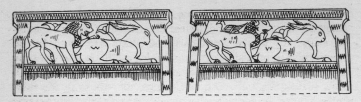

Fig 74 *Ivory comb from a tomb at La Cruz del Negro near Carmona, Spain. L. 0·135 m. Sixth century* BC

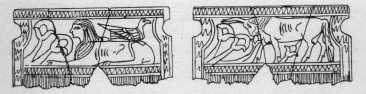

Fig 75 *Ivory comb from a tomb on the hill of Juno, Carthage. L. 0·10 m. Sixth century* BC

Fig·76 *Ivory plaque from a tomb at Bencarron near Carmona, Spain. L. 0·124 m. Sixth century* BC

of Egypto-Phoenician style with hair imitating the Egyptian wig, cut off sharply all round at the shoulders; the hands hold the breasts. Delattre found a similar piece in another seventh-century tomb at Douimes. In general stance and garb these resemble the female-figure vases from Sidon and Beirut (p. 176 f,), but they are more Egyptian in style.[277]

Much ivory-work, particularly combs, has been found in Spain, especially in the tumuli excavated by Bonsor in the Carmona district. Though found with Iberian interments, they are clearly Phoenician in style, however debased that style has become in its western factories. A comb from El Acebuchal,[278] the handle decorated with incised work on both sides, shows debased Phoenician palmettes flanked by squatting rams. Another, from La Cruz del Negro, Carmona [Fig 74], depicts on each face a not particularly bellicose lion attacking an apparently oblivious hare! It resembles in shape one from the hill of Juno at Carthage depicting a sphinx and a bull with lotus plants [Fig 75]: each has semicircular nicks in the sides of the handle. A plaque from a box or a piece of furniture seems to show Greek connections, for it depicts a kneeling Greek warrior with typical helmet, spear and shield, fighting a lion and a gryphon [Fig 76]; but there is no reason why it should not be of western Phoenician make. Greek soldiers were well known at Carthage, and indeed even in Spain, from the sixth century onwards, and this piece need be placed no earlier. Ibiza has yielded only a few minor items of this type. One, a pretty little panel (said to be of bone) with a crouching sphinx, cannot be later than the sixth century BC.

SHELL

Allied to ivory work, but painted and not carved, are the decorated cups and dishes or palettes made from ostrich-egg shells.[279] Such things do not seem to occur in the east, but they abound on many western Phoenician sites. At Carthage they are frequent, especially during the sixth and again during the third century BC, either in the form of cups made from more or less complete eggs, or as roughly cut-out dishes with a face, no doubt prophylactic, painted on them. A dish from Ste Monique [Fig 77] must fall late in the series; its face is crudely drawn, but in a lively style. Cups are better exemplified

Fig 77 *Ostrich-egg shell dish with painted design, Ste Monique, Carthage. W.* c. *0·07 m. Third century* BC

elsewhere, especially in Ibiza and at Villaricos [Plate 52], a mixed Iberian and Punic site in Spain. That they are not as common in Sicily and Sardinia may be fortuitous. Normally they bear only geometric decoration and the palmette, or ornament based on it. Animals rarely appear, and then only in schematic fashion. At Ibiza we find the lotus and a typically Greek palmette, as well as the Punic crescent and disk. Such things must have been produced in many places. They also occur along the north African coast at Djidjelli and Gouraya and elsewhere. Theirs is a dull art, on the whole. Given the nice, smooth surface of an ostrich-egg shell to work on, one might have expected a more venturesome artistic approach.[280]

6. PHOENICIAN JEWELLERY

It is so difficult to distinguish eastern from western styles in jewellery that it is best to consider all the examples together. Such small objects must have been the stock-in-trade of travelling salesmen, and though at times in the west, especially in Spain, local origin is manifest, we often cannot say whether a particular object was made in the Levant or in some other Mediterranean area. It may be that, down to the fifth century at least, much of this jewellery (though not all, p. 204 f.) was made in Phoenicia, Cyprus or Egypt. The close similarity of the individual pieces in design and technique would seem to indicate that they were made at no great distance from each other.

Most of the decorative Phoenician jewellery that has survived in good state is gold: silver jewellery does not often withstand burial in the salty milieux in which the coastal sites lay, while bronze seems chiefly to have been used for utilitarian items like fibulae (which were never so current in Phoenician lands as they were in Greece and Italy), and plain bangles, earrings and hoops of finger-rings. But of gold jewellery there is a mass, and much of it is technically and artistically very good indeed. We can only indicate here the main styles and illustrate them with a few choice examples.

The Phoenicians learnt their gold-working partly from the Mycenaeans and partly from Egypt. They were skilled (p. 138) in repoussé work and in granulation – techniques which, by the seventh century, had become current in Etruria also, perhaps by direct borrowing from Phoenicia. Though technique may help, it is mainly style that differentiates Phoenician work from that of their contemporaries elsewhere. We have seen how the Phoenician style in other media, such as ivories, is characterized by a mixture of Egyptian, Mycenaean and Assyrian or other Asiatic motifs. There is to some extent a predilection for animal, plant and geometric designs, rather than the human figure, and when humans are portrayed they are often the least successful part of an individual composition.

Little jewellery of our period seems to be extant from eastern sites. Among the rare examples we may instance a nice, not too elaborate, leech ear-ring with granulation [Plate 107], found at Marathus and probably to be dated not later than the sixth century BC. The Joan Evans ear-ring in the Ashmolean [Plate 106] and several other examples which closely resemble it from Carthage and Tharros may also be of eastern origin. All were perhaps made by Phoenicians in the Delta, since the Egyptian hawk element takes such a prominent place on them.[281] They must be roughly contemporary with the Marathus piece.

A group of tiny pendant figurines of gold must also be eastern work. Six come from Cyprus, five being in the Cesnola collection in New York and the other in Düsseldorf.[282] The origin of a seventh, now in the Ashmolean Museum, is not known, but it clearly belongs with the others [Plate 95,a, b]. They have two loops for suspension at the back. Myres identifies them as depicting the mother-goddess, but the figures are perhaps male, and if so are probably adorants. They are well made in a typical Egypto-Phoenician style and must belong to the seventh or sixth century BC.

A very different Cypriote piece, which shows many Phoenician characteristics, is a gold plaque depicting two men in a chariot,[283] and, above, two women in high head-dresses. The island has also yielded many examples of the simpler type of ear-ring, such as those illustrated from Carthage [Fig 78,b–d].

From the west we start with an early piece from Malta [Plate 92]. It is a small fragment of leather covered with gold foil on which is embossed a very pretty Phoenician design of two rampant gryphons flanking a multiple palmette, with a winged disk above. We have noted such a design on other works of art, such as an alabaster relief from Aradus (p.

183), but rarely is it so finely and tastefully fashioned as on this piece, which must be part of the cover of a wooden chest or a remnant of some item of ceremonial clothing. It cannot be later than the seventh century.

Tombs at Carthage and Tharros in Sardinia have yielded many circular pendants with fine granulation, such as two from Douimes, both bearing a winged disk, a crescent and disk, and two *uraei* [Fig 78,a]. Details vary, but granulation and chasing are superb on both. Plainer disks of this type and a small pendant Hathor-headed bust can be seen on two

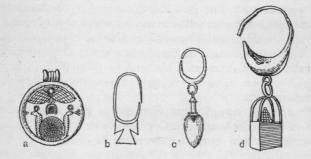

Fig 78 *Gold pendant and ear-rings from Douimes, Carthage. H. (a) 0·022, (b) 0·039, (c) 0·056, (d) 0·044 m. Late eighth to sixth century* B C

necklaces from Tharros [Plate 104]. The plainer disks were sometimes inscribed, like the famous Yadamilk piece [Fig 35] from Douimes (p. 109). A more elaborate pendant from Tharros, showing much Egyptian influence, is in the form of a bust of Isis-Astarte pressing her breasts and wearing a curious head-dress of horns within which are what seem to be three *cippi* crowned with balls [Fig 79]. These pendant types, all fairly early, seem, with the possible exception of the last, to be wholly western and were perhaps made in Carthage.

As an undoubted example of eastern work of this early period found on western sites we may instance the well-known bracelet from Tharros formed of six linked plates bearing Phoenician palmettes or lotus capitals, with an eye-amulet plate at each end [Plate 105]. The design is embossed and tricked out with granulation and chasing and is of the highest standard of craftsmanship. The ends were linked together by a pair of silver cords now partly lost through corrosion. An equally fine Tharros piece in Cagliari has the central plate decorated with a winged hawk-headed scarab.

Ear-rings are very varied in type. Some plainer ones take the form of a Maltese cross or a pendant box or acorn, for example [Fig 78,b–d]. A fine pair from Tharros has finials imitating spherical glass eye-beads [Plate 108].

There are also many ear-rings of complicated design, not unlike the Joan Evans piece, from early tombs at Carthage and Tharros. A pair with a hawk and a pendant box hanging from a 'leech' ring was found in grave 6 at Tharros;[284] and in grave 8, with the palmette bracelet, was one in the form of a double Horus pectoral, from which hangs a vase covered with granulation. Similar ear-rings, but usually simpler, occurred in the Douimes tombs at Carthage. A particularly good one from Tharros, now in Cagliari, is made up of three parts: a stylized Horus pectoral, a hawk and an elaborate vase-pendant. This probably contained a magic text, like the numerous hollow pendants which

Fig 79 *Gold ear-ring with bust of Isis-Astarte, from Tharros, Sardinia. H. c. 0·045 m. Sixth or fifth century BC*

occur on many of the western sites. Two fine ones, in gold, are in the form of columns, one topped by the lion-head of Sekhmet and the other by the ram-head of Amon-Re [Plates 91, 96]. All have a suspension-ring and a few have been found on necklaces. Some, both in Carthage and in Sardinia, have yielded metal plates [Fig 80] embossed with long magical friezes of Egyptian gods and symbols that derive from Egyptian friezes on the walls of temples at Dendereh and Edfu. Two of the plates bear small inscriptions in Punic characters, and for this and other reasons we may believe that, though they follow their Egyptian prototypes pretty slavishly, they were probably made by a Phoenician at Carthage. The pendants in precious metal belong to the seventh, sixth or fifth century: the type lasts, however, in baser metal and even in faience until the third century B C. Variant forms, other than those cited, occur, e.g. one in the shape of a *cippus* with pyramidal top, from Tharros, grave 1, which is duplicated by one from Gades.

The story of Phoenician jewellery in Spain must revolve round the treasure from La Aliseda, near Caceres, even if that treasure may not be wholly Phoenician in content. It is now

Fig 80 *Amuletic silver strip from an amulet-case, Tharros, Sardinia. W. c. 0·015 m. Sixth or fifth century* B C

generally accepted as being of the seventh or sixth century at latest, and it provides, perhaps, more first-class jewellery than any other single find within the Phoenician sphere of influence in the west. Its chief contents were:[285]

1. A belt [Plate 97], 68·3 cm. long and 7·1 cm. wide, formed of many separate plates, not all of which may have been preserved. The plates are granulated and embossed and bear repeated motifs of a debased Phoenician palmette, of a man fighting a lion, and of a gryphon passant.

2. A pair of ear-rings [Plate 98], each 8 cm. in diameter, based on the 'leech' type, with a ring of open-work lotus flowers flanked by hawks facing outwards, alternating with blooms resembling palmettes. The pieces are covered all over with the finest granulation. Joining the ends of the 'leech' bow is a wire for piercing the ear-lobe, and the ear-rings carry besides a small chain to hang over the ear for greater security. Blanco remarks that in this pair the ancient goldsmith shows his whole technical virtuosity and his taste for recurrent ornament.

3. A diadem, 20 cm. long, built of plates, rosettes and pendant spheres on chains between triangular end-plates, which shows mixed influences, not wholly Phoenician. Compare its rosettes and spheres with the Phoenician volutes in the centre of the end-plates.

4. A pair of penannular bracelets, 6·6 cm. in diameter and 2 cm. wide, on which the central band consists of finely designed open-work spirals and is flanked by a plain moulding between cable borders, while the end-plates have embossed palmettes above a large lotus design and are again tricked out with granulation.

Besides these superb pieces, the glass already referred to (p. 145), and two metal utensils, this treasure contained three necklaces of gold beads and pendants, including several amulet-cases, two crescents and disks (both so typically Phoenician), and a number of rings, including a fine broken-backed signet ring of solid gold [Plate 99] in which is mounted an amethyst scarab [Fig 81] engraved with two seated deities facing an altar surmounted by a palmette and a winged disk. The scarab and its mount swivel loosely in the ring, which was not worn on the finger, but on a cord round the neck.

Fig 81 *Design on the amethyst scarab mounted in a signet-ring (Plate 99) in the 'Aliseda treasure'. L. 0·022 m. Seventh or sixth century* BC

Though some of these jewels, such as the signet ring, are purely Phoenician, others, while showing many Phoenician elements, reveal certain alien traits as well. The necklaces may perhaps come from Carthage, and the signet ring from Phoenicia, but the other items are now thought by Blanco to be Tartessian, a culture which had, he thinks, by this time become a mixture of indigenous and oriental influences. This is just what we might expect, since Phoenician dominance in the Spanish hinterland in these early years was not strong: their settlements were but trading-posts exercising no suzerainty but only an artistic and cultural influence on the native population upon whose shores they were permitted to live.[286]

Gades, the chief colony in Spain, has yielded little early jewellery, except one group found in 1887 in a grave near that of the anthropoid coffin (cf. p. 195). This contained two rings, one mounted with an agate signet depicting a woman carrying a jug and a floral branch,[287] two ear-rings and a short necklace of beads with a rosette pendant of Carthaginian type. The group seems to belong at latest to the sixth century, but since it was found near the coffin, its date of deposition is more likely to be the fifth century. Ear-rings in the form of a circular granulated and filigree band with a rosette applied in relief, that occur frequently in tombs at Gades, are also probably sixth-century.

Later Punic jewellery everywhere shows so much Greek influence in its design that it deserves no place in a discussion of Phoenician art. These Greek motifs, however, are often accompanied by the sign of Tanit or the crescent and disk, or other Phoenician emblems to give us proof that, even if Greeks made it, they were working in Carthage or some other Punic centre.

7. PHOENICIAN SEALS AND SCARABS

Allied to jewellery are the seals and scarabs which form such a constant feature of Phoenician tomb-furniture. By the beginning of the Iron Age the two main varieties of near-eastern seals, the cylinder and the stamp, had both had long histories. Even in Mesopotamia the stamp was by this time gradually ousting the cylinder in popularity, but the latter was not yet dead and in fact remained current in Mesopotamia down to Persian times. But in Phoenicia by the beginning of the first millennium BC the cylinder was virtually outmoded. A few belonging to the early part of that millennium have been found in Phoenician surroundings in the east, both in Cyprus and on the mainland. Types are allied to contemporary Syrian ones, and are on the whole debased and dull. In the west the rare examples that have been found are not later than the seventh century and are direct eastern imports (not necessarily from Phoenicia).[288] The cylinder-seal was specially adapted for sealing clay tablets, on which, when soft, its design could be readily rolled, and the abandonment of such tablets in Phoenicia (they were current in Persia down to the end of the fourth century, at least) and the adoption of papyrus, potsherds or

parchment as a medium on which to write,[289] must have led to
their rapid disappearance.

With the abandonment of the cylinder in the east the scarab,
scaraboid and conoid became easily the most popular and predominant types of seal, but the very common Asiatic conoid
does not seem to have spread westwards, and thus it is scarabs
and scaraboids which we find on all western Phoenician sites
of the seventh and later centuries. At first they are mainly
Egyptian in style; most if not all of them must have been made
in Egypt, and this egyptianizing phase lasted till the end of the
sixth century BC (p. 146).

Fig 82 *Two scarabs from Sardinia with (a) The king attacking a lion,
and (b) A king or Baal seated before an altar. Sc.* c. ⅔. *Fifth or fourth
century* BC

Six scarabs and scaraboids [Plate 109,a–f], five from eastern
sites, one with no locality, and all dating between the ninth
and the fifth century, well illustrate this phase. Only one of
them [Plate 109,a] is purely Asiatic and none is Greek in style.
After this Greek influence became predominant, and scarab
designs followed the new fashion. We may note the very Greek
style of the other two examples illustrated [Plate 109,g,h].
Pure Phoenician subjects, however, still occurred, as on two
Sardinian examples, one showing a king attacking a lion, the
other a king or Baal enthroned beside a burning altar [Fig 82].

Cintas has shown in graphic form that at Carthage scarabs
and scaraboids of the seventh and early sixth centuries were of
faience in Egyptian style; from the sixth to the early fourth
century the predominant materials – again in Egyptian style –

were hard stones (especially cornelian), glass, frit and faience; and from the late fifth to the early third century the Sardinian type of green jasper scarab, either in a Greek or in a truly Phoenician style, held the field, to be finally succeeded there-after by faience or frit scarabs and scaraboids of decadent mixed styles.[290] This general pattern also holds good elsewhere in the west, and these scarabs can be of great help in dating tombs and other deposits.

It is thought that there were factories for green jasper scarabs in Sardinia, since so many have been found there, including unfinished pieces. That they are so often Greek in style argues, to my mind, against a Sardinian origin for the majority, for by this time the Carthaginians controlled Sardinia very jealously. We might, rather, believe that they were made at Carthage or in Sicily. However the site of a factory for these little amuletic seals in either of these places eludes us. Some may even have been eastern.

They were worn mounted in rings or strung on necklaces or bracelets. Not all of them were used as seals; but at least those that are mounted in plain gold or silver rings with swivel attachment must certainly have had sphragistic intent, and were not merely ornamental or prophylactic.

Even when they were used as seals their owners usually con-tented themselves with the device and did not inscribe their names on them. Some scarabs, however, both eastern and western, carry Phoenician nominal inscriptions. When this happens there can be no question but that the object is a seal and not merely an amulet.

8. SUMMARY

In this chapter it has only been possible to draw attention to the main trends of Phoenician art in the east and west and no one aspect of it could be discussed as fully as it deserved. The very nature of the Phoenician artistic tradition, with its bor-rowed motifs and mixture of styles, makes analysis doubly difficult, and at the same time exceedingly subjective. Those who know the material intimately may, perhaps, feel that much of interest has been left out and that what is included does not provide the picture they would have wished to see.

There are two basic difficulties. On the one hand, scholars are widely divided in their opinions as to where, in the eastern area, Phoenician art ceases and Syrian, shall we say, or Cypriote, art begins. When the objects in question are found far away from their place of origin – in Greece for example or in Italy – the problem becomes even more acute. It is equally difficult to decide what is truly Phoenician amongst the many art objects found on Phoenician sites, especially in the west, and to separate what is likely to have been made by the Phoenicians themselves from that made by others, chiefly Greeks, working for them.

Yet, when all is said, a picture of the Phoenician as an artist of no mean skill does arise from at least some of the items we have discussed. The ivory carvings and figured metal bowls of the east show his skill in composition and his great sense of artistic style. There can be no doubt that had we been fortunate enough to find some of his textile fabrics this facet of his genius would have appeared to even greater advantage. So, too, the jewels from Carthage and Tharros and other sites show his capacity for taking infinite pains in craftsmanship and design and his ability in fitting the object to its purpose. The work is excellent and the decoration is not overloaded.

In sculpture and figurines, whether of stone, metal or clay, the Phoenician artist is not nearly so adept. Most of the best works we have described – such as the sculptured coffins – are unlikely to have been made by Phoenicians, for they belong to the later period when Greek artists had got a foothold both on the Phoenician coast and at Carthage. The poorer objects, such as metal statuettes and the great mass of terracotta figurines, are cheap, mass-produced items for religious usage, displaying only the most meagre merit as art.

Thus our Phoenician art is not only a mixture of styles, it is a mixture of skills: the best is very good, the worst is unworthy to be called art and the fact that, to paint the picture properly, we have had to include it makes it clear that the Phoenician, though he possessed an artistic bent, was less interested in art for his own purposes than for the price he could get for it abroad.

Notes

1. THE PEOPLE, THEIR ORIGIN AND AFFINITIES

1. Plutarch, *Praecepta gerendae reipublicae*, iii, 6 (*Moralia*, Didot, II, p. 796); Appian, viii (Libyca), p. 62; Pomponius Mela, i, 12.

2. Herodotus (i, 1) says that the Phoenicians came from the coasts of the Indian Ocean, and it is interesting to see that the suggestion that the Semites came from the south had gained ground so early.

3. Mark vii, 26.

4. Matthew xv, 22.

5. Augustine, *Epistolae ad Romanos inchoata expositio*, 13 (Migne, *Patr. Lat.*, XXXV, col. 2096): 'Unde interrogati rustici nostri quid sint, punice respondentes, Chanani, corrupta scilicet, sicut in talibus solet, una littera, quid aliud respondent quam Chananaei?'

6. T. J. Dunbabin, *The Greeks and their Eastern Neighbours*, 1957, pp. 24 ff. He maintains, however (p. 35), that the actual presence of Greeks in the eighth and seventh centuries has so far not been proved in Phoenicia, but only in Cilicia, north Syria (especially at Al Mina, a real Greek colony), Palestine and, of course, Cyprus. Yet this absence of Greek objects of that period in Phoenicia is paralleled by an almost equal absence of Phoenician objects. The fact is that there has not been enough excavation in the appropriate town levels, since they are so difficult to reach (p. 172 below). On this problem see also, now, P. J. Riis, *Sūkas I, The N.E. Sanctuary and the First Settling of Greeks in Syria and*

Palestine, Copenhagen, 1970, pp. 126–75 and map, fig. 46.
He dates the earliest Greek settlement from the ninth century.

2.   GEOGRAPHY

7. Pliny, v, 14 and 17, places the boundary between Phoenicia
   and Palestine at Caesarea, a Herodian foundation on the
   site of the former Tower of Straton, and for him Dor was
   the most southerly important town of Phoenicia. But yet
   he calls Jaffa 'Joppe Phoenicum'. Much interest attaches
   to the claim Eshmunazar of Sidon makes on his coffin text
   of the sixth century B C (see p. 111), that he added Dor and
   Joppa to the Sidonian territory 'for ever'. This suggests
   that they were already Phoenician towns, for conditions in
   the sixth century would not have favoured Sidonian expansion outside the Phoenician area.

8. Strabo, xvi, 2, 13. A portion of the walls, possibly Phoenician, is illustrated in Perrot and Chipiez (1885), fig. 7,
   after Renan. Considerable traces of the harbour works are
   also discernible, and have recently been studied by Miss
   Honor Frost, using both air and under-water survey. Her
   report, now being prepared, will be of great interest and
   value.

9. For a brief account of this fortress see M. Dunand in Ward
   ed. (1968), p. 45.

10. See R. Mouterde *et al.*, *Sidon, aménagements antiques du
    port de Saïda*, Beyrouth, 1951, and for a useful summary
    with key plans, H. Frost, *Under the Mediterranean*, 1963,
    pp. 88–96, figs. 19–23. Of special interest are the sluice-
    gates and tanks provided for admitting a strong flow of
    sea-water to flush away the silt in the closed ports, a system
    which certainly goes back to Roman times, and very
    probably earlier, since some method of getting rid of the
    silt would always have been necessary to enable the ports
    to function properly.

11. Strabo, xvi, 2, 23.

12. Poidebard (1939), pp. 23 ff., pls. 8 ff. For a brief account of Poidebard's work, with a useful plan, see Frost, op. cit. in note 10, pp. 70–88, figs. 17–18, who shows how well Poidebard solved the problems of the closed port and the Egyptian harbour on the south side, although the Sidonian harbour on the north side needs further investigation.

13. Appian, viii (Libyca), 96; Strabo, xvii, 3, 14; and see further Harden (1939), pp. 1 ff.

14. Gsell, II, p. 77, citing Appian and Polybius. A. Audollent, *Carthage romaine*, 1901, p. 224, says that up to the sixth century AD large ships could enter the lake.

15. Gsell, II, pp. 8 ff. and notes ad loc. He cites, however, some ancient texts which indicate that Byrsa, the upper town, had a wider expanse than the hill of St Louis, and Picard, G. and C. (1958), p. 26, note 10, and p. 35, suggest that the three hills of St Louis, Juno and the Odeon/Theatre were all included in it. The hint (p. 78 below, note 90) that the temple of Eshmun may have been on the Odeon hill would confirm this. For the Appian texts about Byrsa see Harden (1939), p. 8.

16. Gsell, II, p. 443 and references ad loc.

17. G. Picard, *Rev. archéol.* 1958, i, p. 30; Picard, G. and C. (1958), p. 30. Two layers of paving, one Punic perhaps, one Roman, have been recognized. Traces of a mole linking the island in the circular port to the mainland and of a channel linking the circular port with the sea have also been found.

18. The great Zaghouan aqueduct, which brought water from the Zaghouan mountain, some 75 km. to the S.W., was not built until Hadrian's time.

19. *Comptes rendus Acad. Inscr.* 1950, pp. 53–9, with map showing position and two photographs; Picard, G. and C. (1958), p. 33; Picard, G. (1956), p. 74, pl. 73.

20. The region had already, by a happy chance, been named 'Salammbo' after the heroine of Flaubert's novel.

21. That by the end of the eighth century Carthage was power-ful enough for the Sicilian settlements to look to her for leadership is suggested by Thucydides' remark (vi, 2, 6), if we can take it at its face value, that when the Greeks came

to Sicily in the 730s the Phoenicians withdrew to the west 'for from there the distance to Carthage was shortest'. The reason for her rapid increase in size and prosperity may have been that she, unlike many of the other settlements, was founded by an aristocratic and influential group of Tyrians, rather than as a mere venture of merchants. She might thus more readily attract new waves of colonists, not only from Tyre, during the unsettled time of the Assyrian attacks from the middle of the eighth century onwards.

22. For a map showing the change in the shore-line at and near Utica see Gsell, III, p. 109.

23. Cintas (1949), pp. 8 ff. and id. (1954), pp. 11 ff., 61 and fig. 80 (map of sites in Morocco).

24. It should be noted, however, that, as on so many Phoenician sites, the coast-line has altered since antiquity: see the two maps in A. Jodin, *Mogador, comptoir phénicien*, 1966, figs. 2 and 3, showing that the headland on which modern Mogador stands was formerly an island and the coast at the mouth of the river Ksob did not curve into a bay. Even so, the island site, so close to the mainland, was a good 'Phoenician' one.

25. Cintas (1954), pp. 35 ff.; Jodin, op. cit. in note 24. Jodin proves (op. cit. pp. 187–9), from pottery and other evidence, that there was an active Phoenician settlement here from the mid seventh to the early sixth century B C, but there was then a gap in occupation until the third century, when Punic amphorae reveal further activity on the site.

26. Recent under-water survey of the lagoons around Motya and of the line of the causeway by Miss du Plat Taylor and others (*Ann. Leeds Oriental Soc.*, IV, 1962–3, pp. 84 ff.; B. S. J. Isserlin, *Not. Scavi*, 1970, pp. 561 ff.) has shown that the surface of the causeway where it can be traced (it disappears for some as yet unaccountable reason *c*. 550 m. before it reaches the mainland shore) lies on average *c*. 5–15 cm. below low-water mark, and also that certain harbour walls and quays outside the north gate of Motya, as well as the ancient shore-line at Birgi, are now submerged. It is clear, therefore, that the water level has risen, perhaps by about half a metre, and that when the Phoenician town existed the island may have been slightly larger and the

distance from it to the mainland shorter. I am grateful to Miss Taylor for help with this problem.

27. J. I. S. Whitaker, Motya, 1921; and, for recent excavations, S. Moscati, *The World of the Phoenicians*, 1968, pp. 200–4, and id. in Ward ed. (1968), pp. 65 ff., and ref. ad loc. to the preliminary reports (cited below, p. 268, *s.n.* A. Ciasca).

28. Full reports on the Tanit precincts at Sulcis and Tharros are still awaited. For important new sites at Monte Sirai and elsewhere on the island see Moscati, *The World of the Phoenicians*, 1968, pp. 211–27 and id. in Ward ed. (1968), pp. 65 ff. and ref. ad loc. to the preliminary reports (cited below, p. 268, *s.n.* F. Barreca). Monte Sirai is specially interesting as the first Phoenician inland site in Sardinia, being two and a half miles from the S.W. coast.

29. For recent work on Phoenician sites in Malta, Gozo and Pantelleria see Moscati, *The World of the Phoenicians*, 1968, pp. 191–3, and id. in Ward ed. (1968), pp. 65 ff. and ref. ad loc. to the preliminary reports (cited below, p. 268, *s.n.* V. Bonello).

30. Strabo, iii, 5, 3 ff.

31. Polybius, x, 10, 1 ff.

3. HISTORY OF THE PHOENICIANS IN THEIR HOMELAND

32. Contenau (1949), p. 121, pl. 1, b.

33. Many objects bearing the names of these and other early pharaohs have been found at Byblos. See M. Chéhab in Ward ed. (1968), pp. 1 ff., pls. 1–3.

34. For recent English translations of the text and short commentaries see B. Gunn in *Land of Enchanters*, ed. B. Lewis, 1948, pp. 29 ff. and John A. Wilson in *Ancient Near Eastern Texts*, ed. J. B. Pritchard, 1955, pp. 18 ff.

35. What ancient authors tell of the foundation of these towns does not, of course, tally with this account, and some of their stories are contradictory. Herodotus (ii, 44), for

example, writing about 450 BC, says he was told by the priests of Melqart at Tyre that the city and temple were founded 2,300 years before, i.e. in 2750 BC, while Justin's estimate (xviii, 3) of one year before the sack of Troy, and Josephus' (*Ant. Jud.*, viii, 3, 1 and *Contra Apionem*, 1, 18) of 240 years before Solomon's temple was built, both work back to the early twelfth century only. When we know that Byblos existed from the fourth millennium BC at least, there is no reason to laugh at Herodotus' date for Tyre, and it is certainly out of the question to accept the early twelfth century as the date of its original foundation, in view of its occurrence in the el Amarna letters. But Justin's story might well refer to a refoundation, for he says that the Sidonians founded Tyre after being expelled from their own city by the men of Askelon, i.e. the Philistines – no doubt during their war of conquest. Perhaps the story can be accepted as a symbol of the rebirth that led Tyre into the ascendancy amongst her neighbours which she possessed from the twelfth century until her defeat by Nebuchadnezzar in 574. As to Sidon, though she may have suffered temporary eclipse, she rose to greatness on her proper site once more in future years, as we shall see (p. 50).

36. This idea was first adumbrated, I believe, by the late Sir Leonard Woolley in a perspicacious article in *Syria*, II, 1921, pp. 177–94.

37. Justin, xviii, 4.

38. See K. M. Kenyon, *Archaeology in the Holy Land*, 1960, pp. 262 ff., pls. 52 and 54.

39. E. A. Wallis Budge and L. W. King, *Annals of Kings of Assyria*, 1902, I, p. 199 f. The inscriptions occur on the colossal bulls and lions, and the text, as published, is based on the version on bull no. 76 in the British Museum.

40. Contenau (1949), p. 271 f.; *C.I.S.*, I, i, no. 5.

41. For a long discussion suggesting that Luli was king of Sidon only, not of Tyre also, see P. Cintas, *Manuel d'archéol. punique*, 1970, pp. 94 ff.

42. Contenau (1949), p. 62. Esarhaddon had sacked Sidon and beheaded its king Abdmilkut six years earlier (ibid. p. 61), founding instead a new town which he called Esarhaddon, of which we have no archaeological knowledge.

For an alternative view, however, identifying the Phoenician figure on the Sinjirli relief as Abdmilkut of Sidon and the Egyptian one as Usharahuru, a son of Taharqa, see J. Leclant in Ward ed. (1968), p. 16. This involves a minor change in the dating of the relief, but such a change does not vitiate the main argument here put forward about the failure of Egypt and Phoenicia when jointly pitted against Assyria.

43. Diodorus Siculus, xvii, 40.

4. THE PHOENICIAN EXPANSION OVERSEAS

44. Herodotus, ii, 49; v, 57.

45. V. Karageorghis, *Cyprus*, 1968, pp. 40, 61 ff.

46. Sir John Myres in *Ann. Brit. School Athens*, XLI, 1939–40, pp. 85 ff.

47. For a summary of results up to 1967 see Karageorghis, op. cit. in note 45, pp. 62–4, 144–9, and his interim reports in the *Bulletin de correspondance hellénique*, LXXXIV, 1960; LXXXVII, 1963, and annually thereafter. The discovery of the Mycenaean and Phoenician temples in 1969 was reported in *The Times* and other newspapers.

48. For a summary account of this find see Seton Lloyd, *Early Anatolia*, 1956, pp. 177 ff. The generally accepted date for the Phoenician inscription on palaeographic grounds is late eighth century, but D. Ussiskhin (*Anatolian Studies*, XIX, 1969, pp. 121–37), though accepting this, is inclined to believe that the inscription may belong to the ninth century, since in his view that is what the rest of the dating of the site suggests.

49. C. N. Johns in *Pal. Expl. Quart.* 1948, pp. 86 ff., pl. ii, fig. 1.

50. Herodotus, ii, 112.

51. For early Phoenician influences in Rhodes see J. N. Coldstream, 'The Phoenicians of Ialysos', *University of London, Inst. of Class. Stud., Bulletin* no. 16, 1969, pp. 1–8.

52. Dunbabin, op. cit. in note 6, p. 40 f.

53. Information kindly supplied by Mr S. Chiappisi, who published the statuette in the Italian journal *Essere*, II, no. 6, June 1958, pp. 16 ff. and more fully in his *Il Melqart di Sciacca e la questione fenicia in Sicilia*, 1961. It is difficult to date the figurine, in origin, as late as the twelfth–ninth century BC, as Chiappisi did. It must surely have been made in the late Bronze Age.

54. T. J. Dunbabin in *Papers of Brit. School Rome*, XVI, 1948, pp. 1 ff.

55. Thucydides, vi, 2, 6. There are no archaeological finds to support the view that Phoenicians ever settled in eastern Sicily. Indeed there is no evidence even for Aegean traders there between *c.* 1300, when the Mycenaean contacts seem to have been broken, and the founding of the Greek colonies in the eighth century. We must not, therefore, try to explain Thucydides' statement by suggesting that he may have confused Mycenaean settlements with Phoenician ones.

56. Harden in *Amer. J. Archaeol.* XXXI, 1927, pp. 306 ff. It is proper to add, however, that some of the recent excavators at Motya, judging from the pottery found in their earliest strata, are disinclined to accept a date earlier than the end of the eighth century for the first settlement on the site (B. Isserlin *et al.*, *Antiquity*, XXX, 1956, p. 112 f.). They also see some Greek influence in the earliest Motyan pottery styles (W. Culican in *Abr-Nahrain*, I, 1961, p. 47 f.) as well as some eastern Phoenician.

57. The original Punic Soloeis was probably not at modern Soli, but at Pizzo (or Cozzo) Carnita, *c.* 7 km. S.W., on a site near where the two anthropoid sarcophagi (p. 195, note 272) and other early Punic sculptures have been found. It is thought that this town was destroyed by Dionysius at the beginning of the fourth century BC and the town at Soli founded some fifty years later. See C. Citro in *Atti Accad. di Scienze Lettere e Arte di Palermo*, XII, 1952–3, pp. 265 ff.; V. Tusa in *Karthago*, XII, 1965, pp. 8 ff.; and M. Guido, *Sicily: An Archaeological Guide*, 1967, p. 54.

58. Strabo (i, 3, 2), writing in the early first century AD, says that the Phoenicians founded colonies outside the Pillars of Heracles shortly after the Trojan War, and this must include Gades. But the chief authority for the traditional date of

both Utica and Gades is Velleius Paterculus in his *Historia Romana*, published in AD 30, who says (i, 2, 4) that the Tyrian fleet which ruled the seas founded Gades about eighty years after the fall of Troy (which elsewhere he puts at *c*. 1190 BC) and that Utica was founded soon afterwards. This would give *c*. 1110 for Gades and perhaps *c*. 1100 BC for Utica. Pliny's version (xvi, 216) concurs, when he says that Numidian cedar beams, placed in the temple of Apollo at Utica 1,178 years ago, were still, in his day, in their pristine state. As Pliny's *Historia Naturalis* appeared in AD 77, this gives 1101 as Utica's date. The pseudo-Aristotelian *De Mirabilibus Auscultationibus* (perhaps not written earlier than the second century AD) cites (ch. 134) Phoenician historians for the statement that Utica was founded 287 years before Carthage, and this, if Carthage is put at its generally agreed date of 814–13, again brings us to 1101 BC.

No fixed dates are given for any other western colonies except one called Auza (site not identified), which a writer called Menander of Ephesus says was founded by Ithobaal of Tyre in the ninth century BC. Sallust says that Lepcis Magna was a colony of Sidonian refugees. Others attribute both it and Hadrumetum to Tyrians. On all these points see Gsell, I, p. 362 f.

For the most recent archaeological evidence about Phoenician (or Punic) settlements at Lepcis Magna, Sabratha and Oea, see A. di Vita in Ward ed. (1968), pp. 77 ff. On present information (ibid. note 9, and refs. there cited) the permanent settlement at Lepcis goes back at least to the seventh century, and those at Sabratha and (possibly) Oea to the fifth century. Firm evidence for this dating at Lepcis was found by Theresa Carter at the Forum Vetus, where the fourth level, securely ascribed to the second half of the seventh century, contained a Punic building of considerable size and style (T. H. Carter in *Amer. J. Archaeol.* LXIX, 1965, pp. 123 ff.).

59. E.g W. F. Albright in *Bull. Amer. Sch. Orient. Res.* no. 83, 1941, pp. 16 ff. believes it is: but others put it in the eighth century or even later. See Driver (1948), p. 107, note 5.

60. Diodorus Siculus, v, 16, stating that it was 160 years after the foundation of Carthage, which he ascribes to 814–13.

61. For a useful up-to-date treatment of Tartessos and its contacts with Phoenician trade and influence see J. M. Bláz-

quez, *Tartessos y los Origenes de la Colonizacion fenicia en Occidente*, 1968.

62. One very important site is the early Phoenician cemetery at Cerro de San Cristóbal, Almuñécar, the ancient Sexi, some 70 km. east of Malaga, excavated by Pellicer Catalán. This yielded, *inter alia*, a series of alabaster jars, two with genuine Egyptian cartouches of Osorkon II (870–47) and Takelothis II (847–23) and two others with imitation cartouches of Osorkon II and Sheshonq II (847); see J. Leclant in Ward ed. (1968), p. 13, note 31. Despite the presence, however, of these apparently ninth-century vessels, the cemetery is not thought to be earlier than the late eighth and early seventh centuries B C, since two early protocorinthian *kotylai* of the first quarter of the seventh century were found in tomb 19 (M. Pellicer Catalán, *Excavaciones en la necrópolis púnica 'Laurita' del Cerro de San Cristóbal (Almuñécar, Granada)*, Excavaciones arqueologicas en España, 17, Madrid, 1963; id. 'Ein altpunisches Gräberfeld bei Almuñécar', *Madrider Mitteilungen*, IV, 1963, pp. 9–38). At the same time trial excavations by H. G. Niemeyer, H. Schubart, and Pellicer Catalán at Toscanos, at the mouth of the river Vélez, 1–2 km. west of Torre del Mar and *c.* 25 km. east of Malaga revealed constructions and Phoenician pottery of the late eighth century and onwards (H. G. Niemeyer *et al.*, 'Eine altpunische Kolonie an der Mündung des Río Vélez', *Archäol. Anzeiger*, III, 1964, cols. 476–93, and H. G. Niemeyer and H. Schubart, *Toscanos, die altpunische Faktorei an der Mündung des Río de Vélez*, I, 1964, Berlin, 1969. Some km. to the east, at Trayamar, near the mouth of the river Algarrobo, a grave with a number of jugs and other vessels of early Phoenician forms was found many years ago, and a mound near by, called La Mezquitilla, where early Phoenician sherds lie on the surface, may be another early Phoenician station; see H. G. Niemeyer *et al.*, 'Altpunische Funde von der Mündung des Río Algarrobo', *Madrider Mitteilungen*, V, 1964, pp. 73–90. Farther west, in Huelva province, A. Blanco and J. M. Luzon have excavated a mining settlement of the eighth and seventh centuries at Solomon's Hill, Riotinto, whose inhabitants either were Phoenicians or were in close contact with Phoenicians, since pottery of Phoenician type was found in the houses (*Antiquity*, XLIII, 1969, pp.

124 ff.; A. Blanco *et al.*, *Excavaciones arqueologicas en el Cerro Salomon, Riotinto, Huelva*, Sevilla, 1970). Other excavations at Huelva itself (Cabeza de San Pedro, etc.), and at Aljaraque near Huelva, have confirmed that there was much Phoenician contact in this area; see J. M. Blázquez *et al.*, *Huelva Arqueologica, Las Cerámicas del Cabeza de San Pedro*, Huelva, 1970, and J. M. Blázquez *et al.*, 'La Factura punica de Aljaraque ...', *Noticiario arqueol. hispanico*, XIII–XIV, 1971, pp. 304 ff., in which see espec. p. 306 for a map showing all early Phoenician sites in south Spain, and notes 1–5 for a full bibliog. of the many relevant reports.

63. Cintas (1954), pp. 35 ff.; A. Jodin in *Bull. d'archéol. marocaine*, II, 1957, pp. 9 ff.; id., op. cit. in note 24, pp. 53 ff. (full discussion and summary of the evidence); M. Tarradell, *Lixus*, 1959; id., *Marruecos púnico*, 1960; F. Villard, 'Céramique grecque du Maroc', *Bull. d'archéol. marocaine*, IV, 1960, pp. 1 ff.

5. CARTHAGE: HER ORIGIN AND HISTORY

64. The date appears in several ancient authors, e.g. Dionysius of Halicarnassus (*Antiq. Rom.*, i, 74), who puts it thirty-eight years before the first Olympiad (776), and Velleius Paterculus (i, 12), who gives the city a life of 667 years. See Gsell, I, p. 397 f.; Harden (1939), p. 4.

Many modern scholars, notably Forrer and Rhys Carpenter, do not accept a date as early as this, and would lower it by a century or even a century and a half. Others, e.g. Cintas, Picard and Albright, take the conservative line. It would be wearisome to argue the matter in detail here, but it can be said that in very recent years the tendency to accept the traditional date, or something very close to it, has become more widespread. The bibliography on this topic is extensive. Consult, *inter alios*, W. F. Albright in *Bull. Amer. Sch. Orient. Res.* no. 83, 1941, pp. 14–22, and id. in *J. Amer. Orient. Soc.* LXVII, 1947, pp. 153 ff.; A. Akerström, *Der geometrische Stil in Italien*, 1943, p. 163 f.; E. O. Forrer, 'Karthago wurde erst 673–663 v. Christ gegründet', in *Festschrift Franz Dornsieff*, Leipzig, 1953, pp. 85–93; E. Frézouls in *Bull. de corresp. hellénique*, LXXIX, 1955, pp. 153–76; Rhys Carpenter, 'The Phoenicians in the west', *Amer. J. Archaeol*. LXII, 1958, pp. 35–53, and id. LXVIII, 1964, p. 178; W. Culican in *Abr-Nahrain*, I, 1961, pp. 36–55; Picard, G. (1964), pp. 31–9, 191 f.; G. Garbini, 'I Fenici in occidente', *Studi Etruschi*, XXXIV, 1966, pp. 111–47; J. Heurgon in *J. Rom. Studies*, LVI, 1966, pp. 1–3; and now, above all, Cintas, op. cit. in note 41, who provides an elaborate and well-argued exposition of the sources and other evidence.

65. The account appears in several authors and most fully in Justin, xviii, 5.

66. See A. Audollent, *Carthage romaine*, 1901, p. 269, note 2; and Gsell, II, p. 8, who calls this a '*hypothèse contestable*'.

67. For the probability that the Byrsa had a wider expanse than the St Louis hill see p. 29, note 15, and map, Fig 4.

68. The founder of the well-known Magonid family, so long the most powerful influence in Punic politics.

69. According to Herodotus (i, 166) the Phocaeans won this battle, but their fleet was so badly mauled that it was a sort of Cadmeian victory (as he says). The surviving Phocaeans returned to Alalia, collected their wives and children, and sailed from Corsica to Rhegium, never to return.

70. See notes 240–1.

71. For 398 and not 397 as the correct date see E. A. Freeman, *History of Sicily*, IV, 1894, p. 127, note 2 (by A. J. Evans); Gsell, III, p. 7. It is certain that the town never fully recovered, though some traces of later occupation, with fourth-century coins, have recently been found by Isserlin near the south gate and by the Italian excavators at Cappidazzu and elsewhere on the island.

72. F. W. Kelsey, *Excavations at Carthage*, 1925, p. 17, fig. 8; Picard, G. (1956), p. 74 f.; Cintas (1950), p. 16, fig. 2; G. Picard in *Rev. archéol*. 1958, i, p. 25 f.

73. Plutarch, *Marius*, 40: ἐν τοῖς Καρχηδόνος ἐρειπίοις φυγάδα καθεζόμενον εἶδες.

6. GOVERNMENT, CONSTITUTION, SOCIAL STRUCTURE

74. Herodotus, vii, 98.

75. Gsell, II, p. 297.

76. Gsell, II, p. 101 f., citing Appian, viii (Libyca), 54, etc., and a statement of Eumachus in *Frag. Hist. Graeca*, ed. Müller, III, pp. 102 (no. 2) and 622 (no. 47), which mentions skeletons found when the ditch was dug.

77. Some think that it is these Berber inhabitants of the *territorium* who are the Libyphoenicians so frequently mentioned in ancient texts; but this term seems to imply different things in different contexts. At times, for example, it seems to mean African Phoenicians in contrast to those of other areas; at others, Berbers living in any north African area where Phoenicians held sway – not only the Carthage *territorium*.

78. Gsell, I, p. 428 f.; II, p. 312.

79. In the fifth century Carthage signed a formal alliance with Utica and in the second treaty with Rome in 348 (p. 64) and the treaty with Philip of Macedon in 215, Utica, alone of all the western allies, is mentioned specifically. Except for a time during the Mercenary war in 241–38 BC (see p. 64 above and Gsell, III, pp. 116 ff.) she remained faithful to Carthage until the outbreak of the third Punic war, when she sided with Rome and was rewarded by being made the capital of the new province of Africa.

7. RELIGION

80. For a short general account in English of this archive, as found in the earlier years' digging, see C. F. A. Schaeffer, *The Cuneiform Texts of Ras Shamra/Ugarit*, British Academy, 1939. See also J. Gray, *The Canaanites*, 1964, pp. 119 ff.

81. Previously I was misled into interpreting Aliyan as Baal's son; but this is wholly unacceptable, as Professor Sir Godfrey Driver has pointed out to me. The word is a standing epithet of Baal, describing him as 'the victor Baal'. See also Gray, op. cit. in note 80, p. 122, who translates it 'the mighty' Baal.

82. Schaeffer, op. cit. in note 80, p. 71.

83. ibid. p. 72.

84. Gsell, IV, p. 230.

85. 'Greece, conquered Greece, her conqueror subdued
    And Rome grew polished who till then was rude.'
        Horace, *Epistles*, ii, 1, 156 (Conington's translation).

86. An element which also appears in the name Carthage (*Qarthadasht*, New Town).

87. According to Pomponius Mela, iii, 46 (Gsell, IV, p. 304). Whether the term 'Pillars of Heracles' was the Phoenician as well as the Greek name for the Straits of Gibraltar is not known. The Greek version of Hanno uses it, but we do not know what words it was translating. According to Strabo (iii, 5, 5) the Libyans and Iberians affirmed that the Pillars were not at the straits, but were stelae with Phoenician inscriptions in the temple of Heracles at Gades.

88. Vulgatum (nec cassa fides) ab origine fani
    Impositas durare trabes, solasque per aeuum
    Condentum nouisse manus . . .
                    . . . velantur corpora lino
    Et Pelusiaco praefulget stamine uertex.
    Discinctis mos thura dare, atque e lege parentum
    Sacrificam lato uestem distinguere clauo.
    Pes nudus, tonsaeque comae, castumque cubile:
    Irrestincta focis seruant altaria flammae.
    Sed nulla effigies, simulacraue nota deorum
    Maiestate locum et sacro impleuere timore.
                        Silius Italicus, iii, 17–31.

89. The temple of Eshmun at Sidon has been excavated; see, e.g. M. Dunand in *Bull. Mus. de Beyrouth*, XVIII, 1965, pp. 107 ff.

90. For the probability that Byrsa spread over neighbouring

hills as well as that of St Louis see note 15; for the Aesculapius dedication found on the summit of the hill west of the
Roman theatre see Picard, C. (1951), p. 42, plan V.

91. Gsell, IV, p. 282.

92. See Giselle Halff, 'L'Onomastique de Carthage', *Karthago*,
XII, 1965, pp. 63–146. The individual occurrences of
names which she lists must run into several thousands, but
they include only ten compounded with TNT (op. cit.
p. 65).

93. Gsell, II, pp. 20, note 1, and 82; P. Berger, *Catal. Mus.
Lavigerie*, I, 1900, p. 33, pl. 5, fig. 3. For the text of this
inscription in French see Lapeyre (1942), p. 202.

94. Dr E. Oren kindly informs me that during his recent survey
and excavation of third- and second-century BC caves and
other sites near Beit Jibrin and Marisa in southern Palestine
he found a weight bearing the name of Tanit in Phoenician
script, and a number of conical pillars, one of which closely
resembled in shape the sign of Tanit. Hellenistic lamps
bearing her sign are also found on eastern sites, and a late
Hellenistic mosaic in the House of the Dolphins at Delos,
signed by its artist Asklepiades of Aradus, has the Tanit
emblem as its central decoration (W. A. Laidlaw, *History
of Delos*, 1933, p. 248; P. Roussel, *Délos, colonie athénienne*,
Paris, 1916, p. 85, note 2).

95. Picard, G. (1956), pp. 34, 41; Picard, G. and C. (1958), p.
60 f. For an essay stressing the African origin of Tanit and
her attributes, and postulating the spread of her cult at
Carthage, in place of that of Astarte, from the sixth century
onwards, see V. Giustolisi, *Le Origini della Dea Tanit*,
Saggi e Monografie, I, Palermo, 1970.

96. Diodorus Siculus, xiv, 77, 5.

97. Gsell, IV, 350.

98. N, Avigad in *Israel Exploration J.* X, 1960, 90-96. Tel
Makmish lies between Dor and Tel Aviv.

99. 1 Kings vii. Barnett (1957), p. 59, points out that the description of the decoration of the temple, with carved
cherubim, palm-trees, and flowers, recalls the motifs we
meet on Phoenician ivories and bronzes (pp. 184 ff.). For a

detailed description of what the temple of Solomon may
have looked like, inside and outside, see G. E. Wright,
Biblical Archaeol. 1957, pp. 136 ff.

100. Sir John Myres, *Pal. Expl. Quart.* 1948, pp. 28 ff.

101. Found in 1957. Yadin (1958), pp. 13 ff.; *Ill. Lond. News*,
21 and 28 March 1959. See also id. *Hazor* III–IV, 1961,
pl. 115, no. 2; since only the plates of this double volume
have so far appeared, a final account of this temple is still
awaited.

102. Herodotus, ii, 44.

103. For the date here adopted for this shrine see M. Dunand
in Ward ed. (1968), p. 44, fig. 1 (N.–S. section through
enclosure) and pl. 14,a. He ascribes it to the Persian period.
For a fuller architectural description and reconstruction see
A. Lézine, *Architecture punique*, 1961, pp. 19 ff., who, however, suggests that the monument is Hellenistic, early third
to mid second century B C.

104. For a careful description and reconstruction see Lézine,
op. cit. in note 103, pp. 7–24.

105. Tacitus, *Histories*, ii, 78.

106. 2 Kings xxiii, 10.

107. Cintas (1947). L. Foucher, *Hadrumetum*, 1964, pp. 33 ff.
The existence of 'topheths' at Nora and Motya and many
sites in north Africa has long been known. Recent work by
Italian archaeologists has added four new Sardinian
examples, at Sulcis (though this one could be inferred from
the number of stelae found years ago), Monte Sirai,
Tharros and Su Cardulinu near Bithia, and has also continued the uncovering of the one at Motya, begun many
years ago by Whitaker. For summary notes on all these
finds see S. Moscati, *The World of the Phoenicians*, 1968, pp.
202 ff., 215 ff., and id. in Ward ed. (1968), pp. 65 ff. For
interim reports on the work at Monte Sirai and Motya see
below, p. 268, *s.nn.* F. Barreca and A. Ciasca respectively.

108. To the bibliography of the site in Cintas (1950), p. 490,
should be added Harden in *Iraq*, IV, 1937, pp. 59 ff. and
Lapeyre in *Comptes rendus Acad. Inscr.* 1939, pp. 294 ff.
For the inscribed stelae found during the first few years of

work see *C.I.S.* I, iii, fasc. 1, 1926, nos. 3709–3905, pp. 104 ff. For those found by Cintas in 1945–50 see ibid. fasc. 3, 1962, nos. 5684–5940, pp. 468 ff.

For a very full account of the origin and growth of this precinct see now Cintas, op. cit. in note 41, pp. 311–423, which discusses, *inter alia*, the pottery sequence in great detail.

109. For preliminary accounts of this find see *Rev. tunisienne*, 1948, pp. 1 ff.; Cintas (1950), pp. 490 ff.; Picard, G. and C. (1958), p. 36 f.; Picard, G. (1956), p. 24 f., pls. 8–9 (=ibid. 1964, p. 37 f., pl. 6); Picard, C. (1951), p. 26 and sections on pp. 24–5. A natural hollow in the native rock was widened and deepened to make a small pit covered with a slab, over which was built a vaulted chamber with an outer wall enclosing a corridor. Against the N. wall was a stone-built altar, and to the N.E. three concentric winding walls forming a '*labyrinthe*'. Several objects were found in this area, and as a foundation-deposit under one wall there was a late geometric amphora with twisted handles (probably Cycladic) and a one-beaked Punic lamp. In the central pit were a number of Punic saucers and imported Greek, mainly protocorinthian, pots, an early Iron Age Cypriote (?) painted *askos* in the form of a duck, and a Punic amphora of an eighth-century form. The complex had fallen into decay fairly soon, because in and around its debris were urn-burials of the lowest stratum of the sanctuary. Cintas at first claimed some of this pottery to be twelfth century or earlier; later he brought the date down to *c.* 1000. But the earliest piece is probably the Cypriote (?) *askos*, which may be late ninth century; none of the rest can be placed earlier than the middle of the eighth century B C. See P. Demargne in *Rev. archéol.* XXXVIII, 1951, pp. 44 ff., Rhys Carpenter in *Amer. J. Archaeol.* LXII, 1958, pp. 39 ff., and W. Culican in *Abr-Nahrain*, I, 1961, p. 47 f.

110. A study of the forms of all the Punic stelae from these sanctuaries would be well worth while, and might prove helpful chronologically. Mme Hours's introductory essay (1950) deals only with those from Carthage; Lilliu (1944), cols. 293 ff., has studied those from Sulcis. The ones from Nora (G. Patroni, *Mon. Antichi*, XIV, 1904, cols. 228 ff.) and Motya (J. I. S. Whitaker, *Motya*, 1921, pp. 271 ff.) are less well known. Some of the forms could be traced back to

eastern prototypes. Many more of these stelae have, of course, since been published in the reports on the work of the Italian Missions in Sicily and Sardinia; for refs. see notes 27–8.

111. M. J. Lagrange, *Études sur les religions sémitiques*, 2 ed. 1905, p. 480 – an inscription from the tomb of Himilkat, priest of Baal Hammon, found by Delattre at Ste Monique in 1901.

112. Picard, G. and C. (1958), p. 77 f.

113. See F. Poulsen, *Ny Carlsberg Glyptotek, Ancient Sculpture*, 1951, no. 837; G. Contenau, *Manuel d'archéol. orientale*, III, fig. 897. Bossert (1951), no. 511, p. 35, purporting to be the same stele, is in fact a different one, though closely akin, and is in the Louvre (G. Contenau, *Antiq. orientales Mus. Louvre*, p. 202, pl. 34 B).

114. Herodotus, i, 199.

115. Perrot and Chipiez (1885), fig. 327; Hours (1950), pl. 33, b and g (from Tanit precinct). Cf. also an ivory amulet in the form of a 'temple boy' from Ste Monique: A. L. Delattre, *La Nécropole des Rabs* (Fouilles de Ste Monique, 3me. année), extr. du *Cosmos*, 1906, p. 16, fig. 26.

116. See R. Dussaud in *Comptes rendus Acad. Inscr.* 1946, pp. 371 ff., espec. pp. 382–4. Note, too, that the word 'moloch' or 'molk' is now thought to mean – at least sometimes – 'sacrifice' and not the deity to whom it is offered. For this point and the meaning and content of the burials in the Tanit precinct and elsewhere see Picard, G. and C. (1958), ch. ii, note 15.

117. Diodorus Siculus, xx, 14, 6.

118. See Picard, G. and C. (1958), loc. cit. in note 116, where it is suggested from evidence at Sousse (Cintas, 1947) that substitution of animals for human infants perhaps began in the fourth century. Lapeyre (*Comptes rendus Acad. Inscr.* 1939, p. 297) also found animal bones in some Tanit urns.

119. For discussion of the text see Gsell, IV, pp. 41 ff.; for the text in French (after Lagrange) see Lapeyre (1942), p. 200 f.

120. Hours (1950), pls. 28–31, and elsewhere.

121. See P. J. Riis, *Hama*, II, 3, *Les Cimetières à crémation*, Copenhagen, 1948; C. L. Woolley, 'Hittite burial customs', *Annals Archaeol. and Anthrop.*, *Univ. Liverpool*, VI, 1914, pp. 87 ff. (Carchemish cemeteries and Deve Huyuk); C. N. Johns in *Quart. Dept. Antiq. Palestine*, VI, 1937, pp. 121 ff. (Atlit); and W. Culican in *Abr-Nahrain*, I, 1959–60, pp. 41 ff. (Ecdippa).

   At Khaldé, near Beirut (M. Saidah in *Bull. Mus. de Beyrouth*, XIX, 1966, pp. 60, 66, 85) there may be a mixture of the two rites, since amphorae, which contained cremated bones thought to be human, were found in some of the inhumation-graves of the later level (end ninth to end eighth century BC). This may also have happened at Ecdippa (Culican, loc. cit.). It is specially interesting to note that these cremation-amphorae at Khaldé are very close parallels to some of the types [Plate 58,c] found in the earliest stratum of the precinct of Tanit at Carthage.

122. Other than the Mycenaeans, of course, who did not practise cremation.

123. Perrot and Chipiez (1885), fig. 94; Contenau (1949), p. 219, fig. 57. But see Bossert (1951), figs. 379–80, who ascribes these monuments to the first century AD, Dunand in *Bull. Mus. de Beyrouth*, VII, 1944-5, pp. 99 ff., dating them not long before the destruction of Marathus by Aradus in the first century BC and Lézine, op. cit. in note 103, p. 24, who adopts Dunand's dating.

124. For the Dougga monument see L. Poinssot in *Comptes rendus Acad. Inscr.* 1910, pp. 780 ff. (describing its reconstruction), Gsell, VI, pp. 251 ff., and for a good, brief description, C. Poinssot, *Les Ruines de Dougga*, Tunis, 1958, pp. 58–61, pls. 16 and 17, a. The inscriptions were placed side by side (Punic on left), but their original position on the monument is uncertain. For Massinissa's tomb see A. Ballu in *Bull. archéol.* 1917, pp. 226–9; Picard, G. and C. (1958), p. 55.

125. Cintas and Gobert (1939), pp. 190 ff. Only the west wall is here illustrated (Fig 31,a): the east wall (op. cit. fig. 93) showed similar designs.

126. A. Caruana, *Report on Phoen. and Rom. Antiq. . . . in Malta*, 1882, p. 29.

127. The three appropriate times for which the Sidonian king-lists cite no other monarchs.

128. Indeed Dunand (*Bull. Mus. de Beyrouth*, XVIII, 1965, p. 107 f.) has now proved that this dynasty belongs to the late sixth century; see J. Leclant in Ward ed. (1968), p. 19, note 104.

8. LANGUAGE, SCRIPT, TEXTS

129. Gsell, IV, p. 183.

130. See p. 20 and note 5. On the extent of this survival, about which modern scholars hold divergent views, see E. F. Gautier, *Le Passé de l'Afrique du Nord*, 1937, pp. 134 ff.; C. Courtois in *Rev. africaine*, XCIII, 1950, pp. 259 ff.; W. M. Green, 'Augustine's use of Punic' in *Semitic and Oriental Studies presented to W. Popper*, Berkeley, 1951, pp. 179 ff.; W. H. C. Frend, *The Donatist Church*, 1952, pp. 57 ff.; and M. Simon, 'Punique ou berbère' in *Annuaire de l'Institut de Philol. et d'Hist. Orientales et Slaves* (Mélanges I. Lévy), XIII, 1953, pp. 613 ff. Simon, who sums up the views of previous writers, suggests that both Berber and Punic survived, the former merely as a negligible patois, but with some inscriptions, the latter more literary, perhaps, but still far from on a cultural par with Latin.

131. For the alphabet and its development see, e.g. C. Singer *et al.*, *A History of Technology*, I, 1954, pp. 762 ff.; Driver (1948); and Diringer (*c.* 1948). The normal Ugaritic script runs from left to right, whereas the Phoenician, like Hebrew, goes from right to left. There are, however, instances (a tablet from Ugarit and two short inscriptions from Palestine) of Ugaritic written from right to left (Albright (1949), p. 187), no doubt in imitation of the Phoenician method. As Ugaritic script was not suitable for everyday use on any other medium than clay, it could never become a serious and lasting rival to the Phoenician.

132. Dunand (1945), 'postscriptum'. The coffin was found with objects of the thirteenth century BC, including an ivory plaque and two vases bearing cartouches of Ramesses II, and

its sculptured decoration fits well with such a date. There were, however, early Iron Age potsherds in the tomb. Acceptance of Sidney Smith's suggestion that the coffin is an earlier one reused by Ahiram in the tenth century would remove all difficulties: S. Smith, *Alalakh and Chronology*, 1940, p. 46, note 117.

One fact which strongly supports the view that Ahiram reused an earlier coffin seems hitherto to have escaped notice: this is that in parts Ahiram's Phoenician inscription is carved on fractured areas, where quite large chips of the edge of the coffin-lid are broken off. This is unlikely to have happened when the coffin was new. A very clear instance (Plate 38) occurs near the left-hand end of the lid (see Plate 15), involving at least ten of the letters at the left-hand end of line 3 of the inscription as set out in Fig 34.

133. Dunand (1945), pp. 158 ff. (but see also his 'postscriptum'); W. F. Albright in *J. Amer. Orient. Soc.*, LXVII, 1947, pp. 153 ff.; Driver (1948), pp. 104 ff. and table on p. 127, pls. 45 ff.; Diringer (*c.* 1948), pp. 211 ff.; J. T. Milik and F. M. Cross in *Bull. Amer. Sch. Orient. Res.* no. 134, April 1954, pp. 5 ff.

134. *Iraq*, VI, 1939, pp. 106 ff.

135. For the pendant (Carthage Mus. no. 894.2.1) see J. Ferron, 'Le médaillon de Carthage', *Cahiers de Byrsa*, VIII, 1958–9, pp. 45–56, pls. 1–2, and *C.I.S.* I, iii, fasc. 3, 1962, no. 6057, pl. 118, and earlier refs. ad loc. The tomb in which it was found (see A. L. Delattre, 'La nécropole de Douimes, fouilles de 1893–4', *Cosmos*, 1897, no. 5, p. 721 f. = p. 13 f. of offprint) contained, *inter alia*, a protocorinthian skyphos which Mme Boucher (*Cahiers de Byrsa*, III, 1953, p. 15, no. 18, pl. 2), though not recognizing it as coming from this tomb, ascribes to the second quarter of the seventh century, and which is most unlikely to be much earlier than that.

I am grateful to Father B. Peckham, S.J., for help with dating the script. In his view it 'seems to require at least an eighth-century date', although he compares it with that of *C.I.S.*, loc. cit. nos. 5684–5, pls. 98–9, two stelae in the form of thrones found by Cintas in the Carthage precinct, which, according to Cintas (1950), p. 581, note 631, cannot, by their context, be older than the late seventh century. For a similar inscription from a fragmentary third stele of this

type see J. Ferron in *Mél. de Carthage*, 1964–5, pp. 55 ff.
Rhys Carpenter (op. cit. in note 109, p. 47) demonstrates
that the script is identical with that of the Nora stone, which
some (p. 57 above) ascribe to the ninth century and for
which Rhys Carpenter, who is against high dating, is never-
theless prepared to accept a late eighth-century date. He
recognizes the difficulty about the later dating of the tomb-
deposit and the two Tanit stelae, but solves it ingeniously
by suggesting that this early script, once introduced into the
west, could have had a long life there until replaced by a
new eastern variety. See also Culican, op. cit. in note 109,
p. 40 and id. *The First Merchant Venturers*, 1966, p. 104 f.,
fig. 116, who accepts an eighth-century date. Ferron, loc.
cit., on the other hand, believes it cannot be later than the
ninth century, and suggests it is a Cypriote piece, brought to
Carthage by Yadamilk (who would then be an ancestor of
the occupant of the tomb), since neither Astarte nor Pygmalion is at home as a deity at Carthage but both would be
in Cyprus. But even if we followed him in deriving it from
Cyprus, that does not, of course, make it necessary to put it
as far back as the ninth century.

136. See, e.g. G. A. Cooke, *A Text-book of North Semitic
Inscriptions*, 1903, pp. 1–4; R. Dussaud, *Les Monuments
palestiniens et judaïques*, 1912, pp. 4 ff.; W. F. Albright in
J. B. Pritchard, *Ancient Near Eastern Texts*, 1955, pp. 320
ff.; and E. Ullendorff in *Documents from Old Testament
Times*, ed. D. Winton Thomas, 1958, pp. 195 ff.

137. See notes 7 and 128. For Tabnit's and Eshmunazar's coffin
texts see, e.g. Lagrange, op. cit. in note 111, pp. 481 ff.;
Contenau (1949), pp. 116 and 272 ff.; and F. Rosenthal in
Pritchard, op. cit. in note 136, p. 505.

138. But see note 48.

139. The inscriptions were first published in M. Pallottino,
G. Colonna, G. Garbini, L. Borrelli, 'Scavi nel santuario
etrusco di Pyrgi . . .', *Archaeol. Classica*, XVI, 1964, pp.
39–117. For an admirable account of the find and its importance see J. Heurgon, 'The inscriptions of Pyrgi', *J.
Rom. Studies*, LVI, 1966, pp. 1–15. The inscriptions lay in
a niche between two temples, hidden beneath fragments of
terracotta sculptures from temple B. Temple A, dated
480–70, was typically Tuscan in style; temple B, the smaller,

was wholly Greek in plan and is dated about twenty-five years earlier. For the temples and the circumstances of the discovery see G. Colonna in *Archaeol. Classica*, XVI, 1964, pp. 53 ff., and id. in *Studi Etruschi*, XXXIII, 1965, pp. 92 ff., 202 ff. For the inscriptions and their interpretation see M. Pallottino and G. Garbini in *Archaeol. Classica*, XVI, 1964, pp. 66 ff., 86 ff.; A. I. Kharsekin in *Vestnik Drevnei Istorii*, IV, 1965, pp. 108 ff.; A. J. Pfiffig, *Uni-Hera-Astarte, Studien zu den Goldblechen von S. Severa-Pyrgi mit etruskischer und punischer Inschrift*, Oster. Akad. der Wissen-schaften, Philos.-Hist. Kl., 88, 2, 1965; and other articles cited by Heurgon, op. cit.

140. Gsell, IV, pp. 212 ff.

141. Contenau (1949), p. 266.

142.   'He knows all lingos, but pretends he doesn't:
        He must be Punic; need we labour it?'
                                    Plautus, *Poenulus*, 112–13.

9. WARFARE

143. Ezekiel xxvi, 7–12.

144. Clement of Alexandria, *Stromateis*, i, 16, 76.

145. L. Basch, 'Phoenician oared ships', *Mariner's Mirror*, LV, 1969, no. 2, pp. 139–62, and no. 3, pp. 227–45. This is a basic analysis of the evidence which no one studying ancient Mediterranean ships can afford to neglect.

146. Herodotus, ii, 159.

147. We may believe Thucydides when he says (i, 13) that the Corinthians were the first Greeks to build such vessels, but cannot now accept his date (*c.* 700 BC) for their first use of them.

148. Basch, op. cit. in note 145, p. 240, and refs. ad loc. The suggestion that Carthage invented the quadrireme derives from Aristotle as cited by Pliny (*H.N.*vii, 57), and the belief is also mentioned by Clement of Alexandria (*Stromateis*, i, 16, 75).

149. Basch, op. cit. in note 145, p. 141 f.

150. Ezekiel xxvii, 10. For a plausible identification of Phut (Put) as covering both Somaliland and Yemen see T. G. Pinches, *s.v.* Put, *International Standard Bible Encyclopedia*, Chicago, 1930.

151. Diodorus Siculus, xi, 1.

152. See, e.g. Lapeyre (1942), pl. 9, and Picard, G. (1964), pl. 74, p. 146.

153. Diodorus Siculus, xvi, 67, 2.

154. Gsell, II, p. 400, citing Livy, xxxvii, 41, 6–7.

155. See note 19.

156. B. Isserlin in *Ill. Lond. News*, 18 October 1969, p. 26 f., id. in *Not. Scavi*, 1970, p. 564 f. and (too recent to have been fully taken account of here) id. in *Antiquity*, XLV, Sept. 1971, pp. 178 ff. I am most grateful to Dr Isserlin for providing me with details of his recent work.

157. There is no archaeological evidence for cothons anywhere except at Carthage and Motya. An alleged cothon at Lepcis Magna (S. Aurigemma in *Notiz. archeol.* I, 1915, p. 46, fig. 12) was probably no more than a normal harbour at a river's mouth. The author of the *Bellum Africanum* mentions one at Hadrumetum (Sousse) in 46 BC, but its emplacement has not been identified, and L. Foucher (*Hadrumetum*, 1964, pp. 80–85) shows that existing evidence at this site points to a normal harbour rather than a cothon. An interior basin at Mahdia between Sousse and Sfax, 72 by 56 m., is accepted by some as Phoenician. Gsell believed it might be medieval.

10. TOWNS

158. For Sisera, Judges v, 28; for Jezebel, 2 Kings ix, 30.

159. Strabo, xvi, 2, 13 (Aradus) and 23 (Tyre).

160. Appian, viii (Libyca), 128.

161. Picard, G. (1956), p. 54, pl. 50,b; Picard, G. and C. (1958), p. 47. These excavations, begun by Cintas, have been

continued by the Tunisian National Institute of Archaeology in recent years, revealing large areas of the town.

162. As, for example, at Delos; see note 94.

163. C. Picard in *Karthago*, III, 1953, pp. 117 ff.; J. Ferron and M. Pinard in *Cahiers de Byrsa*, V, 1955, pp. 31 ff., and IX, 1960–61, pp. 77 ff.; *Bull. archeol.* 1957, p. 35 f. (Seance 11 février); *Rev. archéol.* 1958, i, pp. 21 ff.; Picard, G. and C. (1958), pp. 42 and 47; Warmington (1960), p. 118, pl. 4. The claim of two of the excavators writing in *Cahiers de Byrsa*, locc. citt., that these houses are to be dated after 146 BC is rightly refuted by G. Picard (*Rev. archéol.* loc. cit., and elsewhere).

11. INDUSTRY

164. Gsell, IV, pp. 3 ff.

165. Diodorus Siculus, xx, 8, 3–4.

166. Livy, xxx, 16, 11.

167. Hours (1950), p. 45, pl. 19,d; Lapeyre (1942), pl. 4; Gsell, IV, p. 369.

168. Columella, vi, 1, 3.

169. *Monuments Piot*, XVII, 1909, p. 128 and plates; and see refs. in note 152.

170. Barnett (1957), pp. 116 ff.

171. ibid. fig. 18.

172. The head is of cedar, and gilded; see Picard, G. and C. (1961), p. 106.

173. Gsell, IV, p. 56; Hours (1950), p. 65, pl. 37.

174. Contenau (1949), p. 242.

175. 'Who is this bird who comes here in his shirt-sleeves? D'you think his coat's been stolen at the baths?'
                                        Plautus, *Poenulus*, 975–6.

176. 'You there without a belt!' ibid. 1008.

177. Diodorus Siculus, v, 12, 2.

178. Cintas (1954), p. 88, note 1, suggests, indeed, that the shell debris of dye-extracting establishments were so pestilential that they were usually thrown into the sea. He thinks the existing heaps are normally kitchen-refuse, or the remains of small, private dye-works.

179. 1 Samuel xiii, 19.

180. See J. Déchelette, *Manuel d'archéol.* II, 1, pp. 397 ff. For an actual ingot from Cyprus see Bossert (1951), no. 285, after *Swedish Cyp. Exped.* III, 1937, p. 641, fig. 328. Compare the ingot depicted on a pot-stand of the twelfth or eleventh century BC (p. 185 f.) and numerous ingots of the late thirteenth century BC recently found in a wreck off the coast of Asia Minor at Cape Gelidonya (P. Throckmorton in *Nat. Geographic*, May 1960, p. 682; G. Bass and P. Throckmorton in *Archaeology*, XIV, 1961, pp. 78 ff.). The hide shape for slabs of metal, at least in miniature, is also found in Roman days: [R. A. Smith], *Guide to the Antiq. of Rom. Brit.*, British Mus., 1922, p. 72 f., figs. 93-4.

181. For brief notices about the Egyptian temples see 'Notes and news', in *Pal. Expl. Quart.* 1969, pp. 57-9, and B. Rothenberg in *Ill. Lond. News*, 16 November 1969, pp. 32-3 and 29 November 1969, pp. 28-9. Rothenberg's previous work in Timna is recorded fully in his 'Ancient copper industries in the western Arabah, I', *Pal. Expl. Quart.* 1962, pp. 5-71. For his belief, then, in a Solomonic date for the industry (which he thought was short-lived and of relatively restricted importance) see espec. pp. 40 ff. In the second part of this article (pp. 44 ff.) Rothenberg critically examines the evidence Nelson Glueck put forward in the late 1930s for a Solomonic copper-smelting industry of large proportions at Tell el Kheleifeh, a few km. east of Eilat, to work ore mined in Timna (see, e.g. N. Glueck in *Bull. Amer. Sch. Orient. Res.* nos. 71 (1938), 75 (1939), and 79 (1940), and id. *The Other Side of the Jordan*, New Haven, 1940, pp. 50-113, espec. pp. 91 ff., figs. 43 ff.). He concludes that the structures found by Glueck had no connection with copper-working, but represented, rather, a 'large store and central stronghold of a fortress and caravanserai'.

182. The Solomonic date, in 1962, was based mainly, if not entirely, on the pottery, for which Y. Aharoni postulated

a tenth-century date (*ap*. Rothenberg, *P.E.Q.* 1962, p. 66 f.).
One cannot but wonder how it comes about that pottery,
thus dated in 1962, is now so unequivocally transferred to
the periods of Sethos I and Ramesses III that it gainsays
any possibility of there having been, also, some Solomonic
activity at these sites. We must await fuller publication of
the 1969 discoveries.

182a. But see note 62 for a newly-found mining site at Riotinto
with which the Phoenicians had connections.

183. 1 Kings vii, 13–46.

184. For the La Aliseda treasure and this glass jug see A. Blanco
Freijeiro in *Archivo español de Arqueol*. XXIX, 1956, pp.
3 ff. For alabaster examples of this shape see D. Dunham,
The Royal Cemeteries of Kush, I, *El Kurru*, Cambridge,
Mass., 1950, pp. 30 ff., tomb 4, no. 562, figs. 11,c,j, pl. 39,
E/3 (nearly complete, bearing cartouches of Q. Khensa,
stepmother of Taharqa), and ibid. pp. 27 ff., tomb 3, no.
404, fig. 10,c, and p. 76 f., tomb 22, no. 630, fig. 26,c, pl.
38, B (fragments of shoulder of another, with band of
hieroglyphs). All three tombs are of the seventh century B C.

185. See Blanco, op. cit. in note 184; A. García y Bellido in
Archivo español de Arqueol. XXIX, 1956, pp. 85 ff., and
XXXIII, 1960, pp. 44 ff.

186. A. L. Delattre in *Mém. Antiq. France*, LVI, 1897, p. 384,
fig. 83 (ivory) and p. 392, fig. 88 (bronze).

187. See J. du Plat Taylor in *Iraq*, XXI, 1959, pp. 79–86, and
M. Saidah, 'Fouilles de Khaldé ...', *Bull. Mus. de
Beyrouth*, XIX, 1966, pp. 85 ff. Miss Taylor dates the ware
from *c*. 800 B C at Al Mina, though citing earlier examples
from other places. Saidah's red-slip burnished ware comes
from graves of his upper level, dated end ninth to end
eighth century. The ware also occurs in Rhodes; see Coldstream, op. cit. in note 51, p. 2 f. Some of the Khaldé tombs
have produced amphorae of a shape closely parallel to one
[Plate 58,c] from the lowest stratum in the Tanit precinct
at Carthage (see note 121).

188. Cintas (1950).

189. J. G. Baldacchino in *Papers Brit. Sch. Rome*, XIX, 1951, p.
7, fig. 9, pl. 2, no. 2.

190. Recent excavations in the Malaga and Huelva districts (refs. in note 62) have yielded much early red-slip and other pottery and confirmed earlier indications that Phoenician stations were flourishing in these areas from the eighth century BC, if not the ninth. The protocorinthian pottery, and the alabaster vases of Egyptian type with cartouches, found with eighth-century and later red-slip Phoenician ware at Almuñécar made this certain once and for all. Many of these stations, first founded, it seems, from east Phoenicia, were later resettled under Carthaginian influence. At Mogador and other places on the Moroccan coast (refs. in note 63) Phoenicians were active from at least the mid-seventh century BC, as is again proved by Phoenician red-slip and contemporary Greek pottery. When the Moroccan finds at Mogador, etc., first came to light, Cintas and others were loath to date them so early and they postulated a peripheral retardation, or a rebirth, of this red-slip ware there several centuries after it was in use in the east. But this is wholly untenable, as Jodin shows (op. cit. in note 24, p. 74 f.), even had early Greek pottery not been found there.

    Another suggestion of Cintas's is that this ware was made only in the east and was, at least in early days, brought by trade even to Carthage. He suggests that Phoenician ships carried pottery cargoes westwards as ballast in holds that were to bring back loads of metal ores. This is fanciful, and in any case the red-slip burnished pots at Carthage, though allied in style and shape to the eastern ones, are sufficiently distinct from them to indicate local manufacture. In particular the black triglyph designs on the pots from the lowest level of the Tanit precinct have no eastern parallels.

191. The one-beaked lamps were very rare, it seems, in north Africa. None occurred at Mogador (Jodin, op. cit. in note 24, p. 96), though there was one at Mersa Madakh in western Algeria (ibid. p. 101). J. Deneauve, *Lampes de Carthage*, 1969, p. 23, type I, cites one from a tomb excavated by Delattre on the hill of Juno, and three were found by Cintas in the early shrine in the precinct of Tanit (see note 109 and Cintas (1950), p. 522). The type seems to be commoner in Spain, principally, if not solely, in early contexts. A number have come from Toscanos, Carmona and elsewhere; see H. G. Niemeyer and H. Schubart, op. cit. in note 62, pp. 100–104.

192. L. Carton, *Rev. archéol.* 1894, ii, pp. 180 ff.; A. L. Delattre, *Bull. Antiq. France*, 1896, p. 234; id. in *Mém. Antiq. France*, LVI, 1897, p. 272 f.

193. P. Gauckler, *Nécrop. puniques*, 1915, pp. 513 ff., and pls.; Cintas (1950), pp. 24 ff., fig. 4.

194. Cintas (1950), p. 23 and refs. ad loc.

195. *Bull. archéol.* 1926, p. 231.

196. *C.I.S.*, I, i, no. 137.

197. Too often, especially in older books, glass and glazed ware are frequently confused, and the confusion is aggravated by the misguided custom, copied from the French, of calling the opaque glasses of this early time '*pâte de verre*' or 'glass paste'. These terms should be abandoned for all ancient glassware. The core-made and other glasses that occur so frequently on all Phoenician sites are basically the same in composition as the clear blown glass of imperial days. Their opacity is often more apparent than real, for they would be translucent, at least, if not transparent, if their walls were sufficiently thin.

198. Speaking of ambassadors from Athens going to the Persian court:

> ξενιζόμενοι δὲ πρὸς βίαν ἐπίνομεν
> ἐξ ὑαλίνων ἐκπωμάτων καὶ χρυσίδων
> ἄκρατον οἶνον ἡδύν.

> 'And oft they fêted us, and we perforce
> Out of their gold and crystal cups must drink
> The pure sweet wine.'
>   *Acharnians*, 73–5 (B. B. Rogers's translation).

199. P. Gauckler, *Nécropoles puniques*, p. 10, pls. 19, 120.

200. For this view see J. Vercoutter, *Les Objets égyptiens et égyptisants du mobilier funéraire carthaginois*, 1945, pp. 49, 75, citing H. R. Hall, *Scarabs*, 1913, p. 13, and others. Yet Vercoutter, op. cit. p. 93, perhaps through an oversight, gives the end of the fifth century as the date when scarabs ceased to be made in Egypt.

201. Barnett (1957), p. 114 f.

12. COMMERCE, TRADE AND EXPLORATION

202. The R.V. of 1 Kings v, 9 uses the word 'raft' and the A.V. the word 'float' for the method by which Hiram sent timber to Solomon (see p. 150).

203. Even if we hesitate to accept a Mycenaean origin for the dagger carved on Stonehenge, we must take into account the faience beads of east Mediterranean late Bronze Age type (though probably not of east Mediterranean manufacture, as is now becoming clear) which have been found in Spain, France and Britain, and the Mycenaean dagger-hilt from Cornwall, as well as the spread of curvilinear decorative motifs of Aegean origin via Malta and Spain to New Grange and elsewhere in Britain and Ireland. All these hint at some trade and cultural connections, however indirect, between the Mediterranean and these distant lands.

204. 2 Samuel v, 11 and cf. 1 Chron. xiv, 1. We must assume this was a commercial transaction, not a present, since there seems to be no reason why Hiram should treat David more generously than he treated Solomon.

205. 1 Kings v, 2. The date of Solomon's reign may be put *c.* 960–20 BC. Besides the annual payment mentioned here, we read in 1 Kings ix, 11–13 that Solomon ceded twenty cities of Galilee, but when Hiram went to see them 'they pleased him not'.

206. 2 Chron. viii, 17. Note the spelling Huram, as always in this second Book of Chronicles.

207. 1 Kings ix, 26 and x, 11.

208. 1 Kings xxii, 48.

209. See B. Maisler (now Mazar) in *Israel Expl. J.* I, 1950–51, p. 209 f., pl. 38A, fig. 13,f. Barnett and others would connect Ophir etymologically with Suppara, near Bombay, saying that initial S is frequently dropped in the Gujarati dialect of that district; Barnett (1957), pp. 59 f., 168.

210. 1 Kings x, 22.

211. 2 Chron. ix, 21.

212. Jonah i, 3.

213. Ezekiel xxvii, 12. The terms 'ships of Tarshish' and 'navy of Tarshish' used in connection with voyages to Tarshish and to Ophir merely indicate the kind of ship used for these long journeys, and imply nothing regarding Tarshish itself. For the Tartessos evidence, both literary and archaeological, see now J. M. Blázquez, op. cit. in note 61, *passim*.

214. Ezekiel xxvii, 27.

215. *Iliad*, xxiii, 741 ff. A similar bowl given to Menelaus by the king of the Sidonians is mentioned in the *Odyssey* (iv, 615 and xv, 115).

216.   δὴ τότε Φοῖνιξ ἦλθεν, ἀνὴρ ἀπατήλια εἰδώς,
    τρώκτης, ὃς δὴ πολλὰ κάκ' ἀνθρώποισιν ἐώργει.

                      Odyssey, xiv, 288–9.

217. *Odyssey*, xv, 415 ff.

218. Herodotus, i, 1. The Phoenicians, he says, as soon as they had settled on the Phoenician coast, took to making long trading voyages. Loaded with Egyptian and Assyrian goods they called at ... Argos ... and, after selling most of their wares, seized and carried off a number of Greek women, including Io, daughter of Inachus.

219. Ionian and Attic pottery of the seventh and early sixth centuries has been found as far west as Mogador in Morocco (F. Villard, op. cit. in note 63, pp. 1 ff.; Jodin, op. cit. in note 24, pp. 53 ff.). It was the battle of Alalia in 535 (p. 61) and its consequences which finally ended Greek activities in south-east Spain.

220. For the suggestion that it was based on this play of Alexis see W. G. Arnott in *Rheinisches Museum für Philologie*, CII (3), 1959, pp. 252 ff. Others derive it from Menander, who also wrote a Καρχηδόνιος. The Punic passages are in Act V, lines 930 ff. I am grateful to Mr Arnott for help on this point. A full, critical discussion of the Punic passages in the play may be found in M. Sznycer, *Les Passages puniques en transcription latine dans le 'Poenulus' de Plaute*, Collection 'Etudes et Commentaires', LXV, Paris, 1967 (reviewed at length by B. Delavault in *Karthago*, XV, 1969, pp. 102–6).

221. For an analysis of the pottery evidence see E. Boucher in *Cahiers de Byrsa*, III, 1953, pp. 11 ff., pls. 1–24; also H. Payne, *Necrocorinthia*, 1931, p. 188. According to Mme

Boucher the main flow of imports ceased after the middle of the sixth century B C, having begun at the end of the eighth.

222. D. van Berchem, 'Hercule-Melqart à l'Ara Maxima', *Rendic. Pontif. Accad. Rom. di Archeol.* XXXII, 1959–60, pp. 61–8; R. Rebuffat, 'Les Phéniciens à Rome', *Mél. d'archéol. et d'histoire de l'Ecole Fr. de Rome*, LXXVIII, 1966, pp. 7–48.

223. See note 139 above.

224. Herodotus, iv, 196.

225. Text in C. Müller, *Geog. Graec. Minores*, I, pp. 15 ff. The author is known as pseudo-Scylax, his work having been wrongly attributed to the real Scylax, a Greek explorer of the sixth century B C.

226. For the eastern Phoenician coinage see G. F. Hill, *Catal. Greek Coins in British Museum: Phoenicia*, 1910.

227. See H. Seyrig in *Syria*, XXXVI, 1959, pp. 52 ff.

228. These identifications, first suggested by E. S. G. Robinson as long ago as 1930, are put forward more fully by him in *Essays in Roman Coinage presented to Harold Mattingly*, 1956, pp. 34–53. All the heads except Scipio's are wreathed. Hamilcar's is bearded, the rest are clean-shaven. The Punic generals have Semitic features, Scipio's are much more Roman in character. A. Beltrán, 'Acuñaciones punicas de Cartagena', *Crónica del III Congreso Arqueol. del Sudeste Español*, Cartagena, 1948, pp. 224–38, has propounded similar views. For totally opposed arguments see J. M. de Navascués, 'Ni Barquidas ni Escipion' in *Homenaje al Profesor Cayetano de Mergelina*, Murcia, 1961–2, pp. 1–22.

Fully endorsing, however, Robinson's views, G. Ch. Picard uses the 'Hannibal' coin-portraits to support his belief, which may not be shared by all, that a bronze head from Volubilis (of which two marble versions exist in Copenhagen and Madrid) provides a contemporary portrait of Hannibal by a late third-century B C Greek (Sikeliote?) artist. See G. Ch. Picard, 'Le Problème du portrait d'Hannibal', *Karthago*, XII, 1965, pp. 31–41.

229. For this relief see R. D. Barnett in *Archaeol. News Letter*, Jan. 1956, p. 156; *Archaeology*, IX, 1956, pp. 87 ff., fig. 9 (the

two parts of the relief incorrectly adjusted); *Antiquity*, XXXII, 1958, p. 226, pl. 22,b. For a skilful, detailed analysis of the ships on this relief see Basch, op. cit. in note 145.

230. Barnett, *Antiquity*, XXXII, 1958, p. 227, pl. 24, a (a terracotta model from Amathus in the British Museum).

231. Basch, op. cit. in note 145, p. 142, fig. 2.

232. Contenau (1949), p. 214, pl. 16. For extant anchors (some doubtless Phoenician) and methods of anchoring ships in ancient times see H. Frost, op. cit. in note 10, pp. 29–63.

233. Barnett, op. cit. in note 230, p. 228, pl. 24, b; but Blanco, op. cit. in note 184, p. 45 (no. 16) calls the scene Nilotic.

234. For a useful account of Phoenician exploration, much fuller than I have space for here, see Picard, G. and C. (1961), pp. 213–52.

235. Herodotus, iv, 42.

236. Avienus, *Ora Maritima*, ed. A. Schulten (Fontes Hisp. Antiquae, fasc. 1, 1922), lines 111–12. There is a French ed. by R. Berthelot (1934).

237. ibid. lines 90–91.

238. A tin ingot found many years ago in Falmouth harbour, Cornwall (H. O'N. Hencken, *The Archaeology of Cornwall and Scilly*, 1932, p. 166), is too doubtful in date to be brought in as evidence, though it vaguely resembles the Bronze Age ingots of Cyprus in shape.

239. See J. G. Milne, *Finds of Greek Coins in the British Isles*, Ashmoleum Museum, Oxford, 1948, pp. 18 ff.

240. Text in C. Müller, *Geog. Graec. Minores*, I, pp. 1 ff. Modern commentaries abound. See the bibliography in A. Diller, *The Traditions of the Minor Greek Geographers* (Amer. Philol. Assoc., Philol. Monog. no. xiv, 1952). Among modern discussions note especially J. Carcopino, *Le Maroc antique*, 1943; 2 ed. with appendix, 1948; M. Rousseau in *Revue africaine*, XCII, 1949, pp. 161 ff.; R. Mauny in *Comptes rendus de la première Conférence Internationale des Africanistes de l'Ouest*, II, 1951, pp. 509 ff.; id. *Rev. étud. anciennes*, LVII, 1955, pp. 92 ff.; Picard, G. (1956), p. 192; Picard, G. and C. (1961), pp. 226 ff. For a refreshing point

of view on the general problem of Hanno's voyage and the impossibility of making concerted sense of the existing text see Cintas (1954), pp. 90 ff.

241. G. Germain, 'Qu'est ce que le périple d'Hannon? Document, amplification littéraire ou faux intégral?', *Hespéris*, XLIV, 1957, pp. 205 ff. This criticizes the text from para. 7 onward as partly borrowed from Herodotus and others and, for the rest, a late compilation, quite unlike paras. 1–6, which are what we should expect in a bald official account of a maritime expedition.

242. He could, however, be basing this description on Hanno's text and it is perhaps wrong to lay much stress on the independent character of what he says.

243. Athenaeus, ii, 44 *e*.

244. Herodotus, ii, 32.

245. This suggestion, first made by K. T. Frost ('The *Critias* and Minoan Crete', *J. Hell. Studies*, XXXIII, 1913, pp. 189 ff.), was restated by S. Marinatos in 1939 ('The volcanic destruction of Minoan Crete', *Antiquity*, XIII, 1939, pp. 425 ff.) and made more positive by him following his excavations in Thera (S. Marinatos, *Excavations at Thera, First Prelim. Report, 1967 Season*, Athens, 1968). For a careful and scholarly assessment of the story of the myth and of its connection with the Thera volcano and Minoan Crete see J. V. Luce, *The End of Atlantis: New Light on an Old Legend*, 1969.

246. Diodorus Siculus, v, 20.

247. Harden (1948), p. 141, note 3, and other refs. cited there. See also G. K. Jenkins and R. B. Lewis, *Carthaginian Gold and Electrum Coins*, 1963, pp. 21, 61, giving further refs. The Carthaginian coins included two small gold of the later fourth century and six fourth- and third-century bronze; the Cyrene coin was an early third-century bronze. The hoard cannot have been deposited much earlier than 200 BC.

13. ART

248. This was the kingdom of Mitanni, where an Indo-European Mitannian aristocracy controlled a Hurrian population. See, e.g. Gray, op. cit. in note 80, p. 42 f.

249. See, e.g. C. Virolleaud in *Syria*, III, 1922, p. 285, pl. 64, no. 11; Sir A. Evans, *Palace of Minos*, II, p. 655, fig. 420.

250. Information kindly supplied by the Emir M. Chéhab.

251. For Khirbet Selm and Qrayé see J. du Plat Taylor, op. cit. in note 187, pp. 62 ff., who discusses pottery from these and many other Levant sites, especially the red-slip wares. For the Khaldé cemetery, which is in two levels (tenth to end ninth, and end ninth to end eighth century) and lies beside the international airport, some 10 km. south of Beirut, see M. Saidah's prelim. report of the first two seasons, op. cit. in note 187, pp. 51–90. On the evidence cited by Miss Taylor and Saidah the red-slip ware belongs to the late ninth and the eighth centuries (i.e. Saidah's upper level).

252. See, e.g. Bossert (1951), nos. 1106 ff.; G. Loud, *Megiddo Ivories*, Chicago Orient. Inst. Publ. no. 52, 1939. For the techniques of ivory working see R. D. Barnett in C. Singer *et al.*, *A History of Technology*, I, 1954, pp. 663 ff.

253. For these Nimrud ivories see Barnett (1957).

254. Renan (1864), pl. 4; after whom Perrot and Chipiez (1885), p. 131, fig. 76 (but top part of carpet pattern missing).

255. Full discussion with illus. in E. Kukahn, *Anthropoide Sarkophage in Beyrouth*, 1955, who briefly mentions the B.M. example on p. 86.

256. Full discussion with illus. in O. Hamdy Bey and T. Reinach, *Une Nécropole royale à Sidon*, 2 vols., 1892.

257. For the Baalyaton stele and its parallels see H. Ingholt in *Kunstmuseets Aarsskrift* (Statens Museum for Kunst, Copenhagen), XIII–XV, pp. 81 ff. For the Yehawmilk stele see, e.g. Perrot and Chipiez (1885), p. 67, fig. 23.

258. Myres (1914), p. 62.

259. A. W. Lawrence (*J. Hell. Studies*, XLVI, 1926, pp. 166 ff.) suggests that the dress on this statuette shows no oriental traits, but is a distant copy of the Ionic himation and chiton of, e.g. many of the Acropolis *korai*; I find it difficult to concur.

260. Albright (1949), fig. 38.

261. For a recent discussion of this type of capital, based on one found at Cadiz, see César Román, 'El capitel di tipo protojonico de Cadiz', *Archivo español de Arqueol*. XXXII, 1959, pp. 58–70. For such capitals at Carthage and elsewhere in north Africa from the fifth century B C onwards see Lézine, op. cit. in note 103, pp. 59–62.

262. Cintas (1946), pp. 32 ff. Previously it seemed that these masks were absent in Sicily and Spain. Some good examples of both types, however, have recently been found at Motya (S. Moscati, *The World of the Phoenicians*, 1968, p. 204, and id. in Ward ed. (1968), p. 72, pl. 32,a–b). Doubtless examples from Spain will soon come to light.

263. R. M. Dawkins (ed.), *The Sanctuary of Artemis Orthia at Sparta*, 1929, pp. 163 ff., espec. type G (grotesques), pls. 57–62. The parallel is not really close and is probably fortuitous.

264. For a recent discussion of the connection of the Hazor and other eastern masks, cult-objects and symbols with their much later western parallels see Y. Yadin, 'Symbols of deities at Zinjirli, Carthage and Hazor' in *Near Eastern Archaeology in the Twentieth Century* (Essays in honour of Nelson Glueck), New York, 1970, pp. 199–231.

265. For this find see García y Bellido (1952), pp. 439 ff., figs. 350–55, who refers to Carlos Román, *Antigüedades ebusitanas*, 1913. A bilingual inscription in bronze with a third-century Punic text on one side and a second-century or later neo-punic one on the other, dedicated to Tanit by Abdeshmun, son of Azarbaal, clinches the identification.

266. See, e.g., for Carthage, Hours (1950), p. 19 f., pls. 2–3; for Nora, G. Patroni in *Mon. Antichi*, XIV, 1904, cols. 228 ff., pls. 21 ff. (some only); for Motya, J. I. S. Whitaker, *Motya*, 1921, p. 272, fig. 50.

267. See Lézine, op. cit. in note 103, pp. 35 ff.

268. See, e.g. Lilliu (1944), pls. 9, no. 97 and 10, no. 115.

269. Cintas (1947), pp. 13 ff., figs. 48–9, and, for the Utica ring, id. (1951), p. 53, figs. 20–21; L. Foucher, *Hadrumetum*, 1964, pp. 39 ff.

270. Perrot and Chipiez (1885), p. 308, fig. 232.

271. For both the statue and the stelae see A. L. Delattre, *La Nécropole des Rabs, prêtres et prêtresses de Carthage* (Fouilles de Ste Monique, 3me année), extr. du *Cosmos*, 1906, p. 21 f., figs. 39–41.

272. For Soloeis (found near Pizzo Cannita, see note 57), Perrot and Chipiez (1885), figs. 133–4, and V. Tusa in *Karthago*, XII, 1965, pls. 2–3; for Gades, Garcia y Bellido (1952), pp. 397 ff., figs. 218–20.

273. See A. L. Delattre, *Les Grandes sarcophages anthropoides du Musée Lavigerie*, extr. du *Cosmos*, 1903, and H. de Villefosse in *Monuments Piot*, XII, 1905, pp. 75 ff., pl. 8 (in colour).

274. For the Corinthian jug see Delattre, 'Nécr. punique, Colline St Louis', *Missions Catholiques*, 1896, pp. 84 ff. For the cuirass and mirror-cover see Lapeyre (1942), pls. 9–10. For the 'Sardus Pater' figurine see Lilliu in *Studi Etruschi*, XVIII, 1944, p. 329 f., pl. 13. There is doubt about the provenience of this piece (ibid. note 58). Gesturi and Genoni are a few km. apart in Nuoro province. Spano in 1884 said it came from Gesturi; others, e.g. Taramelli (*Guida Mus. Naz. di Cagliari*, 1915, p. 34) ascribe it to Genoni. For the Siagu Baal-Hammon see Picard, G. (1956), pl. 35 (= id. 1964, pl. 40); A. Merlin, *Sanctuaire de Baal et de Tanit près de Siagu*, Notes et Documents publ. par la Direction des Antiq. et Arts (Tunis), IV, 1910, pl. 2, no. 2.

275. For a suggestion that this figurine represents Ptah, and is much earlier than the fifth century, see Cintas, op. cit. in note 41, pp. 265 ff., pl. 2, no. 3.

276. They are copper, not bronze; see P. Berger, *Catalogue du Musée Lavigerie*, I, 1900, p. 205, note 4. For a general discussion of these razors see J. Vercoutter, *Les Objets égyptiens et égyptisants du mobilier funéraire carthaginois*, 1945, pp. 302–10, pls. 27–8. For one from Utica showing Heracles on one side and Scylla on the other, Cintas (1951), p. 51, fig. 18.

277. For the Juno and Douimes mirror-handles see the recent study by Anna Maria Bisi in *Mél. de Carthage*, 1964–5, pp. 43 ff., with excellent photographs of both.

278. García y Bellido (1952), p. 484, fig. 424. For these Spanish ivories in general see A. Blanco Freijeiro in *Archivo español de Arqueol.* XXXIII, 1960, pp. 3–25.

279. Sometimes these objects, especially the nearly complete shells, show no traces of decoration and may have been left plain. For a recent discussion, primarily of those from Carthage, see M. Astruc in *Cahiers de Byrsa*, VI, 1956, pp. 29 ff.

280. Another kind of shell, the marine *tridachna*, was also decorated, but by carving, not painting. Examples occur on many Mediterranean sites. Some believe that they were decorated by east Phoenician artists of the seventh and sixth centuries BC, others that they were the work of Naukratite Greeks. Imitations, similarly decorated, exist in stone.

281. I can find no evidence, however, for Culican's statement (*Pal. Expl. Quart.* 1958, pp. 90 ff.) that the Joan Evans ear-ring came from Deltaic Egypt. Dr Evans tells me that when bought in London it was without provenience.

282. For the New York pieces, Myres (1914), nos. 3283–7, p. 386; for Düsseldorf, Bossert (1951), no. 321, after M. Ohnefalsch-Richter, *Kypros, the Bible and Homer*, pl. 217, no. 4.

283. In the British Museum: F. H. Marshall, *Catalogue of Jewellery*, 1911, p. 150, no. 1485.

284. References to Tharros graves are taken from Marshall, op. cit. in note 283.

285. For a detailed discussion of this treasure see A. Blanco, op. cit. in note 184, pp. 11 ff., with many illustrations, but omitting the two metal utensils, for which see E. Quadrado Díaz, ibid. pp. 52 ff. See also J. M. Blázquez, op. cit. in note 61, pp. 115 ff., pls. 36 ff.

286. Two other fine groups of jewellery, both probably sixth century and thus somewhat later than the La Aliseda treasure, have been found in the Tartessian area. Both again show a mixture of eastern (Phoenician) and local

(Tartessian) styles, though the Phoenician influence is less prominent in either of them than it is in the La Aliseda group. One, from El Carambolo (Seville), contained twenty-one pieces of gold-work, including two pectorals, two bracelets, a necklace with pendants in the form of seal-rings, and sixteen flat plates which probably were joined together to form two crowns. This was first published by E. Kukahn and A. Blanco, 'El tesoro di "El Carambolo"', *Archivo español de Arqueol.* XXXII, 1959, pp. 38–49. See also, now, J. M. Blázquez, op. cit. in note 61, pp. 138 ff., pls. 52–3. The other, from Sanlúcar de Barrameda at the mouth of the Guadalquivir, contained ninety-five pieces of gold jewellery of many varieties (bracelet, ear-rings, rings, etc.) found in three parts; see (for first publication, but only of the first part of the find) Concepcion Blanco de Torrecillas, 'El tesoro del cortijo de "Evora" (Sanlúcar de Barrameda)', ibid. pp. 50–57. Both these treasures are now in the Archaeological Museum at Seville (C. Fernandez Chicarro, *Catálogo del Mus. Arqueol. de Sevilla*, Madrid, 1969, pp. 94–6, pls. 61, 66, and refs. ad loc.), and both have recently been republished by J. M. de Carriazo: (a) *El Tesoro y las primeras Excavaciones en 'El Carambolo'* (*Camas, Sevilla*), Excav. Arqueol. en España, no. 68, Madrid, 1970; and (b) *El Tesoro y las primeras Excavaciones de Ebora* (*Sanlúcar de Barrameda*), Excav. Arqueol. en España, no. 69, Madrid, 1970. I am most grateful to Miss Jennifer Price for help with these references.

287. García y Bellido (1952), pp. 404 ff., fig. 222; for other Gades jewellery see ibid., figs. 231 ff.

288. Gsell, IV, p. 93; Cintas (1946), p. 18; P. Amiet, 'Cylindres-sceaux orientaux trouvés à Carthage', *Cahiers de Byrsa*, V, 1955, pp. 11 ff.

289. Driver (1948), pp. 81 ff.

290. Cintas (1946), pl. 5 on p. 19. His graph differs in detail but not in general pattern from one published by Vercoutter (op. cit. in note 276, p. 63, fig. 3). For further discussion of scarabs (and amulets) at Carthage see Cintas, op. cit. in note 41, pp. 442–60.

Key to the references in the notes

ALBRIGHT (1949): W. F. Albright, *The Archaeology of Palestine*, Penguin Books, 1949.

BARNETT (1957): R. D. Barnett, *A Catalogue of the Nimrud Ivories . . . in the British Museum*, London, 1957.

BOSSERT (1951): H. T. Bossert, *Altsyrien*, Tübingen, 1951.

CINTAS and GOBERT (1939): P. Cintas and E. G. Gobert, 'Les tombes du Jbel Mlezza', *Rev. tunisienne*, XXXVIII–XL, 1939, pp. 135 ff.

CINTAS (1946): P. Cintas, *Amulettes puniques*. Inst. Hautes Études, Tunis, I, Tunis, 1946.

CINTAS (1947): P. Cintas, 'Le Sanctuaire punique de Sousse', *Rev. africaine*, XC, 1947, pp. 1 ff. (offprinted).

CINTAS (1949): P. Cintas, 'Fouilles puniques à Tipasa', *Rev. africaine*, XCII, 1949, pp. 1 ff. (offprinted).

CINTAS (1950): P. Cintas, *Céramique punique*. Inst. Hautes Études, Tunis, III, Paris, 1950.

CINTAS (1951): P. Cintas, 'Deux campagnes de recherches à Utique', *Karthago*, II, 1951, pp. 5 ff.

CINTAS (1954): P. Cintas, *Contribution à l'étude de l'expansion carthaginoise au Maroc*. Inst. Hautes-Études Marocaines, LVI, Paris, 1954.

C.I.S.: *Corpus Inscriptionum Semiticarum*, Part I (Phoenicia), vols. i–iii (issued in fascicles from 1881 onwards, the inscriptions being numbered consecutively throughout).

CONTENAU (1949): G. Contenau, *La Civilisation phénicienne*, 2 ed. Paris, 1949.

DIRINGER (c. 1948): D. Diringer, *The Alphabet* (London, no date).

DRIVER (1948): G. R. Driver, *Semitic Writing from Pictograph to Alphabet*. Schweich Lectures, 1944. London, 1948; 2 ed. 1954.

DUNAND (1945): M. Dunand, *Byblia Grammata*, Beyrouth, 1945.

GARCIA Y BELLIDO (1952): A. García y Bellido, 'El mundo de las colonizaciones', *Historia de España*, I, ii, ed. D. R. Menéndez Pidal, Madrid, 1952; 2 ed. 1960.

GSELL: S. Gsell, *Histoire ancienne de l'Afrique du Nord*, 8 vols. Paris, 1913 ff. (see p. 258).

HARDEN (1939): D. B. Harden, 'The topography of Punic Carthage', *Greece and Rome*, IX 1939, pp. 1 ff.

HARDEN (1948): D. B. Harden, 'The Phoenicians on the west coast of Africa', *Antiquity*, XXII, 1948, pp. 141 ff.

HOURS (1950): M. Hours-Miédan, 'Les représentations figurées sur les stèles de Carthage', *Cahiers de Byrsa*, I, 1950–51, pp. 15 ff.

LAPEYRE (1942): G. G. Lapeyre and A. Pellegrin, *Carthage punique*, Paris, 1942.

LILLIU (1944): G. Lilliu, 'Le stele puniche di Sulcis', *Mon. Antichi*, XL, 1944, cols. 293 ff.

MYRES (1914): J. L. Myres, *Handbook of the Cesnola Collection of Antiquities from Cyprus*, Metrop. Museum of Art, New York, 1914.

PERROT and CHIPIEZ (1885): G. Perrot and C. Chipiez, *Histoire de l'art dans l'antiquité*, III, *Phénicie-Cypre*, Paris, 1885.

PICARD, C. (1951): C. Picard, *Carthage*, Paris, 1951.

PICARD, G. (1956): G. Picard, *Le Monde de Carthage*, Paris, 1956 = id. (1964): *Carthage*, London, 1964; an altered and revised edition.

PICARD, G. and C. (1958): G. and C. Charles-Picard, *La Vie quotidienne à Carthage au temps d'Hannibal*, Paris, 1958 = idd. (1961): *Daily Life in Carthage at the Time of Hannibal*, trans. A. E. Foster, London, 1961; an altered and revised edition.

POIDEBARD (1939): A. Poidebard, *Tyr, un grand port disparu*, Paris, 1939.

RENAN (1864): E. Renan, *Mission de Phénicie*, Paris, 1864.

WARD ed. (1968): W. A. Ward ed., *The Role of the Phoenicians in the Interaction of Mediterranean Civilizations*. Papers presented to the Archaeological Symposium at the American University of Beirut, March 1967: Amer. Univ. Beirut, 1968.

WARMINGTON (1960): B. H. Warmington, *Carthage*, London, 1960. For revised editions of this book, see p. 272 below.

YADIN (1958): Y. Yadin, *Hazor . . . an Archaeological Exhibition . . . at the British Museum*, London, 1958.

Bibliography*

Information on the Phoenicians is widely scattered in diverse sources, ancient and modern. Many references are cited in the Notes (see pp. 212–50, with Key to the references, pp. 251–2), but numerous other monographs and articles in periodicals have been used in preparing this book and it is impossible to list them all here. The Phoenicians, by their journeys throughout the ancient world and their contacts with so many people, have ensured that they are studied today in many countries and many languages. A selective bibliography from this mass of material is bound to reflect its author's nationality and native tongue, and if the present one includes what may seem an undue preponderance of works in English, this must be my excuse.

Much of the modern literature is in periodicals and I include here only those articles which I have found to be the most essential, omitting, especially, the large mass of excavation reports. Students will find many important articles, not only in the basic archaeological journals, such as *The Antiquaries Journal*, *Antiquity*, *Iraq*, *Journal of Hellenic Studies*, *Journal of Roman Studies*,

* I have not thought it advisable to alter the general form of this Bibliography, which provided, I hope, a balanced selection of the literature on the Phoenicians which was available up to the time when the revised edition of this book went to press in 1963. A number of titles of books and articles published before that date have, however, been added to fill gaps and make the Bibliography more comprehensive.

Many references to more recent books and articles have been incorporated in the Notes to the present edition, and the more important of these, together with a few other recent publications which I have not had occasion to cite, are collected together in an Addendum, pp. 268–72 below.

American Journal of Archaeology, the *Annual* and the *Bulletin* of the American Schools of Oriental Research, *Journal of the American Oriental Society*, *Journal of Near Eastern Studies*, *Bulletin archéologique du Comité des Travaux hist. et scientifiques*, *Comptes rendus de l'Acad. des Inscr. et Belles-lettres*, *Revue archéologique*, *Revue biblique*, *Revue de l'histoire des religions*, *Syria*, *Mélanges d'archéologie et d'histoire de l'École Française de Rome*, *Monumenti Antichi dei Lincei*, *Notizie degli Scavi*, *Jahrbuch des Deutschen Archäologischen Instituts* (and its *Archäologischen Anzeiger*), *Archivo español de Arqueología*, and the *Papers* and *Annuals* of the foreign schools at Athens, Rome, etc.; but also in the more specialized journals, such as *Israel Exploration Journal*, *Palestine Exploration Quarterly*, *Levant*, *Quarterly of the Department of Antiquities in Palestine*, *Annual of the Department of Antiquities of Jordan*, *Bulletin du Musée de Beyrouth*, *Berytus*, *Cahiers de Byrsa*, *Hespéris*, *Karthago*, *Libyca*, *Notes et Documents* publiées par la Direction des Antiquités et Arts (Tunis), *Revue africaine*, *Revue tunisienne*, *Studi Etruschi*, *Studi Sardi*, *Quadernos de Historia primitiva*, *Sefarad*, *Zephyrus*, and others, such as *Mémoires de la Société Nationale des Antiquaires de France*, *Missions Catholiques* and *Cosmos*, which the R. Père Delattre used to record many of his finds at Carthage. Important contributions on special topics also exist in Pauly-Wissowa, *Realencyclopädie*, and in the relevant sections of the *Cambridge Ancient History* and other similar works of reference.

Good bibliographies already exist in Contenau (1949),* primarily for the eastern Phoenicians, and in Picard, G. (1956), primarily for the western Phoenicians. Some specialized bibliographies are noted below and see also the books by Moscati and Cintas cited in the Addendum (pp. 268–72).

ANCIENT AUTHORS AND TEXTS

Semitic, etc.

THE BIBLE. [Chiefly the books of Kings, Chronicles and Ezekiel.] Citations are from the Revised Version.

*The full titles of works thus cited with author's name and date will be found in the Key to the references, which follows the Notes, p. 251 f. above.

THE EL AMARNA LETTERS. [See Knudtzon, J. A., *Die el Amarna Tafeln*, 2 vols. Leipzig, 1915.]

THE UGARIT TABLETS. [Specially valuable for Canaanite religion and myth.]

MONUMENTAL TEXTS of Egyptian, Assyrian and other monarchs.

PHOENICIAN INSCRIPTIONS, many, but by no means all, published in the *Corpus Inscriptionum Semiticarum*, I, i, 1881–7, ii, 1890–1911, iii, 1926–.

Selections from these Semitic, etc. sources may be found in:

Répertoire d'épigraphie sémitique. Paris, Acad. des Inscr. et Belles Lettres, 1900–.

PRITCHARD, J. B., ed., *Ancient Near-Eastern Texts relating to the Old Testament*, 2 ed. Princeton, 1955.

WINTON THOMAS, D., ed., *Documents from Old Testament Times*, London, 1958.

Greek

Principally HOMER (eighth and seventh century BC), HERODOTUS (fifth century BC), POLYBIUS (second century BC), DIODORUS SICULUS, STRABO (first century BC), JOSEPHUS, PLUTARCH (first century AD), and APPIAN (second century AD).

Latin

Principally PLAUTUS (Poenulus, *c.* 190 BC), LIVY (late first century BC to early first century AD), COLUMELLA, PLINY THE ELDER, POMPONIUS MELA, SILIUS ITALICUS, VELLEIUS PATERCULUS (first century AD), JUSTIN's epitome of Pompeius Trogus (second century AD), and ST AUGUSTINE (later fourth to early fifth century AD).

For HANNO and PSEUDO-SCYLAX (Greek), AVIENUS (Latin) and other geographical texts see MÜLLER, C., *Geographi Graeci Minores*, 3 vols. Paris, 1855–61, and many other editions, including some cited under *Expansion and Exploration* (p. 265).

THE EASTERN PHOENICIANS AND THEIR NEIGHBOURS

History and general

ALBRIGHT (1949).
BÉRARD, V., *Les Phéniciens et l'Odyssée*, 2 vols. Paris, 1902–3.
BOSSERT (1951).
CONTENAU (1949).
DUNAND, M., *De l'Amanus au Sinaï, sites et monuments*, Beyrouth, 1953.
DUNBABIN, T. J., *The Greeks and their Eastern Neighbours*. Soc. for Prom. Hellenic Stud., suppl. paper no. 8, London, 1957.
KENRICK, J., *Phoenicia*, London, 1855.
KENYON, K. M., *Archaeology in the Holy Land*, London, 1960.
RENAN (1864).
SCHAEFFER, C. F. A., *Stratigraphie comparée et chronologie de l'Asie occidentale, III–II millénaires*, London, 1948.
WEILL, R., *La Phénicie et l'Asie occidentale*, Paris, 1939.
WRIGHT, G. E., ed., *The Bible and the Ancient Near East*, London, 1961. [Includes W. F. Albright, 'The role of the Canaanites in the history of civilization', pp. 328 ff.]

Special sites

Mainland

CONTENAU, G., *Mission archéologique à Sidon, 1914*, Paris, 1921; *2me Mission do. 1920*, Paris, 1924.
DUNAND, M., *Fouilles de Byblos*, I, II, Paris, 1939, 1954. [Vol. III not yet published, vol. IV, 1968, concerns Neolithic levels only.]
DUSSAUD, R., *Les Découvertes de Ras Shamra (Ugarit) et l'Ancien Testament*, 2 ed. Paris, 1941.
FLEMING, W. B., *History of Tyre*. Columbia Univ. Orient. Stud. no. 10, New York, 1915.
HAMDY BEY, O. and REINACH, T., *Une Nécropole royale à Sidon*, 2 vols. Paris, 1892.
JOHNS, C. N., 'Excav. at Pilgrims' Castle, 'Atlīt, 1933', *Quart. Dept. Antiq. Palestine*, VI, 1937, pp. 121 ff.
MONTET, P., *Byblos et l'Egypte*, 2 vols. Paris, 1928.

MOUTERDE, R., POIDEBARD, A. and LAUFFRAY, J., *Sidon: aménagements antiques du port de Saïda*, Beyrouth, 1951.

POIDEBARD (1939).

RIIS, P. J., *Hama, Fouilles et Recherches* 1931–1938, II, 3, *Les Cimetières à crémation*. Nationalmus. Skrifter, Copenhagen, 1948.

ROTHENBERG, B., 'Ancient copper industries in the western Arabah, I', *Pal. Expl. Quart.* 1962, pp. 5 ff.

SAVIGNAC, R., in *Revue biblique*, n.s. XIII, 1916, pp. 565 ff. [For Aradus.]

SCHAEFFER, C. F. A., *Ugaritica*, I–IV. Mission de Ras Shamra, nos. 2, 5, 8, 15, Paris, 1939, 1949, 1956, 1962. [See also now V. Miss. R.S. no. 16, 1968 (texts and commentaries), and VI. Miss. R.S. no. 17, 1969 ('Festschrift' commemorating thirty years of excavation on the site).]

WOOLLEY, SIR L., *A Forgotten Kingdom*, Penguin, 1953.

— *Alalakh*. Research Rep. Soc. Antiq. London, no. 18, 1955.

YADIN, Y. *et al.*, *Hazor*, I, II, III–IV, Jerusalem, 1958, 1960, 1961. [Only the plate volume of III–IV has yet been published.]

For Byblos and Ras Shamra see many further titles listed in the bibliography in Contenau (1949), and elsewhere.

Cyprus

CASSON, S., *Ancient Cyprus: its Art and Archaeology*, London, 1937.

CESNOLA, L. P. DI, *Cyprus: its Ancient Cities, Tombs and Temples*, London, 1877.

HILL, SIR GEORGE, *A History of Cyprus*, I, Cambridge, 1940. [Includes a chapter on religion.]

MYRES (1914).

— 'Excav. in Cyprus, 1913', *Ann. Brit. School Athens*, XLI, 1939–40, pp. 60 ff. [Lefkóniko sanct., Bamboula (Kition), etc.]

OHNEFALSCH-RICHTER, M., *Kypros, the Bible and Homer*, 2 vols. London and Berlin, 1893, in contemp. German and English edd.

The Swedish Cyprus Expedition, I–III, Stockholm, 1934–7.

— IV, pts. 2–3, Stockholm, 1948, 1956.

THE WESTERN PHOENICIANS

History and general

Our knowledge of the western Phoenicians must always be founded on the great work of Stéphane Gsell, *Histoire ancienne de l'Afrique du Nord*, 8 vols., Paris, 1913–29 (all the first six vols. exist in more than one edition, all before 1929). The first four volumes deal with the Punic period to the fall of Carthage, the last four with the succeeding native kingdoms down to their final incorporation in the Roman Empire. Though Gsell provides no bibliography as such, his massive footnotes are all-embracing, and it is difficult to find any previous work which he did not know and cite. Though called a 'history', his book covers all aspects of north African civilization of the time and has much to say, too, of the other western Phoenician colonies. It lacks, however, illustrations, except a few maps. For a fuller appreciation of Gsell's work see Picard, G. (1956), p. 188.

ALBRIGHT, W. F., in *Bull. Amer. Schools Orient. Research*, no. 83, 1941, pp. 14 ff. [On chronology of settlements.]

On the dates of treaties between Rome and Carthage see BEAUMONT, R. L., in *J. Rom. Studies*, XXIX, 1939, pp. 74 ff.; also PICARD, G. (1956), p. 193; and, with full bibliog. [Boucher-] COLOZIER, E., 'Les Étrusques et Carthage', *Mél. d'archéol. et d'histoire de l'École Fr. de Rome*, LXV, 1953, pp. 63 ff.

BELOCH, J., in *Rheinisches Museum für Philologie*, XXXIV, 1894, pp. 111 ff.

BOSWORTH-SMITH, R., *Carthage and the Carthaginians*, London, 1902.

CULICAN, W., 'Aspects of Phoenician settlement in the west Mediterranean', *Abr–Nahrain*, I, 1961, pp. 36 ff.

EHRENBERG, V., *Karthago*. Morgenland, Heft 14, Leipzig, 1927.

FORRER, E. O., 'Karthago wurde erst 673–663 v. Christ gegründet', in *Festschrift Franz Dornsieff*, Leipzig, 1953, pp. 85 ff.

FRÉZOULS, E., in *Bull. de corresp. hellénique*, LXXIX, 1955, pp. 153 ff.

HOURS-MIEDAN, M., *Carthage*. 'Que Sais-je?', no. 340, Paris, 1949; 2 ed. 1959.

JULLIEN, C. A., *Hist. de l'Afrique du Nord*, 2 ed. revised by C. Courtois, Paris, 1951. [Contains a good bibliography.]

LAPEYRE (1942).

MELTZER, O. and KAHRSTEDT, U., *Geschichte der Karthager*, 3 vols. Berlin, 1879, 1896, 1913.

PICARD, G. (1956).

VOGT, J., ed., *Rom und Karthago*, Leipzig, 1942.

WARMINGTON (1960).

Though not an archaeological work, but a novel, Gustave Flaubert's *Salammbô*, published in 1862, is noteworthy for its picture of Punic life at the end of the third century BC, based mainly on classical sources.

Special sites

Carthage

AUDOLLENT, A., *Carthage romaine*, Paris, 1901. [Has much of value on earlier topography and (pp. 775 ff.) a résumé of ancient texts on topography and history.]

BARADEZ, J., 'Nouvelles recherches sur les ports antiques de Carthage', *Karthago*, IX, 1958, pp. 47 ff. For an earlier assessment of Baradez's and Poidebard's views on the situation of the ports see Picard G. (1956), p. 192.

BEULÉ, C. E., *Fouilles à Carthage* (extr. du *J. des Savants*), Paris, 1861.

CARTON, L., *Sanct. punique découvert à Carthage*, Paris, 1929.

DUVAL, R., 'Mis au jour de l'enceinte extérieure de la Carthage punique', *Comptes rendus Acad. Inscr.* 1950, pp. 53 ff.

GAUCKLER, P., *Nécropoles puniques de Carthage*, 2 vols. Paris, 1915.

HARDEN (1939).

PICARD, C. (1951). [Guide book to the remains on the site, with bibliography relating to various areas and monuments.]

PICARD, G. and C. (1958).

VERCOUTTER, J., *Les Objets égyptiens et égyptisants du mobilier funéraire carthaginois*, Paris, 1945. [Includes (pp. 16 ff.) a a complete summary, with bibliog. and map, of all the Carthage cemeteries excavated by Gauckler, Delattre, Merlin, Poinssot and others.]

For the precinct of Tanit see note 108, p. 227. The earliest, and still two of the best, accounts of it and its implications are POINSSOT, L. and LANTIER, R., 'Un sanct. de Tanit à Carthage', *Rev. de l'hist. des religions*, LXXXVII, 1923, pp.

32 ff. and KELSEY, F. W., *Excav. at Carthage, 1925*, New York, 1926.
For the late Punic houses on the Hill of St Louis see note 163, p. 236.

Other North African sites

Arae Philenorum
GOODCHILD, R. G., in *Papers Brit. School Rome*, XX, 1952, pp. 94 ff.

Dar Essafi (Kerkouane) and Cape Bon
CINTAS and GOBERT (1939).
CINTAS, P., in *Comptes rendus Acad. Inscr.* 1953, pp. 256 ff.

Gunugu (Gouraya)
ASTRUC, M., in *Libyca*, II, 1954, pp. 9 ff.
GSELL, S., *Fouilles de Gouraya*. Assoc. Hist. pour l'Étude de l'Afr. du Nord, no. 4, Paris, 1903.
MISSONNIER, F., in *Mél. d'archéol. et d'histoire de l'École Fr. de Rome*, L, 1933, pp. 87 ff.

Hadrumetum (Sousse)
CINTAS (1947).

Igilgili (Djidjelli)
ALQUIER, J. and P., in *Rev. archéol.* XXXI, 1930, pp. 1 ff.
ASTRUC, M., in *Rev. africaine*, LXX, 1937, pp. 1 ff.

Lixos
TARRADELL, M., *Lixus*, Tetuan, 1959.

Mogador
CINTAS (1954).
JODIN, A., 'Note prélim. sur l'établissement pré-romain de Mogador (campagnes 1956–7)', *Bull. d'archéol. marocaine*, II, 1957, pp. 9 ff.

Morocco
TARRADELL, M., *Marruecos punico*, Tetuan, 1960.
VILLARD, F., 'Céramique grecque du Maroc', *Bull. d'archéol. marocaine*, IV, 1960, pp. 1 ff.

Rachgoun
VUILLEMOT, G., 'La nécropole punique du phare ... de Rachgoun', *Libyca*, III, 1955, pp. 7 ff.

Tipasa
CINTAS (1949).
LESCHI, L., *Tipasa de Maurétanie*, Algiers, 1950.

Utica
CINTAS (1951). [With bibliog. of site, p. 18.]
—'Nouvelles recherches à Utique', *Karthago*, V, 1954, pp. 89 ff.
MOULARD, J., in *Bull. archéol.* 1925, pp. 225 ff.

For other references to excavations on north African sites see
   Cintas (1950), pp. 45 ff.

Sicily

ACANFORA, M. O., 'Panormos preromana', *Archivio storico
   italiano*, IV, 1950–51, pp. 7 ff.
CITRO, C., 'Topografia, storia, archeologia di Pizzo Cannita',
   Atti Accad. di Scienze Lettere e Arti di Palermo, XII, 1952–3,
   pp. 265 ff.
DUNBABIN, T. J., *The Western Greeks*, Oxford, 1948.
GABRICI, E., 'Stele sepolcrali di Lilibeo a forma di Heroon',
   Mon. Antichi, XXXIII, 1929, cols. 41 ff.
ISSERLIN, B. S. J. *et al.*, 'Excavations at Motya...', *Antiquity*,
   XXX, 1956, pp. 110 ff.; idd. 'Motya 1955', *Papers Brit.
   School Rome*, XXVI, 1958, pp. 1 ff.; idd. 'Motya ... excava-
   tions 1961–3', *Ann. Leeds Oriental Soc.*, IV, 1962–3, pp. 83 ff.;
   and see also *Ill. Lond. News*, 3 March 1962, pp. 328 ff., and
   ibid. 21 September 1963, pp. 425 ff.
MARCONI, P., 'Tombe puniche ... a Palermo', *Not. Scavi*,
   1928, pp. 261 ff., 482 ff.
PACE, B., *Arte e civiltà della Sicilia antica*, I, Milan, 1935; 2 ed.
   1958.
PARETI, L., *Sicilia antica*, Palermo, 1959.
WHITAKER, J. I. S., *Motya, A Phoenician Colony in Sicily*,
   London, 1921.

See also *Guide* to Palermo museum in the series of *Itinerari
   dei Musei e Monumenti d'Italia*.

Sardinia

LEVI, D., 'Le necropoli puniche di Olbia', *Studi Sardi*, IX, 1950,
   pp. 5 ff.

LILLIU (1944).
— 'Rapporti fra la civ. nuragica e la civ. fenicio-punica in Sardegna', *Studi Etruschi*, XVIII, 1944, pp. 323 ff.
PAIS, E., *La Sardegna prima del dominio romano*. Memorie Accad. Naz. dei Lincei, cl. scienze morali, VII, Rome, 1881, pp. 259 ff.
PATRONI, G., 'Nora', *Mon. Antichi*, XIV, 1904, cols. 109 ff.
PESCE, G., 'Il primo scavo di Tharros', *Studi Sardi*, XIV–XV, 1955–7, pp. 507 ff.
— *Nora: guida agli scavi*, Bologna, 1957.
— *Sardegna punica*, Cagliari, 1961.
— 'Il tempio monumentale di Tharros', *Mon. Antichi*, XLV, 1961, cols. 333 ff.
— 'I rasoi punici di Sardegna', *Bollettino d'Arte*, IV, 1961, pp. 293 ff.
TARAMELLI, A., 'La necropoli punica ... a Cagliari', *Mon. Antichi*, XXI, 1912, cols. 45 ff.
— *Guida del Museo Naz. di Cagliari*, Cagliari, 1915.

See also *Guides* to Cagliari and Sassari museums in the series of *Itinerari dei Musei e Monumenti d'Italia*.

Malta

BALDACCHINO, J. G., 'Punic rock tombs near Pawla', *Papers Brit. School Rome*, XIX, 1951, pp. 1 ff.
— and DUNBABIN, T. J., 'Rock tomb at Ghajn Qajjet, near Rabat', ibid. XXI, 1953, pp. 32 ff.
CARUANA, A., *Report on Phoenician and Roman Antiq. ... in Malta*, Valletta, 1882.
MAYR, A., *Die Insel Malta im Altertum*, Munich, 1909.
— 'Aus den phönikischen Necropolen von Malta', *Sitzungb. der K. Bayer. Akad. der Wissenschaften zu München*, 1905, pp. 467 ff.

Spain and Ibiza

ASTRUC, M., *La Necrópolis de Villaricos*. Informes y Memorias de la C.G.E.A., no. 25, Madrid, 1951.
BLANCO FREIJEIRO, A., 'Orientalia', *Archivo español de Arqueol.* XXIX, 1956, pp. 3 ff.
— 'Orientalia II', ibid. XXXIII, 1960, pp. 3 ff.

BONSOR, G., 'Les colonies agricoles pré-romaines de la vallée du Baetis', *Rev. archéol.* XXXV, 1899, pp. 126 ff.

COLOMINES ROCA, J., *Les Terracuites cartagineses d'Eivissa*, Barcelona, 1938.

GARCIA Y BELLIDO, A., *Fenicios y Cartagineses en Occidente*, Madrid, 1942.

— 1952.

— 'Materiales de arqueol. hispano-púnica: jarros de bronce', *Archivo español de Arqueol.* XXIX, 1956, pp. 85 ff.

— 'Inventario de los jarros púnico-tartéssicos', ibid. XXXIII, 1960, pp. 44 ff.

MAÑA DE ANGULO, J. M., *La Isla Plana*, Ibiza, 1954.

— *Guia del Mus. Arqueol. de Ibiza*, Ibiza, 1957.

MELIDA, J. R., *Tesoro de Aliseda*. Mus. Arqueol. Nacional, Madrid, 1921.

QUADRADO DIAZ, E., *Materiales ibéricos: Cerámica roja de Procedencia incierta*. Monografías del Seminario de Arqueologia, Salamanca, 1953.

— 'Los recipientes rituales . . . brasilleros púnicos', *Archivo español de Arqueol.* XXIX, 1956, pp. 52 ff.

QUINTERO, P., *La necrópolis anteromana de Cádiz*, Madrid, 1915.

ROMAN, C., *Antigüedades ebusitanas*, Barcelona, 1913.

ROMAN Y CALVET, J., *Los Nombres e Importancia arqueol. de las Islas Pythiusas*, Barcelona, 1906.

SCHULTEN, A., *Tartessos*, 2 ed. Madrid, 1945.

SIRET, L., *Villaricos y Herrerías*. R. Acad. Hist. Madrid, Memorias, XIV, Madrid, 1909.

VIVES Y ESCUDERO, A., *Estudio de Arqueol. cartaginesa: La Necrópolis de Ibiza*, Madrid, 1917.

WRITING, LANGUAGE AND LITERATURE

ALBRIGHT, W. F., in *J. Amer. Orient. Soc.* LXVII, 1947, pp. 153 ff.

COOKE, G. A., *A Text-book of North Semitic Inscriptions*, Oxford, 1903.

DIRINGER (c. 1948). [Contains an extensive bibliog., p. 221.]

— *Writing*. No. 25 in Ancient Peoples and Places, London, 1962.

DRIVER (1948).

DUNAND (1945).

GARDINER, A. H. and PEET, T. E., *The Inscriptions of Sinai*, London, 1919.

GORDON, C. H., *Ugaritic Grammar*, Rome, 1940.

HARRIS, Z. S., *A Grammar of the Phoenician Language*, New Haven, 1936.

— *Development of Canaanite Dialects*, New Haven, 1939.

SCHAEFFER, C. F. A., *The Cuneiform Texts of Ras Shamra/Ugarit*. Brit. Acad. Schweich Lectures, London, 1939.

For the Kara Tepe inscriptions see GURNEY, O. R., *The Hittites*, Penguin, 1952, bibliog. on p. 221, and add, *inter alios*, BARNETT, R. D. *et al.*, in *Iraq*, X, 1948, pp. 56 ff., BOSSERT, H. T., in *Jahrb. für Kleinasiat. Forschung*, II, 1952–3, pp. 293 ff., ALT, A., in *Die Welt des Orients*, II, 1955, pp. 172 ff., and LLOYD, SETON, *Early Anatolia*, Penguin, 1956, pp. 177 ff.

For the possible survival of Punic into the later Roman Empire in north Africa see bibliog. in note 130, p. 231.

RELIGION

DUSSAUD, R., 'Les religions des Hittites et des Hourrites, des Phéniciens et des Syriens' in DUSSAUD, R. and DHORME, E., *Mana: introd. à l'hist. des religions*, I, *Les anciennes religions orientales*, II, Paris, 1945; 2 ed. 1949.

— 'Précisions épigraphiques sur les sacrifices d'enfants', *Comptes rendus Acad. Inscr.* 1946, pp. 371 ff.

HOURS (1950).

LAGRANGE, M. J., *Études sur les religions sémitiques*, 2 ed. 1905.

PICARD, G.-C., *Les Religions de l'Afrique antique*, Paris, 1954.

See also many of the books and articles cited elsewhere in this bibliography.

EXPANSION AND EXPLORATION

ALY, W., 'Die Entdeckung des Westens', *Hermes*, CCLX, 1927, pp. 299 ff., 485 ff. [Includes text of Hanno's *Periplus*.]

BERTHELOT, R., ed., *Festus Avienus 'Ora Maritima'*, Paris, 1934.

BOVILL, E. W., *The Golden Trade of the Moors*, London, 1958. [Discusses trans-Saharan journeying.]

CARCOPINO, J., *Le Maroc antique*, Paris, 1943; 2 ed. 1948.

CARPENTER, R., 'The Phoenicians in the west', *Amer. J. Archaeol.* LXII, 1958, pp. 35 ff.

CARY, M. and WARMINGTON, E. H., *The Ancient Explorers*, London, 1929.

CINTAS (1954).

GAUTIER, E. F., *Le Passé de l'Afrique du Nord*, Paris, 1942.

HARDEN (1948).

HENCKEN, H. O'N., *The Archaeology of Cornwall and Scilly*, London, 1932.

HENNIG, R., *Terrae Incognitae*, Leyden, 1936.

SCHULTEN, A., ed., *Avieni Ora Maritima*. Fontes Hispaniae Antiquae, I, Barcelona, 1922.

WARMINGTON, E. H., *Greek Geography*, London, 1934.

For Hanno see bibliog. in DILLER, A., 'The traditions of the minor Greek geographers', *Philol. Monographs Amer. Philol. Assoc.* XIV, 1952, and, further, notes 240–1 above, p. 244 f.

ART, INDUSTRY AND COMMERCE

Eastern and general

BARNETT (1957).

— 'Early shipping in the near east', *Antiquity*, XXXII, 1958, pp. 220 ff.

CONTENAU, G., *Manuel d'archéol. orientale*, I–IV, Paris, 1927–47. [See esp. II, 1056 ff., and III, 1456 ff.]

CROWFOOT, J. W. and G. M., *Early Ivories from Samaria*, London, 1938.

CULICAN, W., 'Essay on a Phoenician ear-ring', *Pal. Explor. Quart.* 1958, pp. 90 ff.

DE MERTZENFELD, C. DECAMPS, *Inventaire commenté des ivoires phéniciens et apparentés découverts dans le Proche-Orient*, Paris, 1954.

DUNAND, M., 'Les sculptures de la favissa du temple d'Amrit', *Bull. Mus. de Beyrouth*, VII, 1944–5, pp. 99 ff., and VIII, 1946–8, pp. 81 ff.

DUSSAUD, R., *L'Art phénicien du 2me millénaire*, Paris, 1949.

FÉVRIER, J. G., 'L'ancienne marine phénicienne et les découvertes récentes', *La Nouvelle Clio*, I, 1949, pp. 128 ff.

FRANKFORT, H., *The Art and Architecture of the Ancient Orient*, Penguin, 1954. [See especially ch. 11.]

HEAD, B. V., *Historia Numorum*, 2 ed. Oxford, 1911.

HILL, G. F., *Catal of Greek Coins in British Museum: Cyprus*, London, 1904.

— *Catal. of Greek Coins in British Museum: Phoenicia*, London, 1910.

— *Guide to Greek Coins*, London, 1932.

KING, L. W., *Bronze Reliefs from the Gates of Shalmaneser*, London, 1915.

KIRK, G. S., 'Ships on geometric vases', *Ann. Brit. School Athens*, XLIV, 1949, pp. 93 ff.

KÖSTER, A., *Das antike Seewesen*, Berlin, 1923.

— *Studien zur Geschichte des antiken Seewesens*. Klio Beiheft 32, Leipzig, 1934.

KUKAHN, E., *Anthropoide Sarkophage in Beyrouth*, Berlin, 1955.

LOUD, G., *Megiddo Ivories*. Chicago Orient. Inst. Publication no. 52, 1939.

MARSHALL, F. H., *British Museum Catal. of Jewellery*, London, 1911. [Contains much material from Cyprus and Sardinia.]

PERROT and CHIPIEZ (1885).

POULSEN, F., *Der Orient und die frühgriechische Kunst*, Leipzig, 1912.

TAYLOR, JOAN DU PLAT, 'The Cypriot and Syrian pottery from Al Mina, Syria', *Iraq*, XXI, 1959, pp. 62 ff. [Discusses red-slip and other Phoenician pottery from numerous Levant sites.]

THUREAU-DANGIN, F. *et al.*, *Arslan Tash*, Paris, 1931.

Western

ASTRUC, M., 'Traditions funéraires de Carthage', *Cahiers de Byrsa*, VI, 1956, pp. 29 ff. [For cups, etc., of ostrich-egg shell.]

— 'Exotisme et localisme; études sur les coquilles d'oeufs d'autruche décorées d'Ibiza', *Archivo de Prehistoria levantina*, VI, 1957, pp. 47 ff.

VON BISSING, F. W. FREIHERR, 'Karthago und seine griech. und ital. Beziehungen', *Studi Etruschi*, VII, 1933, pp. 83 ff.

BOUCHER [-COLOZIER], Etiennette, 'Céramique archaïque d'importation au Musée Lavigerie de Carthage', *Cahiers de Byrsa*, III, 1953, pp. 11 ff.

CINTAS (1946).

— (1950).

FOUCHET, M. P., *L'Art à Carthage*, Paris, 1962.

HARDEN, D. B., 'Punic urns from the precinct of Tanit at Carthage', *Amer. J. Archaeol.* XXXI, 1927, pp. 297 ff. [Discusses also the parallels from Sicily, etc.]

— 'Pottery from the precinct of Tanit at Salammbo, Carthage', *Iraq*, IV, 1937, pp. 59 ff. [For the chronological typology of the urns.]

LÉZINE, A., *Architecture punique, recueil de documents*. Publications de l'Univ. de Tunis, Fac. des Lettres, 1 ser. V, Paris. 1961.

PICARD, C.-G., 'Les oinochoés de bronze de Carthage', *Rev, archéol.* XII, i, 1959, pp. 29 ff.

ROBINSON, E. S. G., 'Punic coins of Spain' in *Essays in Roman Coinage presented to H. Mattingly*, Oxford, 1956, pp. 34 ff.

Catal. du Musée Alaoui du Bardo, Tunis, I, 1899, by R. La Blanchère and P. Gauckler; Suppl. 1, 1910, by P. Gauckler *et al.*; Suppl. 2, 1921, by A. Merlin and R. Lantier.

Catal. du Musée Alaoui, n.s. (Collections puniques), I, 1954, by C.-G. Picard. [Some archit. fragments and sculpture, but mainly stelae from the precinct of Tanit and neo-punic sites. Well illustrated.]

Catal. du Musée Lavigerie de Carthage, I, 1900, by P. Berger; Suppl. 1910, by A. Boulanger.

For the anthropomorphic coffins from Ste Monique (pp. 103, 195) see, *inter alios*, the two publications cited in note 273 and, for some recent views, others cited by Picard, G. (1956), p. 193.

* These museums are now called 'National Museum, Bardo, Tunis' and 'National Museum, Carthage' respectively.

Addendum to the Bibliography

The following important books and articles have been published since the revised edition of this work went to press in 1963.

BARRECA, F., *La civiltà di Cartagine*, Cagliari, 1964.
— *et al.*, *Monte Sirai I. Rapporto preliminare della campagna di scavi 1963*, Rome, 1964; and further reports in subsequent years.

BASCH, L., 'Phoenician oared ships', *Mariner's Mirror*, LV, 1969, no. 2, pp. 139 ff., and no. 3, pp. 227 ff.

BLANCO, A., LUZON, J. M., and RUIZ, D., *Excavaciones arqueologicas en el Cerro Salomon, Riotinto, Huelva*. Publicaciones de la Universidad de Sevilla, ser. Fil. y Letras, no. 4, 1970.

BLAZQUEZ, J. M., *Tartessos y los Origenes de la Colonizacion fenicia in Occidente*, Salamanca, 1968.
—, LUZON, J. M., DE RUIZ MATA, D., 'La Factoría púnica de Aljaraque en la Provincia de Huelva', *Noticiario arqueol. hispanico*, XIII–XIV, 1971, pp. 304 ff.

BONELLO, V., BORG, V., CAGIANO DE AZEVEDO, M. *et al.*, *Missione archeologica italiana a Malta. Rapporto preliminare della campagna 1963*, Rome, 1964; and further reports in subsequent years.

CARTER, T. H., 'Western Phoenicians at Lepcis Magna', *Amer. J. Archaeol.* LXIX, 1965, pp. 123 ff.

CIASCA, A. *et al.*, *Mozia I. Rapporto preliminare della Missione archeologica della Soprintendenza alle Antichità della Sicilia occidentale e dell' Università di Roma*, Rome, 1964; and further reports in subsequent years.

CINTAS, P., *Manuel d'archéologie punique*, I, Paris, 1970. [A major work of synthesis dealing with the historical and archaeological evidence for the origin and development of Carthage and other western settlements. Two more volumes, covering aspects such as topography, industry and agriculture, commerce and exploration, religion and language, are promised.]

CULICAN, W., *The First Merchant Venturers: the Ancient Levant in History and Commerce*, London, 1966.

DENEAUVE, J., *Lampes de Carthage*. Centre National de la Recherche Scientifique, Paris, 1969.

DI VITA, A., 'Les Phéniciens de l'occident d'après les découvertes archéologiques de Tripolitaine', in Ward ed. (1968), pp. 77 ff.

DUNAND, M., 'Nouvelles inscriptions du temple d'Echmoun', *Bull. Mus. de Beyrouth*, XVIII, 1965, pp. 107 ff.

FOUCHER, L., *Hadrumetum*. Publications de l'Université de Tunis, Fac. des Lettres, 1 ser. X, Paris, 1964.

GARBINI, G., 'I Fenici in occidente', *Studi Etruschi*, XXXIV, 1966, pp. 111 ff.

GARCIA Y BELLIDO, A., 'Deidades semitas en la España antigua', *Sefarad*, XXIV, 1964, pp. 12 ff., 237 ff.
— 'Hercules Gaditanus', *Archivo español de Arqueol.* XXXVI, 1964, pp. 68 ff.

GRAY, J., *The Canaanites*. No. 38 in Ancient Peoples and Places, 1964. [The complementary volume to the present one, dealing with the Levant area in the Bronze Age.]

GUIDO, MARGARET, *Sardinia*. No. 35 in Ancient Peoples and Places, London, 1963. [For the Phoenician and Punic period see ch. vii.]
— *Sicily: An Archaeological Guide*, London, 1967.

HALFF, GISELLE, 'L'Onomastique punique de Carthage', *Karthago*, XII, 1965, pp. 63 ff.

HEURGON, J., 'The inscriptions of Pyrgi', *J. Rom. Studies*, LVI, 1966, pp. 1 ff.

ISSERLIN, B. S. J., 'Motya (Trapani). – Rapporto prelim sugli. scavi degli anni 1961–5', *Not. Scavi*, 1970, pp. 560 ff.
— 'New light on the "cothon" at Motya', *Antiquity*, XLV, 1971, pp. 178 ff.

JENKINS, G. K. and LEWIS, R. B., *Carthaginian Gold and Electrum Coins*. Roy. Numismatic Soc. special publication no. 2, London, 1963.

JODIN, A., *Mogador, comptoir phénicien du Maroc atlantique*, Tanger, 1966.

KARAGEORGHIS, V., *Cyprus*. Archaeologia Mundi series, Geneva, 1968 = id. *The Ancient Civilizations of Cyprus*, London, 1969.

KHARSEKIN, A. I., in *Vestnik Drevnei Istorii*, III, 1965, pp. 108 ff. [On Pyrgi inscriptions.]

LECLANT, J., 'Les relations entre l'Egypte et la Phénicie du voyage d'Ounamon à l'expédition d'Alexandre', in Ward ed. (1968), pp. 9 ff.

Mélanges de Carthage, offerts à C. Saumagne, L. Poinssot, M. Pinard, Paris, 1964–5. [Contains papers on Punic antiquities, including Anna Maria Bisi, 'Une figurine phénicienne trouvée à Carthage', pp. 43 ff., and J. Ferron, 'Inscription archaïque à Carthage', pp. 55 ff.]

MOSCATI, S., *The World of the Phoenicians*, London, 1968; trans. by A. Hamilton from id. *Il Mondo dei Fenici*, Milan, 1966. [Contains a very extensive bibliography.]
— 'New light on Punic art', in Ward ed. (1968), pp. 65 ff.

MOUTERDE, R., 'Regards sur Beyrouth phénicienne . . .', *Mél. de l'Univ. de St Joseph*, XL, 1964, pp. 145 ff.

NIEMEYER, H. G., PELLICER, M., SCHUBART, H., 'Eine altpunische Kolonie an der Mündung des Río Vélez', *Archäol. Anzeiger*, III, 1964, pp. 476 ff.
— 'Altpunische Funde von der Mündung des Río Algarrobo', *Madrider Mitteilungen d. Deut. Archäol. Inst.*, V, 1964, pp. 73 ff.

NIEMEYER, H. G. and SCHUBART, H., *Toscanos, die altpunische Faktorei an der Mündung des Río de Vélez*, Lief. I: *Grabungskampagne 1964*. Madrider Forschungen, VI, Berlin, 1969.

PALLOTTINO, M., COLONNA, G., GARBINI, G., BORRELLI, L., 'Scavi nel santuario etrusco di Pyrgi . . .', *Archaeol. Classica*, XVI, 1964, pp. 39 ff.

PELLICER CATALAN, M., 'Ein altpunisches Gräberfeld bei Almuñécar', *Madrider Mitteilungen d. Deut. Archäol. Inst.*, IV, 1963, pp. 9 ff.
— *Excavaciones en la necrópolis púnica 'Laurita' del Cerro de San Cristóbal (Almuñécar, Granada)*. Excavaciones arqueologicas en Espana, no. 17, 1963.

PESCE, G., *Le statuette puniche di Bythia*, Rome, 1965.

PFIFFIG, A. J., *Uni-Hera-Astarte, Studien zu den Goldblechen von S. Severa-Pyrgi mit etr. und punischer Inschrift*. Osterr. Akad. der Wissenschaften, Philos.-Hist. Kl. 88, 2, 1965.

PICARD, G., *Carthage*, London, 1964. [Altered and revised ed. of *Le Monde de Carthage*, Paris, 1956: see p. 252 above.]

PICARD, G. C. and C., *The Life and Death of Carthage*, London, 1968.

PONSICH, M., *Nécropoles phéniciennes de la région de Tanger*. Études et travaux d'archéologie marocaine, III, Tanger, 1967. [Tombs dated eighth to early fifth century BC, on basis of the jewellery.]

REBUFFAT, R., 'Les Phéniciens à Rome', *Mél. d'archéol. et d'histoire de l'École Fr. de Rome*, LXXVIII, 1966, pp. 7 ff.

RIIS, P. J., *Sūkas I, The N. E. Sanctuary and the First Settling of Greeks in Syria and Palestine*. Publications of the Carlsberg Exped. to Phoenicia, I, Copenhagen, 1970.

SAIDAH, M., 'Fouilles de Khaldé, rapp. prélim. sur la première et deuxième campagnes (1961–1962)', *Bull. Mus. de Beyrouth*, XIX, 1966, pp. 51 ff.

TAYLOR, JOAN DU PLAT, 'Motya . . .', *Archaeology*, XVII, 1964, pp. 91 ff.

TUSA, V., 'Testimonianze fenicio-puniche in Sicilia', *Kokálos*, XI (1965), pp. 589 ff.

VUILLEMOT, G., *Reconnaissances aux échelles puniques d'Oranie*, Autun, 1965.

WARD, W. A., ed., *The Role of the Phoenicians in the Interaction of Mediterranean Civilizations*. Papers presented to the Archaeological Symposium at the American University of Beirut, March 1967: Amer. Univ. Beirut, 1968. [Here cited as Ward ed. (1968).]

WARMINGTON, B. H., *Carthage*, Pelican Books, 1964; and see also the second hard-cover ed., revised and expanded, 1969. [For first ed. see p. 252 above.]

Sources of Illustrations

Acknowledgement for photographs used in the plates is made to the following: Turk Tarih Kurumu, Ankara: 37; Kelsey Museum of Archaeology, Univ. of Michigan, Ann Arbor: 5, 6, 26, 32; Dept. of Antiquities, Beirut, Lebanon: 15, 38; Institut français d'Archéologie, Beirut: 2, 3, 4; Photo Manoug, Beirut: 1; Museum of Fine Arts, Boston, Mass.: 59, 60; Soprintendenza alle Antichità, Cagliari: 11, 12, 34; National Museum, Carthage (through M. P. Cintas): 19–22; Ny Carlsberg Glyptotek, Copenhagen: 44; Museo Arqueologico, Ibiza: 76, 79; Hebrew University and James A. de Rothschild Expedition to Hazor, Jerusalem (through Prof. Y. Yadin): 28, 29, 77; Trustees of the British Museum, London: 17, 18, 23, 24, 40, 48, 51, 57, 63, 65–7, 83, 101, 102, 104, 105, 108, 110, 116; Museo Arqueologico Nacional, Madrid: 52, 53, 73, 88–90, 97–9; Metropolitan Museum of Art, New York: 46, 54, 62, 68, 71, 72; Dept. of Antiquities, Nicosia, Cyprus: 70, 74, 103; Ashmolean Museum, Oxford: part of 58, 64, 69, 80–2, 84–7, 92, 94, 95, 100, 106, 109, 111, 112, 114, 115; Soprintendenza alle Antichità, Palermo (ph. Randazzo): 14; de Clercq collection, Paris (ph. Séarl, through M. Coche de la Ferté): 107; Musée du Louvre, Paris (ph. Chuzeville): 16, 25, 39, 47, 49, 50, 55, 56, 61; Soprintendenza alle Antichità, Piedmont: 45; Museum Haaretz, Tel Aviv (ph. Prior): 41; National Museum, Bardo, Tunis (through M. P. Cintas): 35, 75, 78, 91, 96; Dept. of Antiquities, Valletta, Malta: 36; Mr S. Chiappisi: 93; M. P. Cintas: 7, 10, 42, 43; Mr B. H. Warmington: 9; the remaining plates are from photographs by the author (8, 13, 27, 30, 33, part of 58, 113) or anon. (31).

The maps have been drawn by Mr H. A. Shelley of Cambridge in collaboration with the author. Fig 2 is based on Nelson's *Atlas of the Bible*, map opp. p. 102; Fig 5 on Cintas (1954), fig. 19; Figs 6 and 7 on J. Whitaker, *Motya*, map facing p. 1 and map at end; Fig 8 on García y Bellido (1952), fig. 215. The remainder are essentially new.

The other text-figures with two exceptions (Fig 21, reprinted with minor amendments from D. B. Harden in *Iraq*, IV, pp. 59 ff., fig. 1; and Fig 68, redrawn by Mr G. A. Manchester from A. L. Delattre, *Ste Monique*, *2 trim.* fig. 8) have been redrawn specially for this book by Mrs Marion Cox of Abingdon, Berks., from the following sources:— 11: G. Maspero, *Passing of Empires*, p. 375; 12, 16: G. Contenau in *Syria*, IV, pl. 44 and C. F. A. Schaeffer in id. X, pl. 67, 7; 17, 32: P. Gauckler, *Nécrop. puniques*, pls. 226 and 113; 18, 20, 40, 53–8, 79, 82,a,b: Perrot and Chipiez (1885), figs. 294, 40, 640, 547, 36, 543, 283, 73, 52, 589, 470, 477 respectively; 19: C. Watzinger, *Denkm. Palästinas*, pl. 16; 22, 23, 42,b: D. B. Harden in *Iraq*, IV, pp. 59 ff., figs. 2, 8,a, 4,l; 24,a, 25,a–n, q–t: Hours (1950), pls. 3,d, etc.; 24,b–f: F. W. Kelsey, *Excav. at Carthage*, figs. 12, 17, 19, 20, 24; 25,o, p, 28, 29, 49: Lapeyre (1942), pl. 4,c,d and figs. 145, 153, 135; 26: C. Picard (1951), fig. on pp. 24–5; 27, 42,a: Cintas (1950), pls. 65, 69; 30, 31: Cintas and Gobert (1939), figs. 92–3; 33: Dunand (1945), and others; 34: Diringer (*c.* 1948), figs. 107–8; 35, 38, 39, 78: *Catal. Mus. Lavigerie*, I, pls. 6, 12, 27, 32; 36: J. Whitaker, *Motya*, plan E; 37: A. H. Layard, *Mon. Nineveh*, I, pl. 40; 41: A. F. de Avilés in *Arqueol. e Hist.* VIII, pl. opp. p. 40; 46, 43: *Papers B.S. Rome*, XIX, figs. 6, 9; 44: C. N. Johns in *Quart. D.A. Palestine*, VI, fig. 4; 48, 45, 77, 66, 47, 64: A. L. Delattre, *Ste Monique*, *1 mois*, figs. 9, 11, 33; id. *2 trim.* fig. 39; id. *2 sem.* fig. 50; id. *3 ann.* fig. 48; 52: G. Loud, *Megiddo Ivories*, no. 107; 51: Bossert (1951), fig. 579; 59, 60, 69: A. L. Delattre in *Mém.Antiq. France*, LVI, figs. 29, 56, 41–2; 61: id. *Douimes*, *1893–4*, fig. 39; 62, 63, 80: Cintas (1946), nos. 70 and 83, 85, 97; 65: A. L. Delattre, *Une Favissa à Carth.*, p. 8; 67: G. Picard (1956), pl. 60; 70–72: J. Vercoutter, *Les Objets égyptiens et égyptisants*, pls. 27–8, nos. 913, 907, 902 respectively; 75, 73: A. Merlin in *Bull. archéol.* 1918, figs. 1–2; 76, 74: G. Bonsor in *Rev. archéol.* 1899, figs. 42, 115–16; 81: A. Blanco Freijeiro in *Archivo español de Arqueol.* XXIX, fig. 47.

Notes on the Plates

1. Cedars of Lebanon. The Lebanon was in ancient times prolific in cedar trees and other useful timber, but only a few
   plantations now remain, carefully preserved. The best lies
   near the source of the Nahr Quadisha, inland from Tripoli.
   See pp. 23, 131.

2. Mouth of the Nahr-el-Kelb (the Dog river), some 15 km.
   north of Beirut. Here the Lebanon foothills come close to
   the shore, especially on the southern side. This narrow pass
   has perforce been traversed by all the great armies moving
   north or south, and many, down to the last war and later,
   have left inscriptions to record their passage. An ancient
   rock-hewn road (no longer passable except on foot) high up
   on the cliff is lined with inscriptions of ancient Egyptian
   and Assyrian conquerors. A lower road, again rock-cut,
   seems from inscriptions to have been constructed during the
   first millennium BC and was remade under Caracalla, as an
   inscription relates. The modern road can be seen lower still,
   almost at sea-level. *See* p. 45.

3. Air-view of Tyre from the north. The modern town is in the
   foreground, with its small harbour to the left (probably on
   the site of the old northern harbour). Behind the harbour is
   the isthmus, formed originally by Alexander's siege-mole
   of 332 BC, but widened by gradual deposition of sand on
   each side. Careful air and ground survey by Père Poidebard
   (*see* note 12. p. 214) has revealed important traces of the
   former topography and fortifications. Excavations by the
   Lebanese Department of Antiquities have been in progress
   recently on vacant ground on the southern side of the
   promontory. *See* p. 26.

4. Air-view of the island of Ruad (anc. Aradus) looking east
   towards Tartus (Antaradus) on the mainland, about 4 km.

distant. Portions of ancient fortifications, some probably Phoenician, others later, exist. *See* p. 25.

5. View, taken in 1925, of the harbour of Carthage from the southern slope of the hill of St Louis, looking south across the bay towards the peak of the Djebel Bou Kornein above Hammam Lif at the landward end of the peninsula of Cape Bon. The area in the foreground is now covered with suburban development. *See* pp. 29 ff., 79, 120.

6. View, taken in 1925, of Carthage peninsula from near Sidi Bou Said, looking south across the hill of Ste Monique towards (right) the hills of Juno and of St Louis (crowned by its modern cathedral), and (left) Le Kram and the peninsula of La Goulette, which divides the bay of Carthage from the lake of Tunis. A similar view, today, would show many more buildings on these hills. *See* pp. 29 ff.

7. Post-holes, as excavated by Général Duval in 1949, of part of the late Punic defences of Carthage which ran from south to north across the peninsula from the lake of Tunis to a point near the Sebkhret er Riana (*see* Fig 3). These post-holes and sleeper gullies for a palisade lay between an outer and an inner ditch. The line of the main defence wall, behind this complex, was not discovered. *See* pp. 31, 119.

8. Spring known as the 'Fountain of a thousand amphorae' on the coast between the Bordj Djedid and the hill of Ste Monique. This, though the vault and arches are not earlier than Roman, shows in its lower part some good Punic stone-work. *See* pp. 31, 125.

9. Remains of late Punic houses on the southern side of the hill of St Louis at Carthage. These belong to the period of the Punic wars. The quarter was well laid out in regular *insulae*. *See* pp. 30, 124 f.

10. Part of the excavations by P. Cintas in the late Punic town (third to second century B C) at Dar Essafi (Kerkouane) near Cape Bon, Tunisia, showing a bath with its own drainage system. Note the four steps on the left, leading to the bath. *See* p. 123 f.

11. View of the site of Nora, Sardinia, taken from the medieval tower of S. Efisio on the high tip of the promontory, looking north-west towards the mainland. Excavations at the

beginning of the present century, and quite recently, have yielded important remains of the Punic town, which stood on the isthmus in the middle of the picture. *See* p. 36 f.

12. View of Punic rock-cut cliff tombs of about the fourth or third century BC at S. Avendrace, Cagliari, Sardinia. *See* pp. 36, 98.

13. Part of the Punic town wall at Motya, Sicily, showing chamfered ashlar masonry of good style in regular courses of headers and stretchers, without cement bonding. Fifth century BC or later. This style of masonry perhaps shows Greek influence. *See* pp. 33, 133.

14. Staircase attached to the west wall of the passage between the inner and outer gates of the north gateway at Motya, Sicily (*see* J. I. S. Whitaker, *Motya*, p. 172, plan C), which led to the upper part of the fortifications. Probably sixth century BC. Note the difference in style between this masonry, which is in the true Phoenician tradition, and that of Plate 13. *See* pp. 33, 133.

15. Coffin of Ahiram, a king of Byblos of the early tenth century BC with a contemporary Phoenician inscription visible along the side of the lid (*see* Plate 38 for detail and Fig 34 for transcription). The coffin, of limestone, is probably two or three centuries earlier, and reused by Ahiram, for a thirteenth-century ivory plaque and two alabaster vases bearing the cartouches of Ramesses II were found in the same tomb. The bas-reliefs are typically Phoenician in character; *see* H. Frankfort, *The Art and Architecture of the Ancient Orient*, 1954, p. 159 f., figs. 76–7. From Byblos. National Museum of Antiquities, Beirut. L. 2·16 m. H. 0·104 m. *See* pp. 102, 107, 173, note 132.

16. Coffin of Eshmunazar II, a king of Sidon of the sixth century BC (p. 102 f.). An imported Egyptian coffin of black basalt, with the king's funerary inscription in Phoenician on the lid. Found at Sidon in 1856. Louvre (AO 4806). L. 2·51 m. W. 1·27 m. *See* pp. 102 f., 111.

17, 18. Top and side views of an anthropoid white marble coffin of Sidonian type; male head with head-dress of Egyptian style. Fifth century BC. Provenience unrecorded. British Museum (no. 125097). L. 2·29 m. W. 0·81 m. *See* pp. 103, 183.

19, 20. Grave monument of limestone in the form of a female statue in the round on a rough-hewn base. Third century BC. From the Ste Monique cemetery, Carthage. National Museum, Carthage (*Cat. Mus. Lavig.* Suppl. 1913, pl. 1, no. 2). H. 1·25 m. *See* pp. 101, 194 f.

21, 22. Views of lid and of upper end of an ossuary of limestone inscribed 'Baalshillek the Rab (prince)'. Third century BC. From the Ste Monique cemetery, Carthage. National Museum, Carthage (*Cat. Mus. Lavig.* 1, 1900, pl. 9, nos. 1–2). L. 0·45 m. W. 0·30 m. *See* pp. 104, 196.

23. Fragmentary limestone inscribed slab dealing with regulations laid down by the 'overseers of payments' about sacrifices; a good example of Punic monumental lettering. Fourth to third century BC. From Carthage. British Museum (no. 125303). H. as extant 0·28 m. *See* pp. 95, 110.

24. Limestone model of a cylindrical watch-tower(?) (top and bottom missing), showing parts of three stories: at the bottom, the rounded arch of a door (there are no other details at this level); above, three shallow round-arched windows; at the top, five deeper and narrower windows (tops missing). Dedicated to Tanit and Baal Hammon by Bodashtart son of Abdmelqart. Fourth to third century BC. From Carthage. British Museum (no. 125324). H. as extant 0·465 m. *See* p. 122 f.

25. Terracotta model of shrine of Phoenician type, the entrance doorway flanked by lotus-capped columns. Heads of votaresses appear at the windows on each side wall and the figure within the *naos* is a human-headed bird. The rows of holes perhaps represent the cavities of a dove-cote, as would be in place in a shrine of Astarte of Paphos. Probably seventh century BC. From Idalion, Cyprus. Louvre (N 3294). H. 0·21 m. *See* pp. 84, 187.

26. Part of the lowest stratum (eighth to early seventh century BC) of the precinct of Tanit at Salammbo, Carthage, after excavation in 1925 by a Franco-American expedition under Prof. F. W. Kelsey of the University of Michigan, showing urns lying under cairns of stones, on bedrock, 5 m. below the surface (*see* Fig 23). The wall in the background is the south wall of a large cement vault of late Roman date, which, when it was constructed, caught up and sealed *in*

situ, as they lay, three of the stelae of the second stratum. In the left-hand top corner is a late Roman or Byzantine grave with covering slab. *See* p. 86

27. Urns and stelae of the second stratum (seventh to fourth century B C) of the precinct of Tanit at Salammbo, Carthage, *in situ*. The level of the lowest stratum is indicated by three fragmentary urns lying at the bottom of the photograph (cf. fig. 23, a schematic section based on this view). *See* pp. 86-8.

28. Remains of the orthostat temple of the thirteenth century B C in area H at Hazor, Israel, looking north, as excavated in 1957-8 by Prof. Yadin of the Hebrew University, Jerusalem (*see* Y. Yadin *et al.*, *Hazor*, III–IV, 1961, pl. 115, no. 2), showing the porch, the main hall (with two basalt column-bases at the entrance) and the holy of holies behind. *See* p. 83 f.

29. The holy of holies of the Canaanite sanctuary of the thirteenth century B C in area C at Hazor, excavated by Prof. Yadin in 1955 (*see* Y. Yadin *et al.*, *Hazor*, I, 1958, pp. 83 ff., pls. 27–31). These stelae are distant prototypes of those found in Punic sanctuaries in the west. *See* pp. 86, 192.

30. Coarse limestone stele in the form of a shrine with Egyptian cornice and a lozenge-shaped betyl on a pedestal within. Late sixth or fifth century B C. From the second stratum of the precinct of Tanit at Salammbo, Carthage, National Museum, Bardo, Tunis. H. *c.* 0·75 m. *See* pp. 76, 85, 88, 192

31. Upper part of a coarse limestone stele in which is inserted a slab of fine-grained dark limestone bearing an inscription recording (including the dedicator) seventeen generations of priests of Tanit, which, as the writer in *C.I.S.* remarks, means *c.* 500 years. The stele stands on a low rectangular pedestal. *See C.I.S.* I, iii, fasc. 1, 1926, no. 3778, pls. 14 (inscription) and 13 (complete stele and pedestal) and P. Cintas, *Manuel d'archéol. punique*, 1970, pp. 466 ff. (Punic text with French translation). Probably late fourth century B C, in which case this long line of priests would reach back to the foundation of Carthage. From the precinct of Tanit at Salammbo, Carthage. National Museum, Bardo, Tunis (Picard, *Catal. Mus. Alaoui*, n.s.I, no. Cb-366). Total H. 0·95 m. H. inscribed slab 0·25 m. *See* pp. 88, 93.

32. Fine-grained limestone obelisk with 'bottle' design indica-
tive of Tanit worship and an inscription recording its
dedication to Tanit and Baal Hammon by Eshmunhillesh
son of Iatonmilk. *See C.I.S.* I, iii, fasc. 1, 1926, no. 3709,
pl. 12. Fourth century BC. From the second stratum of the
precinct of Tanit at Salammbo, Carthage. National
Museum, Bardo, Tunis (Picard, *Catal. Mus. Alaoui*, n.s.I,
no. Cb-404). H. *c.* 0·70 m. *See* pp. 88, 193.

33. Coarse limestone stele of early form with a crudely-engraved
'bottle' image of Tanit. Sixth century BC. From the second
stratum of the precinct of Tanit at Salammbo, Carthage.
National Museum, Bardo, Tunis. H. *c.* 0·80 m. *See* pp.
88, 192.

34. Trachyte stele depicting the goddess Tanit within a *naos*
with Egyptian entablature and volute columns. Fifth
century BC. Lilliu's group A, orientalizing style, *Mon.
Antichi*, XL, 1944, p. 326, pl. 6, no. 56. From Sulcis,
Sardinia. Cagliari Museum. H. 0·46 m. *See* pp. 76, 85, 193.

35. Upper part of a fine-grained limestone obelisk showing a
priest in low, round cap holding an infant in his left arm.
Fourth century BC. From the second stratum of the precinct
of Tanit at Salammbo, Carthage; excavated by the Department of Antiquities, Tunis, in 1922. *See* L. Poinssot and
R. Lantier in *Rev. de l'hist. des religions*, LXXXVII, 1923,
p. 47, pl. 4, no. 2. National Museum, Bardo, Tunis (Picard,
Catal. Mus. Alaoui, n.s.I, no. Cb-229). Total H. 1·15 m.
H. of figure 0·17 m. *See* pp. 88, 94, 193.

36. Pedestal of a marble *cippus* engraved with dedications to
Melqart of Tyre in Phoenician and Greek. Second century
BC. Two identical *cippi* were found in Malta in the seven-
teenth century (*C.I.S.* I, i, nos. 122 A, B). This one is now
in the National Museum, Valletta, Malta, the other is in the
Louvre (AO 4818). These bilingual texts greatly helped
Barthélemy and others to complete the decipherment of the
Phoenician language. H. pedestal 0·34 m. *See* pp. 37, 110.

37. Part of one of the monumental inscriptions set up by
Asitawandas, king of the Danunians, in the south-west
gateway at Kara Tepe in Cilicia in the late eighth century
BC, which bear bilingual texts in Phoenician and in Hittite
hieroglyphs. The picture shows part of the Phoenician

version only. These inscriptions should greatly assist the decipherment of this Hittite form of script. *See* pp. 54, 111 f.

38. Part of the Phoenician inscription on the coffin of Ahiram (*see* Plate 15 for coffin and Fig 34 for full text of inscription). The photograph clearly reveals that a section of the text is carved across a fractured area of the lid, and strongly suggests, therefore, that an earlier coffin was reused for Ahiram's burial, since this damage must have occurred some time before his inscription was carved upon it. *See* pp. 102, 107 f, 173, and note 132.

39. Part of a reddish sandstone statue of Osorkon I of Egypt (last quarter of the tenth century BC) bearing the cartouche of that king and a secondary inscription of Elibaal, king of Byblos, in early Phoenician characters. From Byblos. Louvre (AO 9502). H. as extant 0·60 m. *See* p. 108.

40. Cuneiform clay tablet bearing the text of a letter of the first half of the fourteenth century BC from Ribaddi, governor of Byblos, begging for help from the king of Egypt. From el Amarna, Egypt. British Museum (no. 29795). H. 0·095 m. *See* p. 45.

41. Sherd of a large light grey pot inscribed in Hebrew 'Gold of Ophir to Beth-horon, 30 shekels'. Eighth century BC. From Tel Qasile, Tel Aviv, Israel. Museum Haaretz, Tel Aviv. H. 0·063 m. *See* p. 150.

42. Sculptured panel on a limestone stele depicting Baal confronted by a worshipper. Found in level II (late fifth to early third century BC) in the sanctuary excavated by P. Cintas at Hadrumetum (Sousse), Tunisia. *See* Cintas (1947), pp. 13 ff., figs. 48–9. National Museum, Bardo, Tunis. H. 0·17 m. *See* pp. 78, 193.

43. Part of a panel on a limestone stele of the same date and from the same sanctuary as that on Plate 42, depicting a cloaked and hooded goddess, the head-dress reminiscent of the white crown of upper Egypt. *See* Cintas (1947), p. 21 f., figs. 50–51. National Museum, Bardo, Tunis. H. 0·45 m. *See* p. 193.

44. Limestone stele in Phoenician style but showing Greek influence in its portraiture. Inscribed in Phoenician 'Memorial stele of Baalyaton, son of Baalyaton, the presi-

dent'. Fourth or early third century B C. From Umm el
Amad, south of Tyre. Ny Carlsberg Glyptotek, Copenhagen (no. 837). H. 1·80 m. *See* pp. 94, 184.

45. Limestone stele dedicated to Persephone by Milkyaton the
suffete, son of Maharbaal the suffete (*C.I.S.* I, i, no. 176,
pl. 41.) Third or second century B C. From Carthage.
Museo di Antichità, Turin. H. 0·38 m. *See* pp. 82, 192.

46. Votive limestone stele in the form of a proto-Aeolic capital
on a tapering pedestal. The back is unworked. Later sixth
century B C. From Golgoi, Cyprus. Metropolitan Museum
of Art, New York. Myres (1914), no. 1418. H. 1·38 m. *See*
pp. 185, 187.

47. Silver bowl, gilt on interior, with repoussé and engraved
design showing the mixed Assyrian and Egyptian motifs
typical of Phoenician work. Seventh century B C. From
Idalion, Cyprus. Louvre (AO 20134). D. 0·185 m. *See* pp.
133, 181.

48. Part of one of the repoussé bronze bands from the gates
erected at Balawat, near Nimrud, Iraq, by Shalmaneser III
(859–24 B C), king of Assyria, to record his campaigns.
The scene shows tribute-bearers coming from Tyre
(depicted as an island fortress) to the mainland, where they
advance in a long line, led by Assyrian guards. *See* L. W.
King, *Bronze Reliefs from the Gates of Shalmaneser*, 1915,
pls. 13–14. H. of band (with borders) 0·15 m. *See* pp. 26,
49, 114, 122, 134, 161.

49. Part of a wall relief in gypsum from the palace of Sargon II
(722–05 B C) at Khorsabad, Iraq, depicting river-craft
(*hippoi*) bearing logs of timber and propelled by paddles.
Louvre (AO 19889). *See* pp. 148, 161.

50. Detail of another portion of the relief illustrated in the
previous Plate.

51. Drawing of a wall-relief in gypsum from the palace of
Sennacherib (705–681 B C) at Kouyunjik (Nineveh) showing
the flight from Tyre of Luli, king of Tyre and Sidon, in 701.
Note the two types of ships represented (cf. p. 160 f.). The
left-hand portion is taken from A. H. Layard, *Monuments
of Nineveh*, I, pl. 71, that on the right comes from an
original sketch by Layard, which is now in the Dept. of

Western Asiatic Antiquities, British Museum. Neither
portion is known to be extant and both were probably too
damaged to be saved. The connection between the two was
recently recognized by R. D. Barnett (*see* note 229 and refs.).
The slight discrepancies where the two slabs meet may be
partly due to the gap left by sawing them apart and partly
to inaccuracies by the draughtsmen who made the original
drawings and the published reproduction. *See* pp. 26, 49,
114, 116, 122, 134, 159.

52. Ostrich-egg shell cup with painted design in red. *c.* Fifth to
fourth century BC. From the mixed Ibero-Punic site of
Villaricos, Spain. *See* M. Astruc, *La Necróp. de Villaricos*,
1951, pp. 135 ff., pl. 73, no. 428, series II B. Museo
Arqueol. Nacional, Madrid. H. 0·135 m. *See* pp. 130, 201.

53. Jug (mended but incomplete) of green glass. Eighth to
seventh century BC. Part of the 'Aliseda treasure' found at
La Aliseda near Caceres, Spain, in 1920 (*see also* Plates 97–
9). This treasure, which comprised a great many items of
gold jewellery and trappings, a silver brazier, and this glass,
has been variously dated. Many have thought that the group
contains items of earlier dates collected and buried together
in, perhaps, the third century BC. Blanco (*Archivo español de
Arqueol.* XXIX, 1956, pp. 11 ff.), whose view we follow,
dates all the objects within two centuries (late eighth to late
sixth century BC). Museo Arqueol. Nacional, Madrid (no.
28.583). H. 0·15 m. *See* pp. 138, 145.

54. Bronze jug of Phoenician type (cf. García y Bellido in
Archivo español de Arqueol. XXIX, 1956, pp. 85 ff., type A).
Eighth to seventh century BC. Provenience unknown, but
the distribution of the type is mainly western. Metropolitan
Museum of Art, New York (N.E. Dept. Pulitzer Bequest
Fund, no. 55.121.1). H. 0·353 m. *See* p. 138.

55, 56. Two Phoenician pendant heads of polychrome glass
from necklaces, modelled on a core with added details.
Fourth century BC. From Carthage. Louvre (AO 3783–4).
H. 0·05 m. and 0·04 m. *See* p. 145.

57. Three Phoenician vessels of glass modelled on a core with
added trails: (a) monochrome with all-over buff weathering,
from Cameiros, Rhodes, seventh century BC, H. 0·15 m.;
(b) dark blue with opaque yellow and light blue trails, from

Cameiros, fifth century BC, H. (including handle) 0·12 m.; (c) dark blue with opaque white trails, from Tharros, Sardinia, third century BC, H. 0·123 m. British Museum (nos. (a) 61.10–24.18; (b) 62.5–30.6; (c) 56.12–23.41). *See* pp. 144, 156.

58. Series of urns containing the ashes of cremated infants or small animals or birds from the precinct of Tanit at Salammbo, Carthage: (a–f) from the lowest stratum (eighth to early seventh century BC); (g–k) from the second stratum (late seventh to late fourth century BC); (l–o) from the latest stratum (latest fourth to mid second century BC). The urns from this precinct thus cover the whole history of Punic Carthage and form the basis of our knowledge of the typology and chronology of Punic pottery. a, b, d, f, h–k, m, o, Ashmolean Museum, Oxford (nos. 1934.160, 162, 165, 167, 177, 179, 174, 183, 192, 190); c, e, g, l, Department of Antiquities, Tunisia; n, private possession. Scale *c.* ⅛. *See* pp. 60, 86, 140, 188, notes 121, 187.

59, 60. Two polychrome faience plaques in low relief depicting Asiatics wearing highly decorated garments of Syrian or Phoenician type. Period of Ramesses III (1198–67 BC). From Medinet Habu, Egypt. Museum of Fine Arts, Boston, Mass. (nos. 03.1568, 1570). H. 0·25 and 0·295 m. *See* p. 134.

61. Ivory lid of an unguent-box depicting a goddess flanked by two goats. Thirteenth century BC. From Minet el Beida, Syria. Louvre (AO 11601). H. 0·137 m. *See* pp. 147, 174.

62. Ivory plaque depicting the 'woman at the window' motif. Late ninth century BC. From Arslan Tash, Syria. Metropolitan Museum of Art, New York (N.E. Dept., Fletcher Fund, no. 57.80.11). H. 0·083 m. *See* pp. 122, 147, 176.

63. Fragment of an ivory pyxis depicting parts of two sphinxes flanking a sacred tree. Syrian style. Eighth century BC. From the S.E. (burnt) palace at Nimrud, Iraq. British Museum (no. 126513). Barnett (1957), no. S6b. H. 0·06 m. *See* pp. 147, 176.

64. Fragmentary ivory unguent vase in the form of a female holding her breasts. Syrian style. Eighth or seventh century BC. From Beirut, Lebanon. Ashmolean Museum, Oxford (no. 1920.1). H. 0·18 m. *See* pp. 147, 177.

65. Two ivory heads, both with mortises underneath for tenon-
ing to a larger object; (a) Syrian style, (b) Egyptian style.
Eighth century B C. From the S.E. (burnt) palace at Nimrud,
Iraq. British Museum (nos. 118232 and 118216). Barnett
(1957), nos. S183, 185. H. 0·044 and 0·04 m. *See* pp. 147,
177.

66. Bone unguent vase in the form of a female holding a lotus
flower in each hand. Mixed Asiatic and Egyptian style.
Eighth century B C. From Sidon. British Museum (no.
127136). Barnett (1957), no. U13. H. 0·158 m. *See* pp. 147,
176.

67. Part of an ivory panel in low relief which depicted two male
figures plucking fruits from a winged disk with palmette.
Assyrian style. Eighth century B C. From the N.W. palace at
Nimrud, Iraq. British Museum (no. 118115). H. 0·19 m.
Barnett (1957), no. F2. *See* pp. 147, 176.

68. Openwork ivory figure of a sphinx. Assyrian style, but with
Egyptian head-dress and crown. Eighth century B C. From
Arslan Tash, Syria. Metropolitan Museum of Art, New
York (N.E. Dept., Fletcher Fund, no. 57.80.1). H. 0·12 m.
See pp. 147, 176.

69. Part of an ivory panel from a box with incised design of a
bull and a rosette. Assyrian style. Eighth century B C. From
Nimrud, Iraq. Ashmolean Museum, Oxford (no. 1956.960).
L. 0·102 m. *See* pp. 147, 176.

70. Terracotta statuette of a male votary. Late seventh or early
sixth century B C. From the sanctuary at Ayia Irini, Cyprus.
Cyprus Museum, Nicosia. H. 0·61 m. *See* p. 186.

71. Half of an ivory panel with a female figure in the guise of the
goddess Isis to the right of a sacred tree of Phoenician
aspect. Eighth century B C. From Arslan Tash, Syria.
Metropolitan Museum of Art, New York (N.E. Dept.,
Fletcher Fund, no. 57.80.10). H. 0·08 m. *See* pp. 147, 176.

72. Limestone statuette of a lady, the broken-off handle of a
large vessel. Asiatic style. Later sixth century B C. From
Golgoi, Cyprus. Metropolitan Museum of Art, New York.
Myres (1914), no. 1262. H. 0·203 m. *See* p. 180.

73. Alabaster cult-statue of Astarte. Eastern Phoenician work.
Seventh or sixth century B C. From Tutugi (Galera), near

Granada, Spain. Museo Arqueol. Nacional, Madrid (no. E1). H. 0·178 m. *See* p. 94 f.

74. Snow-man type of terracotta votive figurine from a sanctuary. Eighth to seventh century BC. From Marion (Polis tis Chrysochous), Cyprus. Cyprus Museum, Nicosia. H. 0·13 m. *See* p. 186.

75. Fragmentary terracotta male figurine of primitive, hand-made, type. Eighth to early seventh century BC. From the lowest stratum of the precinct of Tanit at Salammbo, Carthage. National Museum, Bardo, Tunis. H. as extant *c.* 0·12 m. *See* pp. 186, 188.

76. Terracotta female figurine of primitive, hand-made, type, from a deposit of many similarly crude figurines found in a pit. *See* García y Bellido (1952), pp. 426 f., 470 ff., figs. 266–77. Seventh century BC. From Isla Plana, Ibiza. Museo Arqueol., Ibiza. H. *c.* 0·20 m. *See* pp. 39, 186, 188.

77. Terracotta male cult-mask, modelled free-hand, from a potter's workshop near the Canaanite sanctuary (*see* Plate 29) in area C at Hazor, Israel; cf. Y. Yadin *et al.*, *Hazor*, II, 1960, p. 115, pls. 182–3. Thirteenth century BC. A mask of similar date, but wheel-made, came from area D, id. I, 1958, p. 138, pl. 163. Hebrew University, Jerusalem. H. 0·217 m. *See* p. 190.

78. Terracotta female mask with silver nose-ring, decorated with red and blue paint. Late seventh to sixth century BC. From tomb 186 at Dermech, Carthage. National Museum, Bardo, Tunis. H. 0·31 m. *See* pp. 190, 193.

79. Terracotta female figurine of Ibero-Punic type with elaborate head-dress and jewellery. Fourth to third century BC. From Ibiza. Museo Arqueol., Ibiza. H. *c.* 0·30 m. *See* p. 192.

80. Bronze male figurine of a local Baal with pointed cap, brandishing a weapon (now missing). Thirteenth century BC or later. From Beirut, Lebanon. Ashmolean Museum, Oxford (no. 1890.592). H. 0·11 m. (with dowel 0·126 m.). *See* pp. 138, 139, 175.

81, 82. Roughly cast bronze figurines of local deities grouped in a pair and a foursome, for use as votive offerings in a Phoenician shrine. Thirteenth century BC or later. The pair was bought in Aleppo; the other is said to be from 'near Sardis', though this is a most unlikely provenience for this Phoenician type. Ashmolean Museum, Oxford (nos. 1912.80; 1889.775). H. 0·068 m. and 0·118 m. *See* pp. 138, 175.

83. Copper or bronze stand with openwork panels on its four sides depicting respectively a harpist, a man carrying two fish, a man carrying a cup and two rolls of cloth, and (the side shown here) a man bearing a copper ingot in the form of a hide. Asiatic (perhaps Syrian rather than Phoenician) influence. Twelfth to eleventh century B C. From Curium, Cyprus. British Museum (no. 1920.12-20.1). H. 0·125 m. *See* p. 185 f.

84, 85. Bronze female figurine (front and back views) with low head-dress and hair in long plaits; tasselled girdle. Syrian style. Eighth to seventh century B C. Bought in Aleppo, Syria. Ashmolean Museum, Oxford (no. 1889.794). H. 0·082 m. *See* pp. 138, 181, 186.

86. Bronze figurine of a seated lady. Syrian style. Ninth to eighth century B C. From Baalbek, Lebanon. Ashmolean Museum, Oxford (no. 1889.807). H. 0·084 m. *See* pp. 138, 181.

87. Bronze male votive figurine seated on a throne flanked by lions and holding a *patera*. Ninth to eighth century B C (or earlier?). Said to be from Homs, Syria (bought in Athens). Ashmolean Museum, Oxford (no. 1909.371). H. 0·082 m. *See* pp. 138, 182.

88-90. Bronze figurine of a priest, his face covered with gold leaf. Phoenician work with Egyptian influence. Fifth century B C or earlier. Found in 1928, 5 m. deep, on the site of the telephone exchange at Cadiz. Museo Arqueol. Nacional, Madrid. H. 0·13 m. *See* p. 197.

91. Hollow gold pendant, topped by lion-head of Sekhmet crowned by disk and *uraeus*, which contained a charm of thin gold leaf (L. 0·27 m., W. 0·023 m.) bearing tiny engraved figures of deities and animals in four horizontal lines (cf. P. Gauckler, *Nécropoles puniques*, I, p. 92, and II, pp. 451 ff.; J. Vercoutter, *Les Objets égyptiens et égyptisants du mobilier fun. carth.*, ch. 9, espec. pp. 371 ff., pl. 29). Late sixth century B C. From tomb 212 at Dermech, Carthage. National Museum, Bardo, Tunis. H. 0·046 m. *See* p. 205.

92. Fragment of leather covered with gold leaf embossed with a typical Phoenician design of two gryphons flanking a multiple palmette, with winged disk above. Seventh century BC. From Malta. Ashmolean Museum, Oxford (no. G.440). H. 0·044 m. *See* p. 203.

93. Copper statuette of Melqart, of Asiatic pose but wearing Egyptian crown. Fourteenth to thirteenth century BC. Found in the sea off Sciacca on the south coast of Sicily. This figurine must have originated in Phoenicia, and to find such an early piece so far west is a matter of great interest. *See* S. Chiappisi, op. cit. in note 53, for an account of its discovery. Palermo Museum. H. 0·38 m. *See* pp. 56, 175.

94,a, b. Two views of a bronze female figurine in flounced skirt of Aegean affinity; the head and features typically Phoenician. Ninth century BC. Bought in Aleppo, Syria. Ashmolean Museum, Oxford (no. 1913.49). H. 0·078 m. *See* pp. 138, 181.

95,a, b. Two enlarged views of a gold pendant depicting an adorant. Phoenician work. Seventh to sixth century BC. Provenience unrecorded, probably Cypriote. Ashmolean Museum, Oxford (no. 1953.132). H. 0·036 m. *See* p. 203.

96. Hollow gold pendant, topped by ram-head of Amon-Re. Unlike the companion piece (Plate 91) this piece contained only the debris of a silver charm. Fifth century BC. Found by P. Gauckler in a Dermech tomb near Bordj Djedid, Carthage. National Museum, Bardo, Tunis. H. 0·034 m. *See* p. 205.

97. One end (Scale $\frac{2}{3}$) of the embossed gold belt in the 'Aliseda treasure' (cf. Plate 53, caption). The belt consists of separate plates with embossed and granulated decoration showing Phoenician influence in its style and ornament, but with other outside influences (perhaps Etruscan) as well. Seventh to sixth century BC. Tartessian fabric? From La Aliseda, near Caceres, Spain. Museo Arqueol. Nacional, Madrid (no. 28.562). Total length of belt 0·683 m. W. 0·066–0·071 m. *See* pp. 138, 206.

98. Gold ear-ring with safety chain (for hanging over ear), based on the 'leech' type with a ring of openwork lotus

flowers flanked by hawks, covered with the finest granulation. Seventh to sixth century B C. Tartessian fabric? From the 'Aliseda treasure' (*see* Plate 53). Museo Arqueol. Nacional, Madrid (no. 28.536). D. 0·08 m. *See* pp. 138, 206.

99. Gold broken-backed signet ring with amethyst scarab (for the design *see* Fig 81). Seventh to sixth century B C. Phoenician. From the 'Aliseda treasure' (*see* Plate 53). Museo Arqueol. Nacional, Madrid (no. 28.561). W. of hoop 0·043 m. *See* pp. 138, 207.

100. Gold plaque with appliqué ornament in relief, the whole probably a decorative setting from a larger object. The design depicts the Paphian sanctuary in Cyprus (cf. Plate 101), with its triple shrine and an enclosure in front, but apparently with two betyls instead of candelabra in the side chapels. Hellenistic or Roman period. Provenience unrecorded, but probably Cyprus (formerly in the Nelidoff collection). Ashmolean Museum, Oxford (no. 1931.548). H. 0·021 m. *See* pp. 52 f., 85.

101. Reverse of bronze coin of Cyprus, depicting the Paphian sanctuary, inscribed ΚΟΙΝΟΝ ΚΥΠΡΙΩΝ ('Cyprian Confederation'), in very similar guise to that of Plate 100, but with candelabra in the side chapels and doves instead of rosettes on the side-chapel roofs. *See* G. F. Hill, *B.M. Cat. Greek Coins: Cyprus*, 1904, no. 162, pl. 17, no. 9 (Caracalla, A D 211–17) and pp. cxxvii ff. for general discussion of this reverse type, which began under Septimius Severus (A D 193–211). D. 0·034 m. *See* pp. 52 f., 82, 85.

102. Reverse of bronze coin of Byblos depicting a sanctuary precinct with tall betyl, beside which is a smaller shrine. Inscribed ΙΕΡΑC ΒΥΒΛΟΥ (lit. 'of holy Byblos'). *See* G. F. Hill, *B.M. Cat. Greek Coins: Phoenicia*, 1910, no. 38, pl. 12, no. 13 (Macrinus, A D 217–18). D. 0·03 m. *See* pp. 82, 84 f.

103. Limestone statuette of a 'temple boy' – apparently a religious prostitute who also acted as a ministrant in a temple. *See*, e.g. Myres (1914), pp. 186–8. Fourth century B C or later. From Lefkóniko, Cyprus, 1913 (J. L. Myres in *Annual Brit. School Athens*, XLI, 1939–40, p. 66, pl. 18, no. 465). Cyprus Museum, Nicosia. H. 0·29 m. *See* p. 94.

104. Two necklaces of beads and pendants: the outer one gold and coloured glass beads with lotus-flower and Hathor-head pendants; the inner one cornelian, agate and black stone beads, gold heart-pendants, and gold-mounted amber pendant. *See* F. H. Marshall, *B.M. Cat. Jewellery*, 1911, pp. 156, 158, pls. 24–25, nos. 1545, 1551. Sixth century BC. From Tharros, Sardinia. British Museum. L. 0·302 m. and 0·19 m. *See* pp. 138, 204.

105. Gold bracelet of linked plaques with embossed and granulated palmettes, lotuses and eyes of Horus; remains of the silver bands which joined these plaques into a bracelet appear at each end. The middle portion and the two end-pieces of this fine bracelet were published separately by F. H. Marshall (*B.M. Cat. Jewellery*, 1911, p. 155 f., nos. 1539–40, 1542, pls. 24–25), who did not realize that they fitted together and gave them separate numbers. The outer ends of the silver bands overlap, but do not form a real junction. Seventh or sixth century BC. From Tharros, Sardinia. British Museum. L. 0·204 m. *See* pp. 138, 204 f.

106. Gold 'leech' ear-ring with hawk and vase pendant (the top of the ear-ring missing). Seventh to sixth century BC. Bought in London. Ashmolean Museum (Dr Joan Evans loan, 1930). H. as extant 0·083 m. *See* pp. 138, 203.

107. Gold 'leech' ear-ring of simple type with granulation. Sixth century BC or earlier. From Marathus (Amrit), Syria. De Clercq collection (Paris), no. 682. H. 0·021 m. *See* pp. 138, 203.

108. Pair of gold ear-rings with large, plain hoops, and terminals resembling glass 'eye'-beads; and a gold swivel ring set with a sard scarab depicting Bes with antelope and dog. Sixth or fifth century BC. For the ear-rings (which he calls bracelets – I think wrongly: cf. the equally large Aliseda ear-rings, Plate 98) *see* F. H. Marshall, *B.M. Cat. Jewellery*, 1911, p. 156, pl. 24, no. 1543; for the ring and its bezel id. *B.M. Cat. Finger Rings*, 1907, p. 51, pl. 8, no. 288, and H. B. Walters, *B.M. Cat. Engraved Gems*, 1926, p. 45, pl. 7, no. 371. From Tharros, Sardinia. British Museum. D. ear-rings 0·073 m. D. ring 0·028 m. *See* pp. 138, 205.

109. Casts of Phoenician seals, eastern and western (Scale *c.* $\frac{5}{4}$). *See* pp. 82, 209, The original seals are all in the Ashmolean Museum, Oxford:

a   Haematite scaraboid; eagle attacking deer. Ninth or eighth century BC. Bought in Aleppo, Syria. A.M. no. 1920.20.

b   Chalcedony scaraboid; male winged sphinx and *uraeus*. Eighth or seventh century BC. From Beirut, Lebanon. A.M. no. 1889.429.

c   Chalcedony scarab; Horus between Isis and Nephthys. Seventh or sixth century BC. From near Beirut, Lebanon. A.M. no. 1889.420.

d   Chalcedony scaraboid; sphinx, winged scarab, and *uraei* flanking cartouche. Sixth century BC. From Nazareth, Israel. A.M. no. 1889.419.

e   Green jasper scarab; 2 deities (?Isis and Osiris). Fifth century BC. Provenience unknown. A.M. no. 1921.1222.

f   Green jasper scarab; Horus between Isis and Nephthys. Fifth century BC. From Syria. A.M. no. 1890.138.

g   Green jasper scarab; janiform head. Fourth century BC. From Tharros, Sardinia. A.M. no. Fortnum G.20.

h   Green jasper scarab; Triton. Late fifth or fourth century BC. From Tharros, Sardinia. A.M. no. 1889.884.

110. Casts of Phoenician coins, eastern and western (Scale $c. \frac{2}{3}$). The original coins are all in the British Museum, except k, which is in Leningrad:

a   SIDON AR
    Obv. Battlements, galley, 2 lions; Rev. King of Persia slaying lion. G. F. Hill, *B.M. Cat. Phoenicia*, 1910, pl. 18, nos. 6–7. Early fourth century BC. See pp. 26, 114, 123, 157 f.

b   SIDON AR
    Obv. Galley and waves; Rev. King of Persia (or the local Baal) in trap with king of Egypt or of Sidon behind. Hill (1910), pl. 19, no. 5. Second quarter of fourth century BC. See pp. 116, 157 f., 160.

c   ARADUS AR
    Obv. Fish-tailed deity; Rev. Galley and hippocamp. Hill (1910), pl. 1, no. 5. Early fourth century BC. See pp. 25, 78, 157.

d   TYRE AR
    Obv. Dolphin, waves, murex-shell; Rev. Owl in incuse square. Hill (1910), pl. 28, no. 9. Second half of fifth century BC. See p. 157.

e   TYRE AR
    Obv. Melqart on hippocamp, waves, dolphin; Rev. Owl
    in dotted circle. Hill (1910), pl. 29, no. 6. Fourth century
    BC. *See* p. 157.

f   SICULO-PUNIC AR
    Obv. Head of Tanit in Punic head-dress; Rev. Lion,
    palm-tree and Punic inscription 'People of the Camp'.
    G. F. Hill, *Guide to Greek Coins*, 1932, pl. 26, no. 41.
    Mid fourth century BC. *See* pp. 129, 158.

g   SICULO-PUNIC AV
    Obv. Head of Tanit/Persephone; Rev. Horse, sign of
    Tanit. Hill (1932), pl. 26, no. 39. Fourth century BC.
    See p. 158.

h   SICULO-PUNIC AR
    Obv. Head of Tanit/Persephone; Rev. Horse, palm-
    tree. Hill (1932), pl. 31, no. 20. Late fourth century BC.
    See pp. 129, 158.

i   CARTHAGE El.
    Obv. Head of Tanit/Persephone; Rev. Horse, disk
    and *uraei*. Middle or late third century BC. *See* p.
    158.

j   SICULO-PUNIC AR
    Obv. Head of Tanit/Persephone; Rev. Head of horse.
    Hill (1932), pl. 38, no. 31. Mid third century BC. *See* p.
    158.

k   CARTHAGO NOVA AV
    Obv. Male head (Hasdrubal?); Rev. Prow of galley.
    E. S. G. Robinson, 'Punic coins in Spain', *Essays in
    Roman Coinage presented to H. Mattingly*, ed. R. A. G.
    Carson and C. H. V. Sutherland, 1956, p. 49, no. 4(*a*).
    After 228 BC. *See* pp. 65, 159.

l   CARTHAGO NOVA AR
    Obv. Male head (Hannibal?); Rev. Horse, palm-tree.
    Robinson (1956), p. 51, no. 7(*b*). After 218 BC. *See* pp.
    65, 129, 159.

m   CARTHAGO NOVA AR
    Obv. Head of Heracles/Melqart (Hamilcar Barca?); Rev.
    Elephant and rider. Robinson (1956), p. 50, no. 6(*a*).
    After 221 BC. *See* pp. 65, 118, 159.

n   GADES? AR
    Obv. Head of Melqart; Rev. Elephant, letter aleph.
    Robinson (1956), p. 52, no. 8(*a*). After 209 BC. *See* p.
    159.

111. Mushroom-lipped pottery jugs with neck-carinations. Brown ware with over-all red burnish. Ninth to eighth century BC. (a) Cyprus; (b) er-Retabeh, Egypt. Ashmolean Museum, Oxford (nos. 1959.364 and E3472). Scale *c.* $\frac{1}{4}$. *See* pp. 54 f., 139 f., 185.

112. Mushroom-lipped pottery jugs with neck-carinations. (a, c) buff ware with reddish-brown paint on the lip and neck, seventh to sixth century BC; (b) brown ware with black linear decoration, and red paint on lip, fifth century BC. From Cyprus (a), Larnaka, Cyprus (b), and Al Mina, Syria (c). Ashmolean Museum, Oxford (nos. 1959.363; C156; 1937.420). Scale *c.* $\frac{1}{5}$. *See* pp. 139, 185.

113. Mushroom-lipped and trefoil-lipped pottery jugs. Late eighth to sixth century BC. From Carthage. Scale *c.* $\frac{1}{4}$. These two types were regular concomitants of burials of this period at Carthage and are found on almost every contemporary Phoenician or Punic site also. *See* pp. 138, 140.

114. Typical Phoenician saucer lamps with one or two beaks to hold the wicks. (a, c) from Carthage, (b) from Malta, and (d) from Larnaka, Cyprus. (b, d) Fifth to fourth century BC. (a, c) Fourth to third century BC. Ashmolean Museum, Oxford (nos. a, b, Norwich loan; c. 1910.102; d, C182). Scale c. $\frac{1}{5}$. *See* p. 142.

115. Pottery jars and jug, red ware with white colour wash over which are horizontal lines or bands in black paint. Fifth to fourth century BC. From Malta. Ashmolean Museum, Oxford (nos. 1939.79; Newcastle loan; M.1). Scale. *c.* $\frac{1}{7}$. *See* p. 141.

116. Late Punic mausoleum at Dougga, Tunisia, erected in honour of 'Ateban, a Numidian prince of the late third or earlier second century BC. The monument shows much Greek architectural influence. A bilingual inscription in Punic and Libyan, which was removed from the monument in the first half of the nineteenth century, is now in the British Museum (nos. 125225–6). H. of monument 21·0 m. *See* p. 101.

Index

162–9, credibility of, 63, 163, note 241

Hanno, merchant in *Poenulus*, 135, 152–3

harbours, 26, 29, 58, 115; *see also* cothons

Hasdrubal, son-in-law of Hamilcar Barca, 73; in Spain, 64, 70; possible portrait of, on coins, 65, 159, note 228

Hasdrubal, son of Magon, 61

Hathor, goddess, on stele, 184; on vase, 188

Hathor-head, capitals, 82; pendants, 204

Hazor (Israel), Canaanite stronghold, 21, 41, 172; potter's workshop, 190; temples, 83–4, 86; mask, 190; pottery, 139; LBA stelae, 86, 192

Hebrew(s), conquest of Canaan by, 21, 46, 149; language, 107–9; literature, 112

Heracles, on razor, at Carth., 198; *see also* Melqart, *and* Pillars of

Herne Island, 168

Herodotus, cited, 52, 55, 69, 84, 94, 113, 115, 152, 156, 162, 169, notes 2, 35, 218

Hiernorum gens, 163

hieroglyphs, Egyptian, 40–41, 107, on alabaster vases, note 62; on glass jug, 145, on silver bowl, 180; on Hittite, 111

high places, 85

Himera (Sicily), battle of, 62, 117, 152; 'sacrifice' of prisoners at, 95

Himilco, Carth. explorer, 59, 63, 162–3; date of, 162; his voyage in Atlantic, 163

Hippo Diarrhytus (Bizerta, Tunisia), 25

hippoi, see ships

Hiram the Great, K. of Tyre, 47, 71, 115, 149–50

Hiram, K. of Tyre and Sidon, 49, 109

Hiram, Tyrian workman, 137

Hittite(s), 41, 44–6, 172, 185; empire destroyed, 46; language and inscr., 107, 111

Homer, cited, 19, 56, 113, 134, 137, 151, 153

Horns of the South and West, 167

Horus-hawk, on razor, 199; -pectorals, on ear-rings, 205

houses, 26, 30, 34, 122–6, 131

Huelva (Spain), early Phoen. finds, note 62

Hurrian(s) (Horites), 41, 172; language, 107; Mitannian kingdom of, 172; pottery, 172

Hyksos, 41

Iberian(s), art influences, 187, 192; in Punic armies, 114

Ibiza, *see Ebusus*

Idalion (Dali, Cyprus), model shrine, 84, 187; silver-gilt bowl, 181

Igilgili (Djidjelli, Algeria), 202

India, elephant tusks, 146; Ophir in?, 150

industry, Ch. 11

inscriptions, Assyrian, 49; bilingual, 37, 54, 101, 110–12; Bronze Age, 107–8; Gk, 153; hieroglyphic, 40, 44, 103, 145; Moabite, 107, 111; Phoen., 37, 54, 57, 59, 70–71, 73, 75, 88, 91, 95, 101, 103, 105, 107, 108–12, 180, 204–5, 210, note 135

iron, coming of, 136; use of, 136; from Tarshish, 151

Isis, goddess, on ivory panel, 176; on razors at Carth., 82, 199

Isis/Astarte, on pendant, 204

Isis/Hathor, cult at Byblos, 76

Israel, kingdom of, 46–9; wars with Moab, 111; plough, 129

Note

Since this book went to press a monograph by the late John C. Allan, *Considerations on the Antiquity of Mining in the Iberian Peninsula* (Royal Anthropological Institute Occasional Paper no. 27, London, 1970) has come to my attention. It contains much useful information and comment on ancient mining and metals in Spain and Portugal by a metallurgical expert who had a long acquaintance with Iberian mines and their products. Had I known of Mr Allan's monograph in time, I should certainly have made use of it in revising my text.

D.B.H.

More about Penguins and Pelicans

Penguinews, which appears every month, contains details of all the new books issued by Penguins as they are published. From time to time it is supplemented by *Penguins in Print*, which is a complete list of all available books published by Penguins. (There are well over three thousand of these.)

A specimen copy of *Penguinews* will be sent to you free on request, and you can become a subscriber for the price of the postage. For a year's issues (including the complete lists) please send 30p if you live in the United Kingdom, or 60p if you live elsewhere. Just write to Dept EP, Penguin Books Ltd, Harmondsworth, Middlesex, enclosing a cheque or postal order, and your name will be added to the mailing list.

Note: *Penguinews* and *Penguins in Print* are not available in the U.S.A. or Canada

The Greeks

H. D. F. Kitto

This is a study of the character and history of an ancient civilization, and of the people who created it. Since its first publication as a Pelican, *The Greeks* has sold 1,400,000 copies.
The critics have said of it:

'The best introduction I have ever read to Ancient Greece. The author's liveliness of mind and style enabled him to make a mass of information appetizing and digestible' – Raymond Mortimer in the *Sunday Times*

'Very easy to read . . . a triumph of balance and condensation' – Harold Nicolson in the *Observer*

'Professor Kitto is a model historian – lively, accurate, and fully acquainted with the latest developments in the subject . . . never vague . . . often witty and always full of vigour' – *The Times Educational Supplement*

The Vikings

Johannes Brøndsted

Professor Brøndsted's purpose is to shed light upon
the Nordic Viking, that strange phenomenon of
European history from A.D. 800 to 1100. He analyses
the motives of the Viking raids and voyages, and
investigates the reasons why the Vikings could occupy
the North Atlantic islands but could not secure their
settlements in North America; why they were able to
reach all the coast of Western Europe and penetrate
Eastern Europe to Istanbul and Baghdad but could
not penetrate Central Europe. The Vikings'
acceptance of Christianity, a religion quite alien to
their own philosophy, is also considered.
The book, now re-issued in a revised translation,
deals also with the background and origin of the
Vikings, their industries and equipment, ships and
armies, social organization and daily life, ideas and
beliefs as they are reflected in runic inscriptions,
burial customs, and Icelandic medieval literature.

The Hittites

O. R. Gurney

The Hittites as a legendary Palestinian tribe are
familiar to us from our schooldays. In this book the
story is told of the rediscovery of the historical
Hittites during the last eighty years, as the result
of excavation and the decipherment of cuneiform and
hieroglyphic documents. The Hittites of history were
a great nation of Asia Minor, whose kings treated on
equal terms with those of Egypt, Babylon, and
Assyria, during a period of about two hundred years in
the second millennium B.C. There was an Indo-
European strain in them which is revealed in their
language and perhaps in the physical types of some
of the Hittite prisoners represented on Egyptian
monuments. Their earliest social organization also
shows some points of resemblance to that of the
heroic age of Greece. Their religion on the other
hand seems to have been largely that of the indigenous
population, who must be supposed to have inhabited
the country before the Indo-European reached it.
They developed a rupestrian art, which has its roots
in the soil of Mesopotamia, but exhibits a strong and
independent style of its own.
This is an attempt to present a balanced picture of
what is known of the Hittites and in the chapter on
literature to give some impression of the more
important types of documents found among their
archives.